THE W. F. CODY
BUFFALO BILL

COLLECTOR'S GUIDE WITH VALUES

JAMES W. WOJTOWICZ

COLLECTOR BOOKS
A Division of Schroeder Publishing Co., Inc.

The current values of this book should be used only as a guide. They are not intended to set prices, which vary from one section of the country to another. Auction prices as well as dealer prices vary and are affected by condition as well as demand. Neither the Author nor the Publisher assumes responsibility for any losses that might be incurred as a result of consulting this guide.

Searching for a Publisher?

We are always looking for knowledgeable people considered to be experts within their fields. If you feel that there is a real need for a book on your collectible subject and have a large comprehensive collection, contact Collector Books.

On the Cover:

Top: Celluloid pinback button, ca. 1896
Top left: 1892 souvenir medal
Bottom left: 1893 multi-foldout advertisement herald
Bottom right: First cover design for the 1893, Chicago Columbian season,
Wild West show program

Cover design by Beth Summers
Book design by Holly C. Long

Additional copies of this book may be ordered from:
Collector Books
P.O. Box 3009
Paducah, Kentucky 42002 – 3009

@$24.95. Add $2.00 for postage and handling.
Copyright © 1998 by James W. Wojtowicz

CONTENTS

PREFACE

Collecting artifacts associated with our early American West is finally receiving the national recognition it deserves. Numerous reference books are being published that are entertaining, informative, and sophisticated. This of course, is good news to the interested collector, however, little has been published regarding the material that specifically encompasses William Frederick Cody's life. The volume and variety of Buffalo Bill memorabilia available today is remarkable. This fact is yet another tribute to an extraordinary man.

W. F. Cody was born February 26, 1846, near LeClaire, Scott County, Iowa. He passed away January 10, 1917, at his sister's home in Denver, Colorado. His life spanned one of the most exciting periods in American history, literally from the Pony Express to the airplane.

Research reveals without any doubt that Cody was indeed a legitimate frontiersman. This fact coupled with his handsome physique and likable personality, would bring him fame and fortune that few would ever match. Little did he know that when he started his show business career it would be a run of 44 consecutive years. It all started in Chicago, Illinois, in December of 1872.

A stage play by Ned Buntline was the beginning of Cody's amazing show business career. Scouting and guiding for the Army during the summer months and playing on stage during the fall and winter made for a very active life. His stage acting lasted until his Wild West exhibition started in 1883. However, he did in 1884 run The Wild West Show during the day and offer a stage play at night. His acting inspired newspaper articles and advertisements for stage appearances. Stage programs, carte de visites, studio photos, and even lithographs are available from this period. Cody had his autobiography published in 1879, and it is one of the important early collectibles.

Buffalo Bill's famous Wild West exhibition started in May of 1883. He went through several business partners and 34 consecutive years of successes and disappointments. Considering the hardships of travel during those years, it was absolutely an astonishing run.

The profusion of colorful collectibles this entertainment dynasty produced and inspired is staggering. Wild West Show lithographs, colorful programs and couriers, route books, photographs, books, postcards, toys, pinback buttons, medals, paperweights, insert cards, menus, sheet music, and dime novels to start with are still plentiful. Even personally handwritten letters by W. F. Cody are not too difficult to acquire. Occasionally some of his personal belongings appear at auction including guns, clothes, and other Wild West Show trappings.

A unique facet of Cody collecting is the fact that his Wild West Show casts and personnel will lure even veteran collectors into expanding their collections.

A few of Buffalo Bill's companions and related material are included in this book because they help to provide an understanding of Cody and the Wild West.

All examples appearing in this volume, with three exceptions, are original and were made during Cody's lifetime. Since it is apparent no one will ever have access to every Cody-related collectible, this effort is a beginning. It will focus mainly on material that is still available to collectors today.

ABOUT THE AUTHOR

James W. Wojtowicz, pronounced (Voy-tof-veach), was born and raised in Chicago, Illinois. He started collecting at the tender age of seven and has been at it ever since. Coins, stamps, baseball cards, non-sport cards, soda bottle caps, toy soldiers, cowboys, Indians, and comic books were his boyhood pursuits. After an intermission for courting, marriage, and starting a family, it was full speed ahead.

Western items and antique toys are his key areas of interest. Researching your area of interest and sharing that information is vital to the health and welfare of the collecting community. After contributing to two collector reference books and enjoying many others, the author decided to give back something to the collecting fraternity. After 18 years of buying and trading Buffalo Bill material, it was time to share this fascinating information.

ACKNOWLEDGMENTS

In the beginning there was collecting associate and friend Thomas Trychta, whose encouragement, support, and help with photography propelled this project into action. Thomas Glass who graciously agreed to write the Introduction was also instrumental from start to finish.

Many thanks to The Buffalo Bill Historical Center of Cody, Wyoming. I will always be indebted to the advisory board, board of trustees, and to Mr. Paul Fees, the Ernest J. Goppert curator of The Buffalo Bill Museum for the generous grant and other considerations. The museum's library staff is outstanding, especially Christina Stopka, librarian and archivist, Frances Clymer, associate librarian, Joan Murra, library assistant, and Elizabeth Holmes, associate registrar.

The Circus World Museum in Baraboo, Wisconsin, was very helpful and the staff's patience and guidance will always be remembered. The director of the museum's Robert L. Parkinson Library and Research Center, Mr. Fred Dahlinger, Jr., was cooperative and informative.

Dedicated to the Memory of Melvin A. Schulte of Pocahontas, Iowa.

My gratitude is also extended to The Ringling Brothers – Barnum & Bailey Combined Shows, Inc. for allowing the use of all the Sells – Floto Circus titled material.

My sincere appreciation is offered to all contributors, especially to William M. Lentz, Jr., Ken Harch, Bob Johnson, Steve Cash, David Smucker, Sam Logan, Robert Sabia, George T. Jackson, Jack Regan, David Hirsch, Jim Yeager, M. Douglas Parks, Betty Hall, Alfred K. Schreier, Karen Wojtowicz, Scott Hawkinson, Frank Spizzirri, Norbert K. Natzman, Michael Del Castello, and Jimmie Gibbs Munroe, the granddaughter of Zack Miller.

Special acknowledgments to my wife, Kathleen, for all those hours of typing and for her uplifting encouragement and patience. To my son, Joseph, for his help with photography and to my daughter, JoAnn, for her computer input. To my wonderful parents, Lillian and Michael, a big thank you for introducing me to the marvelous world of collecting.

God bless you all.

INTRODUCTION

BUFFALO BILL CODY — SCOUT, SHOWMAN, AMERICAN ICON

THOMAS GLASS, NORTHERN ILLINOIS UNIVERSITY

William Frederick Cody, better known worldwide as "Buffalo Bill," died in 1917, but still today is a hero for many Americans in his role as one of the most important figures in winning the West. Without doubt, Buffalo Bill Cody was one of the most unique and best known Americans of the late nineteenth and early twentieth centuries.

Part of the uniqueness of Cody is that he was a world famous showman depicting on the stage and in the arena historical spectacles in which he had been a featured player. Cody was the real thing, not a phony, but a bonafide hero of Western America during the critical decades of the westward migration, banishment of the American Indian, extermination of the buffalo, growth of railroads, era of cowboys, and agricultural development. During his lifetime Cody played a visible part in each of these epochs.

Very few well-known personages of the West did not know or rub elbows with Buffalo Bill Cody. Many such as Wild Bill Hickok, Generals George Custer and Phil Sheridan were numbered among his friends. The most famous Army officers, politicians, businessmen, scouts, buffalo hunters, gunfighters, and cattlemen were part of his wide network of friends and acquaintances during his event filled life which began in 1846 and lasted nearly 71 years.

Cody was born to parents of modest means at LeClaire, Iowa. The family of two boys and four girls moved to Kansas during the troubled years before the Civil War. Cody's early life near Leavenworth, Kansas, was a typical frontier boyhood.

In 1857, Cody's father died from a wound suffered in a violent conflict with a pro-slavery man. This tragic event caused young Billy to begin early in life to learn the frontier survival skills he would later use so well in scouting and Indian fighting.

Among young Bill Cody's teachers were bull-whackers and wagonmasters working for the firm of Russell, Majors, and Waddell freighting between Leavenworth and western cities and military forts. During his teenage years working on the "bull teams," Cody had the chance to meet and learn frontier skills from older and more experienced frontiersman.

Shortly before the Civil War, Cody rode briefly for the Pony Express. Some skeptics in the past have claimed that Cody never rode for the Pony Express but Alexander Majors, partner in Russell, Majors, and Waddell, owners of this first intercontinental mail service, wrote in 1893 that Cody did indeed ride for them.

The beginning of the Civil War found the young Cody loafing around Fort Leavenworth and Fort Larned doing a bit of dispatch riding, but mostly hunting, drinking, and honoring his widowed mother's pleas to not enlist with the boys in blue. Nonetheless, Cody became mixed up with several Kansas antislavery militia groups who at times rivaled in their brutal behavior the infamous Quantrill's guerillas. Cody owns up to this not too honorable period of his youth in his first autobiography published in 1879 by Frank Bliss.

Shortly, after the death of his mother, Cody enlisted in the 7th Kansas Cavalry and served out the remainder of the war as a private. At the conclusion of hostilities, William F. Cody entered into marriage with Louisa Frederici of St. Louis. The marriage was one of opposites and Louisa never liked living either on the frontier or later on the road following the Wild West Show. It can be fairly said that Cody's marriage was not a success even though it was blessed with one son and three daughters. By the early 1900s Cody accused Louisa of trying to poison him and used this allegation as an excuse to seek a divorce which was never legally granted.

At first the young Codys set up housekeeping, managing a hotel owned by a friend of the Cody family. This venture failed and the young couple then moved on to Army posts such as Fort Hays and Fort McPherson where Cody worked as a scout for generals Hancock and Custer. These years late in the 1860s were the beginning of Cody's scouting and subsequent notoriety.

Scouting for the Army was generally on a contract basis with an approximate pay of $60 per month. At other times when not in the field scouts were expected to be teamsters, haycutters, or perform work assigned by the Post Quartermaster. Many times they were dismissed until new Indian hostilities arose.

During one of these intervals in the late 1860s Cody acquired a contract with the Kansas Pacific Railway to shoot buffalo to feed workers building the railroad toward western destinations. This is the point in his life when the sobriquet of "Buffalo Bill" was laid upon his shoulders for life. Perhaps this nickname (almost everyone in the west had a nickname) was given Cody after a buffalo shooting contest with noted frontiersman and scout Billy Comstock. Or, perhaps by ordinary workers on the railroad who were thankful to have fresh buffalo meat.

At about this same time Buffalo Bill was discovered by "Ned Buntline" also known as "Colonel" E.V.C. Judson, a notorious character and writer of cheap dime novels. Judson published a number of "Buffalo Bill" thrillers, introducing Cody to thousands of readers in the East. In these dime novels Cody was pictured rescuing maidens from fates worse than death, catching criminals, and saving wagon trains from hordes of blood thirsty Indians.

Cody, by the early 1870s, was consistently noticed by the legitimate Eastern press for his scouting activities. These were heavily reported by newspapers in New York and Chicago. Of a non-military nature Cody's name appeared in the press frequently guiding hunting parties such as that of the Earl of Dunraven and other wealthy Englishmen and Americans.

After one of these sorties New York publishing magnate James Gordon Bennett of the *New York Herald* invited Cody to visit New York. While there, Cody, much to his surprise, discovered that "Buffalo Bill" was a very well-known personage thanks to Ned Buntline, the Army, wealthy hunters, and hostile Indian tribes.

In 1872 Cody, along with scouting friend Jack (Texas Jack) Omohundro, left Louisa, children, and Fort McPherson bound for Chicago to meet Ned Buntline. The reason for the trip was the launching of "Scouts of the Prairies," the two scouts first adventure on the stage. And certainly an attempt to capitalize on publicity from dime novels and Indian fighting. The play was an artistic disaster but wildly popular with theater-goers in Chicago and elsewhere.

After the initial season Cody and Omohundro extricated themselves from Buntline and brought in a new partner, James Butler Hickok, better known as Wild Bill. The three partners were successful with their "combination" of two plays, but Hickok did not take well to the stage and departed before the end of the season.

Cody with partners, Texas Jack and later Captain Jack Crawford the "Poet Scout," fielded a different combination every year from 1872 to 1883 when the first Wild West Show went on the road. During these years Cody typically played the boards during the winter and scouted for the Army during the warm months. When not scouting he guided groups of wealthy and famous hunters such as General Sheridan and the Grand Duke Alexis of Russia. These hunts were well publicized in the press and certainly helped augment Cody's reputation as scout and Indian fighter. The summer scouting also helped to draw customers to the winter theatrical season.

His most famous Indian fight during the theatrical combination period was a single-handed duel in 1876 with a minor chief named Yellow Hand, who Cody killed and scalped allegedly crying the "First Scalp for Custer." In addition to this somewhat melodramatic event, Cody, while scouting for the 5th Cavalry, also participated in another action for which he was awarded the Medal of Honor. In the 1900s the Army denied Cody a pension allowed medal holders because he was a contracted civilian scout not a regular enlisted man or officer.

By 1882 Cody was tiring of winters on the road with his combination. During the one winter he began refining an idea of a Wild West exhibition. The idea of depicting or exhibiting historical scenes from the development of the West was not an original concept. However, others had not been able to successfully implement it.

In July 1882, Cody, using his hometown of North Platte, Nebraska, neighbors, and friends, sponsored what might be called the first American rodeo and Wild West show. After further refining his first attempt at a Wild West exhibition and investing in stock, employees, and equipment, the first Buffalo Bill Wild West Show opened in May 1883 in Omaha, Nebraska, in partnership with Dr. W.F. Carver, a world famous marksman. By the end of the season it was evident that a touring show depicting historic scenes of the West with action provided by cowboys, Indians, soldiers, and buffalo was viable but not in partnership with a jealous Dr. Carver.

Not until the winter of 1884 did Cody find the winning management combination. The signing of partnership papers with Nate Salsbury insured the show would have the management it had sorely needed in the first year. Also, part of this second year show were Major Frank North of Pawnee Scout fame (and also ranching partner of Buffalo Bill) and Captain Adam Bogardus, another world famous shot who replaced Dr. Carver. Dr. Carver would for the rest of his life belittle Buffalo Bill Cody at any opportunity.

The Wild West Show, after the 1884 season, acquired perhaps its greatest performer besides Buffalo Bill. This was Annie Oakley, who would remain with the show for most of 16 seasons under a "handshake contract" with Cody. "Little Missie" won the hearts of America and came to epitomize feminity with a rifle or shotgun in an era where women were considered to be much less than equal with men in almost all respects.

The Wild West Show was very successful in the 1885 and 1886 seasons. But Salsbury had his eye on perhaps the jewel in the entertainment crown of the period, namely performing in England before the English aristocracy during Queen Victoria's Golden Jubilee celebration.

Buffalo Bill and the Wild West Show were immensely successful in London performing before Queen Victoria, Prince Albert, and other crowned heads of European nations. The success in England set up later many successful seasons in England, France, and elsewhere in Europe.

After returning to the United States in 1888 the Wild West Show headquartered in the New York area. There were additional seasons scheduled in Europe before the show, in 1893, settled in Chicago outside the gates of the Columbian Exposition. Perhaps more people saw the Wild West Show in 1893 than any other year during its long existence.

Cody, during the late 1880s and in the 1890s, was becoming increasingly wealthy. It is quite likely that at this time Buffalo Bill was the most famous American in the world, certainly the best known show person.

By 1902, Cody's chief partner, Nate Salsbury, died of cancer. His place was taken by James Bailey of circus fame who completed a decade-long transition of the Wild West Show to the more circus-like Wild West and Congress of Rough Riders. This new form of the Wild West Show included a wide array of sideshows which dismayed Cody, who always desired his show to be a historical exhibition rather than a circus. Later in 1909 Cody, was in need of a new partner and found Pawnee Bill Lillie, another wild west show proprietor, who had furnished competition periodically in the past. Lillie, as a young interpreter for Pawnee Indians, had accompanied the show during its maiden year in 1883 and remained a friend of Cody's through thick and thin.

Buffalo Bill and Pawnee Bill remained partners until unwise investments and luxurious spending habits forced Cody into deep debt, ultimately bringing the 'Two Bills Show" into bankruptcy in 1913 at Denver. Until his death in

January 1917 Cody was forced to tour with the Sells Floto Circus and the 101 Ranch Show as a figurehead and salaried employee. During these last years he vainly attempted to regain financial stability through his land investments in the Cody, Wyoming, area as well as in several Arizona mines.

No American western hero or showman has ever matched the worldwide fame of Buffalo Bill Cody who was on the stage and in the arena from 1872 until 1916. Fortunately, for collectors of American and especially western memorabilia the Buffalo Bill Wild West show fully exploited the fame of Buffalo Bill by publishing numerous types of photo-graphic images, souvenir booklets, programs, medals, watchfobs, figurines, and of course books about and by Buffalo Bill.

The variety of Buffalo Bill memorabilia is almost limitless with some being extremely expensive while other such as postcards being quite reasonable. Perhaps most important for a beginning collector is the reading and studying of numerous non-fiction books about Buffalo Bill and his era. The story of the development of western America should not be told without giving a significant role to Buffalo Bill.

The Virginia Reel on horseback was a popular show event and at times Cody joined in.

WILD WEST
SHOW PROGRAMS

Courtesy Circus World Museum, Baraboo, Wisconsin

1883 PROGRAM
Size – 6⅞" x 10"
Pages – 16 full pages
Published by Calhoun Printing
Co., Hartford Conn.

Fortunately, Cody and his Wild West Show had many consistencies. The most important by far was Buffalo Bill himself. Another very significant factor regarding The Wild West Show, will always be the wonderfully colorful and interesting programs. Luckily for collectors today, there is a program for each and every year of the show's existence.

The first program is informative and impressive because of the colorful artwork on the front and back covers. The text is exciting and the use of many illustrations will keep the reader's attention. The 1883 program set the pattern for almost all other Wild West Show programs to follow. It is surprisingly sophisticated for the period.

Cody and The Wild West would have an incredible run of 34 consecutive years. There are actually 36 different programs to collect. In 1893 two different front covers were used. Again in 1903 we have the standard program which was supplemented by a special silk-cover program issued for March 14, 1903. This occurred to honor the visit of King Edward VII and his royal friends. There are 26 distinctly different front covers. All the program front covers are colorful and personify Buffalo Bill and the Wild West. There were other non-western events included with historical characters to match, however, the main theme would always be the American West.

The back covers are all colorful and tastefully exe-cuted. Western scenes and two different Wild West Show lithographs appeared on the back covers until 1899 when general advertising first appeared. Most back cover advertising had a generalized western theme included.

Within the programs we find many illustrations and historical sketches about performers and western related subjects. There is repetition from year to year however, something different always appears. As we read our way through the programs it becomes apparent we are looking at an encyclopedia of the American Wild West Show experience.

One of Cody's better idiosyncrasies was his fondness for quality art in advertising. The program front covers are a testimony to that principle. Even the back cover efforts have a look of quality, although most back covers will not be illustrated. The 1910 and 1911 programs have several different back cover advertisements.

Variations play a key roll in this category. It is common to find small changes made for the same season's second printing. Always check that duplicate simply because you may find an interesting variation. One other important factor to keep in mind is that this program listing may not be complete. Other examples may exist especially for the overseas touring seasons. The limitations of time and travel kept this researcher from visiting England and Europe.

1883 — THE INAUGURAL WILD WEST SEASON

The first program is quite sophisticated for its time. A busy front cover with vivid color displays an array of western figures. The back cover has a very graphic Indian and frontiersman fighting scene.

"Novelty of the Century" is the opening statement on the first page. By many accounts, this declaration turned out to be true. "The Wild West, Cody and Carver's Rocky Mountain and Prairie Exhibition," was the official title of the show. Cody was billed as Buffalo Bill, "the famed scout and Indian fighter." Dr. William F. Carver was called The King of Riflemen and acknowledged champion marksman of the world. The program continues with a camp of Cheyenne, Arappahoe, Sioux, and Pawnee Indians, a group of Mexican Vaqueros, a round-up of western cowboys, a company of prairie scouts, plus a host of western celebrities. Animals were well represented by a herd of wild buffaloes, a corral of Indian ponies, a band of mountain elk, a drove of Texas steers, and a pack of Mexican burros. Together these two groups would present lifelike and thrilling pictures of western life.

We also find in bold print Major Frank North, The White Chief of the Pawnees, "Honored by the officers of the United States Army as their most valuable ally, in their triumphs over the red warriors of the west." North was a partner of Cody's in ranching in Nebraska.

Captain A. H. Bogardus receives special billing in this 1883 program. He is described as an "honored veteran, champion of America, and a scorer of a 1,000 victories." He was a noted shotgun exhibitionist and later a partner of Cody's.

Interestingly, Gordon William Lillie joined the show as interpreter for the Pawnee Indians. He would later become Pawnee Bill and head his own Wild West Show. Sadly, he ended his show business career partnered with Buffalo Bill in 1913. The first management team is listed as follows, Cody and Doc Carver proprietors, Ed C. Woolcott, business manager, Ariel N. Barney, press agent, Josh E. Ogden, general advertising agent, John M. Burke, general manager, Jule Keen, treasurer, Frank Whitiker, superintendent, and Eugene Overton, quartermaster.

Since there is no list of events in the 1883 program proper, it must be speculated that there was an inserted flyer-type used. Research has turned up two different flyer-type inserted lists of events for the 1884 programs.

The show opened in Omaha, Nebraska, on May 19, 1883. Carver was Cody's first business partner, in the Wild West enterprise. He was billed as the "Evil Spirit of the Plains" and unfortunately, had a disposition to match. The two just could not make their relationship work and would part company in November 1883.

The fact that a group of basically undisciplined men put a new entertainment concept on the road at that time is extraordinary in itself. As rough as it was in the beginning, the show did fairly well. Many newspaper reports were complimentary. This new outdoor Wild West entertainment would have a firm grip on the American and foreign publics for years to come.

"The Evil Spirit of the Plains."

Dr. Wm. F. Carver
Cut from 1883 program

1884

The second year of "Buffalo Bill's Wild West – America's National Entertainment," started with a new partnership; W. F. Cody, Nate Salsbury, and wing shot specialist Adam H. Bogardus. The addition of Nate Salsbury was the ingredient Cody needed. He understood the entertainment world. His intellect and business sense coupled with Cody's fame and popularity, was the formula for success.

This program included sixteen full pages with most of the text featuring Cody. Other short sketches portrayed Captain A. H. Bogardus, Champion Wing Shot of the World; Major Frank North, the Pilot of the Prairie; "Oklahoma" Payne, the Progressive Pioneer; Buck Taylor, King of the Cowboys; "Con" Groner, the Cowboy Sheriff of the Platte; Jim Lawson, the Roper; Seth Hathaway, Pony Express Rider; Bill Bullock, Cowboy; and Fred Matthews, the Deadwood Stagecoach Driver.

The actual program of events was a slipped in one-page flyer. A print of Cody on one side with the list of events on the other. There are two variations of this flyer. The program of events are the same, just the artwork and layout are different.

1884 PROGRAM

1. Grand Parade.
2. Grand Equestrian Entree.
3. Grand Quarter Mile Race, among four Mexicans, four Cowboys, and four Indians.
4. Pony Express.
5. 100 Yard Race, between Indian on Horse and Foot.
6. Shooting by **Capt. Bogardus** and his four sons.
7. Bucking Ponies.
8. Shooting on Horseback by **Buffalo Bill**.
9. Stage Coach Attacked by Indians.
10. Half Mile Race with Indian Ponies and Thoroughbreds.
11. Burro Race, Half Mile.
12. **Maj. Frank North** and Pawnees, in Scalp and War Dances.
13. Lassoing and Riding of the Wild Texas Steers.
14. Buffalo Chase by **Buffalo Bill** and Pawnee Indians.
15. Conclude with Attack on Settler's Cabin by Indians and Rescue by **Buffalo Bill** with his Scouts, Cowboys, and Mexicans.

1884 PROGRAM
Size – 6⅞" x 9⅞"
Pages – 16 full pages
Published by Calhoun Printing Co.

1885

Cody and Nate Salsbury are in 1885 the sole proprietors. This combination would carry them to the top of the outdoor entertainment business. Few would ever match their accomplishments or successes.

The list of events are now a part of the program proper. Cody will always be prominently featured in all programs. Johnnie Baker, "the Cowboy Kid," starts his performing career. Annie Oakley and her manager/husband, Frank Butler, join the show. Interestingly, no written sketch about Annie Oakley appears in this program. Other members of the show are "Con" Groner, the Cowboy Sheriff of the Platte; "Buck" Taylor, King of the Cowboys; Bill Irving, Broncho Bill; Tom Clayton; Billie Bullock; Bridle Bill; Coyote Bill; John Higby, the new Deadwood Coach driver; Frank Powell, "White Beaver"; and John Nelson and his Indian family are also part of the show in 1885.

One very important aspect of this season is that Sitting Bull toured with the show for four months. Cody's horses get their first real recognition. Old Buckskin Joe, Brighman, Tallbull, Power Face, Stranger, and Old Charlie are affectionately mentioned.

1885 PROGRAM
Size – 7" x 10"
Pages – 16 full pages
Published by Calhoun Printing Co.

1885 PROGRAM

Subject to Changes and Additions.

1. Grand Processional Parade.
2. Entree.
3. Race between Cowboy, Mexican, and Indian.
4. Pony Express by Billy Johnson.
5. 100 Yard Race between Indian Pony and Indian on Foot.
6. Duel between **Buffalo Bill** and Yellow Hand.
7. Rifle Shooting by Seth Clover.
8. Master Johnnie Baker, the Cowboy Kid.
9. Miss Annie Oakley, Champion Lady Shot.
10. The Cowboy's Fun, or Riding of Bucking Ponies and Mules by Buck Taylor, Broncho Bill, Bill Bullock, Tom Clayton, Coyote Bill, Bridle Bill.
11. Hon. **Wm. F. Cody** (Buffalo Bill), America's Practical All-Round-Shot, Shooting with Rifle, Shot Gun, and Revolver, on Foot and Horseback.
12. The Deadwood Stage Coach.
13. Race between Sioux Boys on Bareback Indian Ponies.
14. Race between Mexican Thoroughbreds.
15. War, Grass, Corn, and Scalp Dances by Pawnee, Wichita, and Sioux Indians.
16. Mustang Jack (Pets-ze-ca-we-cha-cha), the Great Jumper.
17. Roping and Riding of Wild Texas Steers by Cowboys and Mexicans.
18. Hunting of Buffalo by **Buffalo Bill**, Cowboys, and Pawnees.
19. Riding of Wild Elk by Voter Hall.
20. Attack on Settlers' Cabin by Indians, and Repulsed by **Buffalo Bill**, Cowboys, and Mexicans.
21. Salute.

1886

The fourth year program can be confusing. It contains the same salutatory by John M. Burke dated North Platte, Neb., March 1, 1885, that appeared in the 1885 program.

Lillian Smith, "The California Huntress" and "Champion Girl Rifle Shot," was added to the show that year. Also Gabriel Dumont, The Entitled Chieftain of the Canadian Riel Rebellion, toured with the show in 1886.

Two different programs of events have turned up.

One with 22 events and the other with 20. It should be kept in mind that variations are common. There is a possibility that this front cover was used for a short period in 1885.

Performers were Con Groner, Buck Taylor, Dick Johnson, Lillian Smith, Annie Oakley, Johnnie Baker, Mustang Jack, Billy Bullock, Billy Johnson, Fred Mathews, Otto Williams, John Hancock, Antonio Esquivel, John Higby, Capt. C. Pell, Jim Kid, Dick Bean, Bill Irving, Eddie Goodman, and Tod Randall. John Nelson and his Indian family by this season were becoming regulars.

Indian Chiefs mentioned for the first time included Young-Man-Afraid-Of His Horses, American Horse, Rocky Bear, and Lone Wolf of the Sioux, Brave Chief and Young Chief, Pawnee Warriors. Curley, The Crow Scout, only alleged survivor of Custer's command, was also with the show.

1886 PROGRAM

Subject to Changes and Additions.
1. Grand Processional Review.
2. **Entree.** Introduction of Individual Celebrities, Groups, etc.
3. **Race** between Cowboy, Mexican, and Indian on Ponies.
4. **Pony Express,** ridden by Billy Johnson, illustrating Mode of Conveying Mails on the Frontier.
5. **Rifle Shooting** by Johnnie Baker, the "Cowboy Kid."
6. **Duel** between **Buffalo Bill** and Chief Yellow Hand, and Indian Battle, "First Scalp for Custer."
7. **Wing Shooting** by Miss Annie Oakley.
8. **The Cowboy's Fun.** Throwing the Lariat, Riding Bucking Ponies and mules by Buck Taylor, Bill Bullock, Tony Esquivel, Jim Kidd, Dick Johnson, and Cowboys.
9. **Rifle Shooting,** by Miss Lillian F. Smith, "The California Girl."
10. **Race,** ridden by Lady Riders.
11. **Attack Upon the Deadwood Stage Coach** by Indians, Repulsed by Cowboys commanded by **Buffalo Bill.**
12. **Race** between Sioux Boys on bareback Indian Ponies.
13. **Race** between Mexican Thoroughbreds.
14. **Phases of Indian Life.** A nomadic tribe camps upon the prairie, the attack of the hostile tribe, followed by scalp, war, and other dances.
15. **Mustang Jack** (Petz-ze-ka-we-cha-cha), the Wonderful Jumper.
16. Hon. **W.F. Cody, "Buffalo Bill,"** America's Great Practical All-round Shot.
17. **Roping and Riding of Wild Texan Steers** by Cowboys and Mexicans.
18. **The Buffalo Hunt. Buffalo Bill,** assisted by Sioux, Pawnee, Wichita, and Comanche Indians.
19. **The Attack on the Settlers' Cabin** by Marauding Indians; the Battle and Repulse by Buffalo Bill, Leading Cowboys and Mexicans.
20. **Salute.**

1886 PROGRAM
Size – 7" x 10"
Pages – 16 full pages
Published by Calhoun Printing Co.

1887

On March 31, 1887, Cody and The Wild West sailed for England. The success of this season in England was extraordinary. The fact that profits were high is secondary to the fact that The Wild West established a new understanding between our two nations. To better comprehend the impact, I suggest reading "The Wild West in England." This is the last chapter in the 1888 book *Story of The Wild West and Campfire Chats* by Buffalo Bill. Here we have a detailed description of the visit written when facts and names were fresh in Cody's memory.

We have two 1887 programs. The original batch of programs was printed by The Forbes Lithographic Company of Boston, Mass. It is dated 1887 and has 21 events listed including the salute. Event number sixteen was Mustang Jack, The Cowboy Jumper. When the second printing was done in England, Mustang Jack was no longer listed. This was the only difference in the list of events. The front covers are the same, however a few sketches vary.

From May 9 to October 31 the show entertained with a special sense of purpose. A winter stand took place at Manchester, opening on December 17. A large indoor theater was home for four months. On May 6, 1888, the sail for home started.

Please note the simulated autograph on the front cover. This effect will be used on many Cody collectibles. It has come to the author's attention that some new collectors have purchased simulated autographs, thinking they were originals. Please be careful when paying extra for an autographed item.

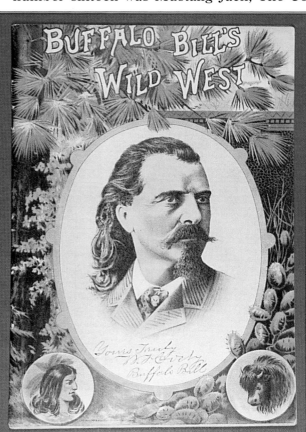

1887 PROGRAM
Size – 7" x 10"
Pages – 40 numbered pages
Published by Allen, Scott & Co., 30 Bouverie St.
E.C., London

1888 PROGRAM
Cover – Same as 1887
Size – 7" x 10⅛"
Pages – 40 numbered pages
Published by Calhoun Printing Co.

1888

Back home for the sixth season, Cody was confident about the future of his exhibition. The successes in England were reported here almost on a daily basis. Many people wanted to see what the Queen was so excited about. More Royalty visited the Wild West Show than anyone would have ever imagined. Cody and Salsbury were setting new standards for the entertainment world.

Annie Oakley did not tour with Cody's Wild West in 1888. Lillian Smith, Buck Taylor, Bill Bullock, Capt. Fred Matthews, Utah Frank, John Nelson, and Dr. D. Frank Powell, also known as White Beaver, were with the show. Miss Emma Hickok becomes a performer. She is none other than James Butler Hickok's stepdaughter.

Indians were now getting some respectability within the program. Positive sketches were appearing and would continue.

Please note that this is the only program between 1885 and 1901 that does not list Annie Oakley in the list of events. A variation program has 20 events listed.

1887 PROGRAM

Overture
1. **Grand Processional Review.**
2. **Entree.** Introduction of Individual Celebrities, Groups, etc.
3. **Race** between Cowboy, Mexican, and Indian on Ponies.
4. **Pony Express.** Illustrating the Mode of Conveying Mails on the Frontier.
5. **Rifle Shooting** by Johnnie Baker, the Cowboy Kid.
6. **Illustrates an Attack** on an Emigrant Train by the Indians, and its Defense by Frontiersmen, after which **A Virginia Reel** on Horseback by Western Girls and Cowboys.
7. **Miss Annie Oakley,** Wing Shooting.
8. **Cowboy's Fun.** Throwing the Lariat. Picking from the Ground while Riding at Full Speed. The Riding of Bucking Ponies and Mules by Cowboys.
9. **Lillian Smith** (The California Girl), Rifle Shooting.
10. **Ladies' Race** by American Frontier Girls.
11. **Attack on the Deadwood Stage Coach** by Indians. Their Repulse by Scouts and Cowboys, commanded by **Buffalo Bill.**
12. **Race** between Sioux Indian Boys on Bareback Indian Ponies.
13. **Race** between Mexican Thoroughbreds.
14. **Horseback Riding** by American Frontier Girls.
15. **Phases of Indian Life.** Nomadic Tribe Camps on the Prairie. Attack by Hostile Tribes, followed by Scalp, War, and other Dances.
16. **Buffalo Bill** (Hon. W. F. Cody). America's Practical All-round Shot.
17. **Roping and Riding** of Wild Texas Steers by Cowboys and Mexicans.
18. **Genuine Buffalo Hunt** by **Buffalo Bill** and Indians.
19. **Attack on a Settler's Cabin** by Hostile Indians. Repulse by Cowboys, under the leadership of **Buffalo Bill.**
20. **Salute.**

1888 PROGRAM

1. **Grand Processional Review.**
2. **Entree.** Introduction of Individual Celebrities, Groups, etc.
3. **Race** between Cowboy, Mexican, and Indian on Ponies.
4. **Pony Express.** Illustrating the Mode of Conveying Mails on the Frontier.
6. **Illustrates an Attack** on an Emigrant Train by the Indians, and its Defense by Frontiersmen, after which **A Virginia Reel** on Horseback by Western Girls and Cowboys.
7. **Wing Shooting** by Master Johnnie Baker.
8. **Cowboy's Fun.** Throwing the Lariat. Picking from the Ground while Riding at Full Speed. The Riding of Bucking Ponies and Mules by Cowboys.
9. **Lillian Smith** (The California Girl), Rifle Shooting.
10. **Ladies' Race** by American Frontier Girls.
11. **Attack on the Deadwood Stage Coach** by Indians. Their Repulse by Scouts and Cowboys, commanded by **Buffalo Bill.**
12. **Race** between Sioux Indian Boys on Bareback Indian Ponies.
13. **An Exhibition of Fancy Riding** by Miss Emma Hickok.
14. **Phases of Indian Life.** Nomadic Tribe Camps on the Prairie. Attack by Hostile Tribes, followed by Scalp, War, and other Dances.
15. **Buffalo Bill** (Hon. W. F. Cody). America's Practical All-round Shot. Shooting on Foot and on Horseback.
16. **Attack on a Settler's Cabin** by Hostile Indians. Repulse by Cowboys, under the leadership of **Buffalo Bill.**
17. **Salute.**

The 1887, 1888, and 1889 programs all have the same back cover artwork.

1889

The first long European tour started in 1889. Annie Oakley was back and Lillian Smith was gone. The "Exposition Universale" arena in Paris, France, was home for The Wild West Show for seven months. This was followed by a tour of Southern France. The success in France surely influenced Cody and Salsbury to tour many other countries in Europe.

Featured performers were Annie Oakley, Johnnie Baker, and M. C. L. Daly, an expert pistol shooter. The French publisher's credit appears just below Cody's simulated autograph. Again, please keep in mind that simulated autographs are common regarding Cody collectibles.

The 1889 program provides written sketches on Cody, Johnnie Baker, Nate Salsbury, Tony Esquival, Buck Taylor, Annie Oakley, Dr. Frank Powell, Gabriel Dumont, and John Nelson with his Indian family.

The 1889 management team was ready to tour Europe. Col. W. F. Cody (**Buffalo Bill**) president, Nate Salsbury vice-president and manager, Jule Keen treasurer, John M. Burke general manager, Lew Parker contract agent, Albert E. Scheible representative, Frank Richmond orator, Carter Coufurier publicity agent.

1889 PROGRAM
Cover – Same as 1887, except for French's publisher's credit
Size – 7¼" x 10¼"
Pages – 47 numbered pages
Published by Lith F. Appel, 12. R. du Delta, Paris

1889 PROGRAM
Translation (from the French)

Frank Richmond, Orator

Notice: The presentation you are going to see is made up solely of a series of exercises shone of the ability one can acquire when it must become a way of life. At first, and without thinking about it, many people have thought that the different phases of our presentation are but the results of a prerehearsed plan: nothing is further from the truth, however, and those who see our exercises for a second time can see that the man as well as the animals performing are subject to the influence of variable circumstances and do not make their success depend on anything but their own ability, bravery, and personal wisdom. **Nate Salsbury, manager.**

1889 Opening

1. **General Introduction.**
2. **Grand Processional** of the whole troupe.
3. **Introduction of Individual Celebrities, Groups, Etc.**
4. **Pony Race** between a Cowboy, a Mexican, and an Indian, make two turns around the track.
5. **Wing Shooting** by Miss Annie Oakley.
6. **Pony Express.** The manner in which letters were conveyed in the Wild West before the construction of the Railroads or Telegraph lines.
7. **Attack on an Emigrant Family** by a band of marauding Indians. Defense of the convoy by Scouts and Cowboys commanded by **Buffalo Bill.** These wagons and harnesses are the same ones used 30 years ago by the emigrants in their travels in the Wild West of America before the railroad crossed the continent.
8. **The Virginia Reel** danced on horseback by Girls and Cowboys of the Frontier.
9. **Wing Shooting** by Mr. Johnnie Baker.
10. **Cowboy's Fun** – Throw up lasso, pick up objects thrown to the ground from horseback at a full gallop. They ride the Broncho Jumpers.
11. **Pistol Shooting** by M.C.L. Daly.
12. **Attack on the Deadwood Stage Coach** by Indians. Defense of the coach by Scouts and Cowboys commanded by **Buffalo Bill.** This vehicle is the authentic vehicle used to carry the mail on the frontier between Deadwood and Cheyenne 35 years ago.
13. **Race Between Young Sioux on Bareback Ponies.**
14. **Indian Dance:** War Dance, Sun Dance, Dance of Love, etc. by Sioux, Arapahoes, Brules, Ogallalas, and Cheyennes.
15. **Colonel W.F. Cody, Buffalo Bill,** the King of the Frontiersmen in various exercises.
16. **Buffalo Hunt.**
17. **Attack on a Settler's Cabin** by maranding Indians. Defense commanded by **Buffalo Bill.**

Translation (from the German)
The Wild West of Buffalo Bill
A Show Portraying the Life of the American Frontiersman
Please read the Program attentively!

The performances presented by Buffalo Bill's Wild West have nothing in common with the usual high-wire act and circus rider shows which depend entirely on skill acquired through practice.

It is our intention to acquaint the public with manners and customs and the daily way of life of the inhabitants of the Western United States by portraying scenes and actual events occurring there. Each member of the troupe stands out through the skill and courage distinguishing his kind. Whatever the audience's critical judgment may be regarding the performance, we wish to assure you that every scene presents a picture of the customs of the population which is accurate in the smallest detail.

All horses are descended from the Spanish breed introduced into Mexico by Ferdinand Cortez and his companions. Every piece of equipment such as harnesses etc. is authentic and has been in use for many years. We consider ourselves to be the first to have succeeded in combining, through many years of experience, so many original and truly historical elements.

Having earned the acclaim of press and public at home as well as in London, Paris, Barcelona, Naples, Rome, Milan etc., we are honored today to introduce ourselves to the public of Vienna.

Vienna, May 1890 Nate Salsbury, Director

1890 PROGRAM

1. Entry of Celebrities and Groups as follows:
   Group of Arrapahoe (sic) Indians Their Chief Black Heart
   Group of Cowboys (American Cow Hands or Cow Punchers) Buck Taylor, King of the Cowboys,
   Group of Brules Indians Little Chief, their Chief,
   Group of the Indian Tribe Cutt (sic) Off Brave Bear, Chief,
   Group of Mexican Vaqueros Sr. Antonio Esquival,
   Group of Cheyenne Indians Eagle Horn, Chief
   Group of American Frontierswomen
   Young Bennie Irving, smallest cowboy in the world
   The Boy Chiefs, young chiefs of the Sioux
   Flags of Friendly Nations
   Group of Ogallala Sioux Indians Low Neck, Chief
   Rockey (sic) Bear, "Medicine Man" of the Sioux
   "Buffalo Bill" (Col. W. F. Cody), Head of Army Scouts of the United States Army
2. Horse Races between a cowboy, a Mexican, and an Indian, on Spanish-Mexican horses.
3. Miss Annie Oakley famous markswoman showing her fabulous virtuosity in the use of firearms.

Italy sees the show and is impressed. Even a Papal blessing by Pope Leo the XIII was included while playing Italy. Rome, Naples, Florence, Bologna, Milan, and Verona were important and profitable tour stops.

In Venice, Buffalo Bill and a few show Indians were photographed in a gondola. This publicity photo was one of the shows best and would appear in many Wild West programs in years to come. The show moved on to Austria and then into Germany to finish the 1890 campaign.

1890 GERMAN PROGRAM
Size – 6¾" x 9¾"
Printed in Germany

1890 PROGRAM

Translation (from the German)

4. **Former Pony-Express Rider** demonstrating how Government letters and telegrams formerly were transmitted across the vast prairies before the arrival of railroad and telegraph. Every 10 miles the rider had to change mounts and had to travel 50 miles without stopping.

5. **Surprise Attack on an Immigrant Wagon Train** by Indians and its defense by frontiersmen. After beating back the attack, cowboys and frontierswomen perform the Virginia Reel dance on horseback. Please note: The wagons are the same that were used 35 years ago.

6. Historical Events from the Life of **Buffalo Bill**. The famous hand-to-hand combat with Yellow Hand, Chief of the Sioux, at War Bonnet Creek, Dakota, and his defeat and death on July 17, 1875, in the presence of Indian and American Troops. In America, this combat between representatives of two different human races is of the same historical importance as the famous combat between the Horatii and the Curatii.

7. **Little John Baker**. The cowboy marksman, decorated with the medals of the Young Marksmen of the World.

8. Picking up Objects from the Floor. Done by cowboys while riding at full gallop; casting a lasso, which shows how cattle and wild horses are captured; executing various equestrian feats. Riding of bucking broncos, the wildest and most untamable horses in existence today. It is impossible to tame them and break them of their habit of throwing a rider.

9. Shooting with Pistol and Revolver by Mr. **C. L. Daly.**

10. **Race** between American Frontierswomen.

11. **Attack by Indians on the Deadwood Stage Coach** which is repulsed by Buffalo Bill and the cowboys under the command of Buffalo Bill. Please note that this is the original old stage coach called [Translation from the German] "Old Deadwood Coach" which is famous because so many people lost their lives riding in it, and which 18 years ago traveled the route between Deadwood and Cheyenne. Two U.S. presidents, four kings, and other members of Royalty who attended the Queen of England's Jubilee, have ridden in this coach because they considered it to be a very important and historical rarity, bestowing an interesting quality on the performance.

12. **Race** between Indian Boys on Horseback using no saddles.

13. **Col. W.F. Cody** (Buffalo Bill) shoots while galloping on horseback.

14. Indian Customs. Indian camp on the plains and foot races; various special dances.

15. Buffalo Hunt as done in North America's Wild West, "Buffalo Bill" and the Indians.

16. Attack on a Frontier Village carried out by hostile Indians. Cowboys under the command of Buffalo Bill defend the village.

17. **Final. Salute.**

Important Note: The spectator should imagine himself transported into a country where such scenes and events are actually happening, and should realize that these are true and authentic groups of people.

Management, in the presentation of this performance, intends to instruct and entertain and to depict the events in such a manner as they have happened and have been handed down in history. The presence of Col. W. F. Cody ("Buffalo Bill") whose past is vividly brought to life in these scenes, should be of great interest. He has been Pony Express Rider, Stage Coach and Wagon Train Driver, Wild Horse Hunter, Buffalo Hunter, Indian Fighter, and Head of the Leaders of the American Army.

Civilization's ultimate triumph over the vast American Continent will be celebrated in Chicago in 1893 in a large-scale International Exhibition in honor of Christopher Columbus. This exhibition is meant to signify the end of that bloody portion of world history in which dramatic happenings Col. W. F. Cody and his company were the last participants. They now are honored to present — as far as circumstances permit — a vivid portrayal of history, during which German explorers and descendants have contributed so honorably to glory, law, and order, wealth, and good fortune of the country.

John M. Burke General Manager

1891

The European tour continued. Many large German cities were stops, and the love affair the Germans had with our American West started with Cody's Wild West Exhibition. After Holland and Belgium the Wild West headed back to tour Great Britain.

A reunion of the veterans of The Charge of the Light Brigade at Balaclava was held in conjunction with a Wild West performance. There is a wonderful paperweight showing these survivors lined up in front of the show's tents. Another very successful season was recorded by The Wild West Show.

1891 PROGRAM
Size – 7¼" x 9¾"
Pages – 64
Published by Stafford & Co., Netherfield, Nottingham

Two-page flyer program
inserted with full program for 1891.

A typical Wild
West show scene.

With a return to Earl's Court in London would the Wild West match the success of the 1887 engagement? The answer came when Queen Victoria wanted a command performance at Windsor Castle.

The hard riding cossacks, in their first season with the show, were receiving most of the attention.

During the 1891 and 1892 touring seasons, the program proper didn't include the list of events. The slipped-in flyer type was used. A folded two-page flyer was available for the equivalent of one cent. These had different images of Cody on the front with advertising on the back.

1892 PROGRAM
Size – 7⅛" x 8½"
Pages – 64 numbered pages
Published by Stafford & Co., Netherfield, Nottingham

1892 PROGRAM

Overture: "Star Spangled Banner"
Cowboy Band: Wm. Sweeny, leader.

1. **Grand Processional Review** and introduction of Groups and Individual Characters.
2. **Miss Annie Oakley**, Celebrated Shot, who will illustrate her dexterity in the use of Fire-arms.
3. **Horse Race** between a Cowboy, a Mexican, and an Indian, on Spanish-Mexican Horses .
4. **Pony Express**, The Former Pony Post Rider will show how the Letters and Telegrams of the Republic were distributed across the immense Continent previous to the Railways and Telegraph.
5. **Attack on an Emigrant Train by Indians & Repulse by the Cowboys.** N.B. – The Wagons are the same as used 35 years ago.
6. **Captain Jack Burtz's** Lightning Drill.
7. **Cowboy Fun,** Picking objects from the Ground. Lassoing Wild Horses. Riding the Buckers.
8. **Across Country**, with Riders of all Nations.
9. **Johnny Baker,** Celebrated Young American Marksman.
10. **Russian Cossacks**, in Feats of Horsemanship, Native Dances.
11. **Racing Between American Back-Woods Women.**
12. **Capture of the Deadwood Mail Coach** by the Indians, which will be rescued by **"Buffalo Bill"** and his Attendant Cowboys. N.B. – This is the identical old **Deadwood Coach**, called the Mail Coach, which is famous on account of having carried the great number of people who lost their lives on the road between **Deadwood** and Cheyenne 18 years ago. Now the most Famed Vehicle extant.
13. **Racing Between Indian Boys on Bareback Horses.**
14. **Life Customs of the Indians.** Indian Settlement on the Field and "Path."
15. **Col. W. F. Cody ("Buffalo Bill")**, in his unique Feats of Sharpshooting.
16. **Buffalo Hunt**, as it is in the Far West of North America, **"Buffalo Bill"** and Indians. The last of the only known Native Herd.
17. **Attack on a Settler's Cabin**. Capture by the Indians. Rescue by **"Buffalo Bill"** and the Cowboys.
18. **Salute**
    National Anthem – Conclusion

1893

Chicago hosted the World's Columbian Exposition in 1893. The magnificent architecture, exhibits, displays, and amusements were on over 600 acres of land. The Fair opened on May 1 and closed on October 31. Paid admissions were reported to be over 27 million. Chicago was the place to be in 1893.

Cody and Salisbury tried to be part of the official exposition but they were denied entry. The next best thing then was to set up camp just outside, opposite one of the main entrances to the Fair. The show lot was large and had seating for 18,000. Full houses were a common occurrence. On September 23 a new Chicago consecutive performances record was set at 302. This was without a doubt one of the most successful outdoor show business seasons of all time.

Profits have been reported as high as a million dollars.

We have two distinctly different front covers for 1893. The first is similar to that of 1892, and is somewhat harder to locate. The other is wonderful in design and fortunately is easy to acquire. It is the most common program before 1900.

One other important note is the new title "Buffalo Bill's Wild West and Congress of Rough Riders of The World." This title runs through 1908. The program is now in its most classic form. Cody, Oakley, and Johnny Baker will be the individual stars with the cowboy's, Indians, and other rough riders forming an unbeatable combination.

1893 PROGRAM First
Size – 7¼" x 9¼"
Pages – 64 numbered pages
Published by The Blakely Printing Co., Chicago

1893 PROGRAM Second
Size – 7¼" x 9¼"
Pages – 64 numbered pages
Published by The Blakely Printing Co., Chicago

1893 PROGRAM

Overture: "Star Spangled Banner"
Cowboy Band: Wm. Sweeny, leader.

1. **Grand Review** introducing the Rough Riders of the World and Fully Equipped Regular Soldiers of the Armies of America, England, France, Germany, and Russia.

2. **Miss Annie Oakley**, Celebrated Shot, who will illustrate her dexterity in the use of Fire-arms.

3. **Horse Race** between a Cowboy, a Cossack, a Mexican, an Arab, and an Indian, on Spanish-Mexican, Broncho, Russian, Indian, and Arabian Horses.

4. **Pony Express**. The Former Pony Post Rider will show how the Letters and Telegrams of the Republic were distributed across the immense Continent previous to the Railways and the Telegraph.

5. **Illustrating a Prairie Emigrant Train Crossing the Plains**. Attack by marauding Indians repulsed by "Buffalo Bill," with Scouts and Cowboys. N. B. – The Wagons are the same as used 35 years ago.

6. **A Group of Syrian and Arabian Horsemen** will illustrate their style of Horsemanship, with Native Sports and Pastimes.

7. **Cossacks**, of the Caucasus of Russia, in Feats of Horsemanship, Native Dances, etc.

8. **Johnny Baker**, Celebrated Young American Marksman.

9. **A Group of Mexicans** from Old Mexico, will illustrate the use of the Lasso, and perform various Feats of Horsemanship.

10. **Racing Between Prairie, Spanish and Indian Girls.**

11. **Cowboy Fun.** Picking Objects from the Ground, Lassoing Wild Horses, Riding the Buckers.

12. **Military Evolutions** by a Company of the Sixth Cavalry of the United States Army; a company of the First Guard Uhlan Regiment of His Majesty King William II, German Emperor, popularly known as the "Potsdamer Reds"; a Company of French Chasseurs (Chasseurs a Cheval de la Garde Republique Francaise); and a Company of the 12th Lancers (Prince of Wales' Regiment) of the British Army.

13. **Capture of the Deadwood Mail Coach** by the Indians, which will be rescued by "Buffalo Bill" and his attendant Cowboys. N. B. – This is the identical old Deadwood Coach, called the Mail Coach, which is famous on account of having carried the great number of people who lost their lives on the road between Deadwood and Cheyenne 18 years ago. Now the most famed vehicle extant.

14. **Racing Between Indian Boys on Bareback Horses.**

15. **Life Customs of the Indians**. Indian Settlement on the Field and "Path."

16. **Col. W. F. Cody** ("Buffalo Bill"), in his Unique Feats of Sharpshooting.

17. **Buffalo Hunt**, as it is in the Far West of North America — "Buffalo Bill" and Indians. The last of the only known Native Herd.

18. **The Battle of the Little Big Horn**, Showing with Historical Accuracy the the scene of **Custer's Last Charge**.

19. **Salute – Conclusion**

1894 PROGRAM

Overture, "Star Spangled Banner."
Cowboy Band, Wm. Sweeney, leader.

1. **Grand Review**, introducing the **Rough Riders of the World**. Indians, Cowboys, Mexicans, Cossacks, Gauchos, Arabs, Scouts, Guides, American Negroes, and detachments of fully equipped Regular Soldiers of the Armies of America, England, France, Germany, and Russia.
2. **Miss Annie Oakley**, Celebrated Shot, who will illustrate her dexterity in the use of fire-arms.
3. **Horse Race**, between a Cowboy, a Cossack, a Mexican, an Arab, a Gaucho, and an Indian, on Spanish-Mexican, Broncho, Russian, Indian, and Arabian horses.
4. **Pony Express.** A former Pony Post Rider will show how the letters and telegrams of the Republic were distributed across the immense Continent previous to the building of railways and the telegraph.
5. **Illustrating a Prairie Emigrant Train Crossing the Plains.** It is attacked by marauding Indians, who are in turn repulsed by "Buffalo Bill" and a number of Scouts and Cowboys.
6. **A Group of Riffian Arabian Horseman** will illustrate their style of horsemanship, together with native sports and pastimes.
7. **Johnnie Baker**, Celebrated Young American Marksman.
8. **Cossacks**, of the Caucasus of Russia, in feats of horsemanship, native dances, etc.
9. **A Group of Mexicans** from Old Mexico will illustrate the use of the Lasso, and perform various feats of horsemanship.
10. **Hurdle Race**, between Primitive Riders mounted on Western Broncho Ponies that never jumped a hurdle until three days before the opening of the present exhibition.
11. **Cowboy Fun.** Picking objects from the ground, lassoing wild horses, riding the buckers, etc.
12. **Military Musical Drill** by a detachment from the Seventh United States Cavalry from Fort Riley; detachment from the Fifth Royal Irish Lancers; detachment from French Dragoons of Republic Francaise; detachment from Garde Cuirassiers of His Majesty Kaiser Wilhelm II.
13. **Attack on the Deadwood Mail Coach by Indians**. Repulse of the Indians and rescue of the stage, passengers and mail by "Buffalo Bill" and his attendant Cowboys. N.B. – This is the identical old Deadwood Coach, called the Mail Coach, which is famous on account of having carried the great number of people who lost their lives on the road between Deadwood and Cheyenne 18 years ago. Now the most famed vehicle extant..

Season number 12 was played at Ambrose Park, South Brooklyn, New York. This would be the last of the long stand show efforts. A new arena was built with seating for 20,000. However, show expenses were just too high and there were some financial problems. Nate Salsbury's health problems prevented him from keeping up with his management responsibilities. Some changes took place, including adding the South American Gauchos from Argentina as the new attractions.

1894 PROGRAM
Size – 7" x 9½"
Pages – 64 numbered pages
Printed by Fless & Ridge Printing, Fifth Avenue, New York

14. **Racing Between Indian Boys on Bareback Horses.**
15. **Battle of the Little Big Horn.** Historical picture of Custer's Last Charge. Meeting and consolidation of hostile Sioux on the Little Big Horn under Sitting Bull to give battle to the United States Army then congregating under Generals Terry, Crook, Miles, Custer, Carr, Merritt, Gibbon, Forsythe, Henry, Mills, Whistler, Otis, Reno, Benteen, and others. Assembling in larger numbers than before known in Indian history, they with strategic cunning ambushed the gallant Custer and his command of 328 of the Seventh Cavalry on the 25th day of June, 1876, and the meeting, customs of camping, dances, etc., by the Sioux Indians, several of those present having been in the massacre; and the military are represented by members of the Seventh United States Cavalry, several of whom participated in the battle of Wounded Knee, 1890, between this famous regiment and the same Sioux. The horse ridden by the personator of General Custer was the favorite war horse of the late Chief, Sitting Bull.
16. **South American Gauchos** (First appearance in the United States). Riding, throwing the bolas, etc. These primitive horsemen are of Indian and Spanish descent from the interior plateaus and pampas of the Argentine.
17. **Col. W.F. Cody** ("Buffalo Bill") in his unique feats of sharpshooting at full speed.
18. **Buffalo Hunt**, as it was in the Far West of North America – "Buffalo Bill" and Indians. The last of the only known Native Herd.
19. **Attack on Settlers' Cabins** and rescue by "Buffalo Bill" and a band of Cowboys, Scouts, and Frontiersmen.
20. **Salute.**
Conclusion.

Simulated buffalo hunts by Cody and companions were indeed a thrilling feature of the show.

1895

A pivotal year for Cody and The Wild West Show. James A. Bailey, of the famous Barnum and Bailey shows, adds his expertise and experience to the enterprise. The aggressive barnstorming circus type touring is now the new agenda. Check the route sheets for a complete listing from 1895 through 1916.

The program front differs from the 1894 simply because John M. Burke, the shows publicity agent, slipped his likeness into the cowboy logo.

This program front was used for 1895, 1896, 1897, and 1898. General advertising started with the 1895 program. Interesting ads appear in the front and back portions of the program.

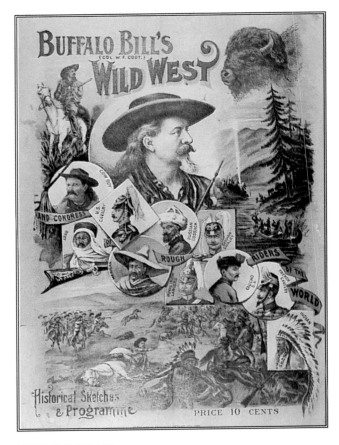

1895 PROGRAM
Size – 7" x 9½"
Pages – 64 numbered pages, 10 for advertisements
Printed by Fless & Ridge Printing Co., Fifth Avenue,
New York

1895 PROGRAM

Overture, "Star Spangled Banner,"
Cowboy Band, Wm. Sweeney, leader.

1. **Grand Review**, introducing the **Rough Riders of the World**, Indians, Cowboys, Mexicans, Cossacks, Gauchos, Arabs, Scouts, Guides, American Negroes, and detachments of fully equipped Regular Soldiers of the Armies of America, England, France, Germany, and Russia.
2. **Miss Annie Oakley**, Celebrated Shot, who will illustrate her dexterity in the use of fire-arms.
3. **Horse Race**, between a Cowboy, a Cossack, a Mexican, an Arab, a Gaucho, and an Indian, on Spanish-Mexican, Broncho, Russian, Indian, and Arabian horses.
4. **Pony Express.** A former Pony Post Rider will show how the letters and telegrams of the Republic were distributed across the immense Continent previous to the building of railways and the telegraph.
5. **Illustrating a Prairie Emigrant Train Crossing the Plains.** It is attacked by marauding Indians, who are in turn repulsed by "Buffalo Bill" and a number of Scouts and Cowboys.
6. **A Group of Riffian Arabian Horseman** will illustrate their style of horsemanship, together with native sports and pastimes.
7. **Johnnie Baker**, Celebrated Young American Marksman.
8. **Cossacks** of the Caucasus of Russia, in feats of horsemanship, native dances, etc.
9. **A Group of Mexicans** from Old Mexico will illustrate the use of the Lasso, and perform various feats of horsemanship.
10. **Hurdle Race**, between Primitive Riders mounted on Western Bronco Ponies that never jumped a hurdle until three days before the opening of the present exhibition.
11. **Cowboy Fun.** Picking objects from the ground, lassoing wild horses, riding the buckers, etc.
12. **Military Musical Drill** by a detachment from the Seventh United States Cavalry from Fort Riley; detachment from the Royal Irish Lancers; detachment from French Dragoons of Republic Francaise; detachment from Garde Cuirassiers of His Majesty Kaiser Wilhelm II.
13. **Attack on the Deadwood Mail Coach by Indians.** Repulse of the Indians and rescue of the stage, passengers and mail by "Buffalo Bill" and his attendant Cowboys.
    N.B. – This is the identical old Deadwood Coach, called the Mail Coach, which is famous on account of having carried the great number of people who lost their lives on the road between Deadwood and Cheyenne 19 years ago. Now the most famed vehicle extant.
14. **Racing Between Indian Boys on Bareback Horses.**
15. **Ten Minutes with the Rough Riders of the World.**
16. **Col. W.F. Cody** ("Buffalo Bill") in his unique feats of sharpshooting at full speed.
17. **Buffalo Hunt**, as it was in the Far West of North America – "Buffalo Bill" and Indians. The last of the only known Native Herd.
18. **Attack on Settlers' Cabins** and rescue by "Buffalo Bill" and a band of Cowboys, Scouts, and Frontiersmen.
19. **Salute.**
    Conclusion.

WILD WEST SHOW PROGRAMS

1896

The circus influence has now become firmly entrenched on Cody and The Wild West. The side show or annex now is a regular part of the show. One may be surprised to know that a female impersonator named Harry St. Julian was in his second season with Buffalo Bill's Annex.

Charles R. Hutchinson of J. A. Bailey's staff compiled and published the first route book for Cody's Wild West. This 1896 route book is a real treasure. It is full of information about the show and personnel. Many fine photos are also included. Daily entrees of the shows engagements are enlightening and fascinating.

Route books have always been eagerly pursued by circus collectors. This group of collectors have saved more Wild West material than any other collecting group.

The 1896 program of events is identical to the 1895.

1896 PROGRAM
Cover – Same as 1895
Size – 7" x 9½"
Pages – 64 numbered pages, 12 for advertisements
Printed by Fless & Ridge Printing Co., Fifth Avenue, New York

1897

John M. Burke was a masterful publicity agent and the show's general manager. He stated the 1897 tour, "Will be celebrated for the excellence of the military features, and the recognition governments, states, and cities, through their martial organizations, are giving to the mission of the Buffalo Bill's Wild West in the entranced interest taken in primitive sports and the acquirement of equestrian skill."

This season will also be noted for the successful inauguration of the Chicago Colosseum, then the largest arena in the world, erected on the Wild West's Chicago Fair campgrounds.

1897 PROGRAM
Cover – Same as 1895
Size – 7" x 9½"
Pages – 64 numbered pages, 10 for advertisements
Printed by Fless & Ridge Printing Co., Fifth Avenue, New York

1897 PROGRAM

Overture, "Star Spangled Banner,"
Cowboy Band, Wm. Sweeney, leader.

1. **Grand Review**, introducing the **Rough Riders of the World,** Indians, Czikos, Cowboys, Mexicans, Cossacks, Gauchos, Arabs, Scouts, Guides, and detachments of fully equipped Regular Soldiers of the Armies of America, England, Germany, and Russia.
2. **U.S. Artillery Drill** by Veterans from Capt. Thorpe's Battery D, Fifth Regiment, U. S. Artillery.
3. **Miss Annie Oakley**, Celebrated Shot, who will illustrate her dexterity in the use of firearms.
4. **Horse Race**, between a Cowboy, a Cossack, a Mexican, an Arab, a Gaucho, and an Indian on Spanish-Mexican, Broncho, Russian, Indian, and Arabian horses.
5. **Pony Express.** A former Pony Post Rider will show how the letters and telegrams of the Republic were distributed across the immense Continent previous to the building of railways and the telegraph.
6. **Illustrating a Prairie Emigrant Train Crossing the Plains**. It is attacked by marauding Indians, who are in turn repulsed by "Buffalo Bill" and a number of Scouts and Cowboys.
7. **A Group of Riffian Arabian Horseman** will illustrate their style of horsemanship, together with native sports and pastimes.
8. **Johnnie Baker**, Celebrated Young American Marksman.
9. **Cossacks** of the Caucasus of Russia, in feats of horsemanship, native dances, etc.
10. **A Group of Mexicans** from Old Mexico will illustrate the use of the Lasso and perform various feats of horsemanship.
11. **Hurdle Race** between Primitive Riders mounted on Western Bronco Ponies.
12. **Cowboy Fun**. Picking objects from the ground, lassoing wild horses, riding the buckers, etc.
13. **Military Musical Drill** by a detachment from the Fifth Royal Irish Lancers and a detachment from the Garde Cuirassiers of His Majesty Kaiser William II.
14. **Sixth U.S. Calvary**. Veterans from Col. Sumner's celebrated Regiment at Fort Myer, Va., in military exercises and an exhibition of athletic sports and horsemanship.
    NOTE — The men will wear the Campaign Uniforms adopted by the U. S. Army on the frontier. The horses are Western Range Bronco Horses, used in this manner for the first time in history, after only two weeks handling at Ambrose Park. The Army and National Guard use the "American" horse.
15. **Attack on the Deadwood Mail Coach by Indians**. Repulse of the Indians and rescue of the stage, passengers and mail by "Buffalo Bill" and his attendant Cowboys.
16. **Racing Between Indian Boys on Bareback Horses.**
17. **Five Minutes with the Rough Riders of the World.**
18. **Indian War Dances.**
19. **Col. W.F. Cody** ("Buffalo Bill") in his unique feats of sharpshooting at full speed.
20. **Buffalo Hunt,**, as it was in the Far West of North America — "Buffalo Bill" and Indians. The last of the only known Native Herd.
21. **Attack on Settlers' Cabins** and rescue by "Buffalo Bill" and a band of Cowboys, Scouts, and Frontiersmen.
22. **Salute**.
    Conclusion.

1898

Another banner season for the Wild West. There is no doubt that the 1890s were the strongest show years for Cody. The State of Nebraska honors its famous son. August 31 was "Cody Day" at the Trans – Mississippi Exposition, held in Omaha. Exposition officials, old friends, and prominent politicians paid tribute to this interesting man.

The Program of Events was basically the same as 1897 except for two features. A bevy of beautiful Rancheras, genuine and famous frontier girls in feats of daring equestrians. The cowgirls were becoming popular attractions. Also new, a color guard of the Cuban Veterans, on leave of absence in order to give their various wounds time to heal, all have fought for the flag of Cuba and will soon return to that country to act as scouts and guides, for which their familiarity with the topography of the island especially commends them.

1898 PROGRAM
Cover same as 1895
Size – 7" x 9½"
Pages – 64 numbered pages
Printed by Fless & Ridge Printing Co., Fifth Avenue, New York

1899

The 1899 program had a wonderful new front cover. Back cover advertising makes its first showing. To keep up with the times, The Battle of San Juan Hill was part of the show. Actual veterans from this engagement participated. Event No. 13 — Gymkana Race — was a curious affair, the program reads. Riders gallop, dismount, turn coat inside out, remount, gallop, dismount, light cigar, put up umbrella, mount, and come in with umbrella up and cigar lighted.

According to the 1899 route book, the show gave 341 performances at 132 different places, and traveled 11,111 miles in 200 days. It well may have been the shows most successful touring season. It also helped close out the nineteenth century.

1899 PROGRAM
Size – 7¼" x 9½"
Pages – 64 pages, plus four for advertisements
Printed by Fless & Ridge

Title page for the 1899 program

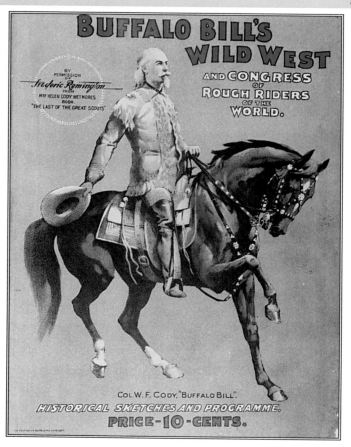

1900 PROGRAM
Size - 7⅜" x 9½"
Pages – 64 pages, plus 8 for advertisements
Published by J&H Mayer, NY, New York

Frederic Remington, the famous western artist, gave permission to Cody to use his painting of *Buffalo Bill in the Spotlight*. The original is oil on canvas (black and white). Cody colorized it to make a very attractive front cover.

Event No. 13 was changed to relay races, four teams, number one a Filipino woman vs. an Indian squaw. Number two a Mexican vs. a Filipino, number three, an Arab woman vs. an American girl, and number four a cowboy vs. a Cossack.

At the end of the list of events were a few management announcements. These appeared in most programs.

– The Management reserves the right to change program according to circumstances, occasion, or accident.

– NOTICE – In order not to disturb the audience all persons are earnestly requested to remain seated until the end.

– Any discourtesy on the part of the ushers or other employees should be at once reported to the Manager. All articles found will be sent to the Manager's office.

– Several experienced detectives are in attendance at every performance for the protection of our patrons.

– Colonel Cody uses Winchester Rifles and ammunition exclusively in all his exhibitions.

– Address all business communications pertaining to the Arenic Dept. of The Wild West Exhibition to Mr. Johnnie Baker.

Wild horse riding was always a popular feature of the Wild West show.

Title page for the 1900 program

1901

A very interesting season for The Wild West. John M. Burke describes it best, as always. "And now, to all that has made this unique entertainment the public's favorite in the past, there is this season added the Battle of TienTsin, the Rescue of the Legations in China last year, participated in by Marines of the Navies of all the world powers; the picturesque Gourkas and Sikhs and Japanese Soldiers, and an Exhibition Drill of United States Life-Saving Service men, by a real life saving crew; a band of Boers direct from DeSmet's army; a squad of the Strathcona Horse, Canada's crack regiment, direct from the South African War, and a squad of Northwest Mounted Police, the pride of the Candian frontier."

This was Annie Oakley's last campaign with Cody. There seems to be some controversy as to why she left the show. A train wreck at the end of the 1901 season may have been the reason. However, it is possible that the Butlers just had had enough of the difficult traveling life style they endured for 17 years.

Annie Oakley was gone like so many others, but Cody's Wild West Show odyssey would continue.

1901 PROGRAM
Size 7¼" x 9½"
Pages 64 pages, plus 8 for advertisements
Published by J.H. Mayer, NY, NY

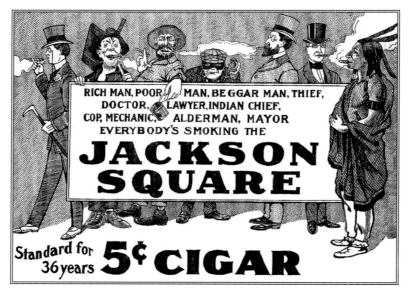

One of the interesting ads from the 1901 program

1902

Cody is 56 years old and still touring. One wonders how he was able to maintain such a hard pace. This twentieth season was a tough one. A coast to coast grueling affair that started in early May and ended in early November.

Coupled with the demands of the tour, he had to hurry to Cody, Wyoming, for the official grand opening of his Irma Hotel. There was very little time for resting, as he had to sail for England and open his show on Dec. 26, 1902, in London.

The show opening was a sad one because word arrived that Nate Salsbury, Cody's friend and most important business partner, passed away just before Christmas. This was a very difficult year for Buffalo Bill.

Staff of "Buffalo Bill's Wild West Company
Col. W.F. Cody ("Buffalo Bill"), president
Nate Salsbury, vice-president, manager
John M. Burke, general manager
Jule Keen, business manager, treasurer
Johnnie Baker, arenic director
Wm. McCune, officer of the day
Joe Esquivel, chief of cowboys
Wm. Sweeney, leader of cowboy band
M.B. Bailey, chief electrician
Harry Clarence, orator

The back cover for 1902

1902 PROGRAM
Size – 7¼" x 9½"
Pages – 64 pages, 11 for advertisements
Published by J.H. Mayer, New York, NY

1903

We find The Wild West Show in London, England, for the start of its final overseas tour. They would travel through Great Britain and much of Europe for four continuous years.

The 1903 front cover is the same as the 1902 except at the bottom the price is six pence. This program utilizes the slipped in two-page program of events type flyer. This idea had some real advantages. First the main complete program could be printed without worry of change. The inserted flyer could be changed without too much expense or extra pages added, as would be the case later. Some people just could not afford the ten-cent complete program, but might buy the insert for the one-cent cost.

So keep in mind, when you find a Buffalo Bill Wild West program and there is no list of events, you will know that it had a slipped in program of events originally.

1903 PROGRAM
Size – 7¼" x 9⅝"
Pages – 64 pages, 9 for advertisements
Printed by Partington Advertising Co., 171 Strand, London, WC

Special Edition Program
This silk covered program was issued to honor the visit of King Edward VII on Satruday, March 14, 1903.
Size – 7" x 10¼"
Pages – 4 pages
Printed & Lithographed by Weiners, Ltd., London

1904

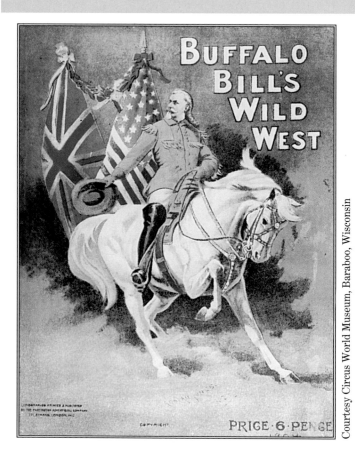

Courtesy Circus World Museum, Baraboo, Wisconsin

The second season touring England, part of Wales, and venturing into Scotland proved to be very successful. Charles Eldridge Griffin, toured with the show as part of the annex, during this four year adventure. He states in his interesting book, *Four Years in Europe With Buffalo Bill,* that while, in Glasgow, Scotland, the show did the largest week's business in the history of The Wild West as a traveling organization.

This tour was one of Cody's last triumphs.

1904 PROGRAM
Size - 7¼" x 9⅝"
Pages - 64 pages plus 9 for advertisements
Printed by Partington Advertising Co., 171 Strand, London, WC

A fine image of Cody on a twentieth century tobacco label.

1904 PROGRAM

1. **Overture,** "The Star Spangled Banner." Cowboy Band. Wm. Sweeney, director.
2. **Grand Review,** led by Col. W. F. Cody, "Buffalo Bill," introducing to the audience the Congress of Rough Riders of the World.
3. **Exhibition of the Various Methods of Riding.** Illustrated by a Cowboy, a Cossack, a Mexican, an Arab, and a North American Indian.
4. **Artillery Drill.** Presenting veterans of the U. S. Artillery, showing the muzzle-loading cannon formerly in use in contradistinction to the modern rapid-fire guns.
5. **Life Saving,** and the demonstration of the use of the mortar, carrying the life line, followed by the breeches-buoy. Illustrated with United States Government apparatus, loaned for the purpose. This number is introduced as a purely instructive one to the younger generation, that they may know the methods they can hope for and rely on if the emergency arises.
6. **Col. W.F. Cody "Buffalo Bill,"** in feats of shooting from on horseback.
7. **Pony Express Riding,** showing how the letters and telegrams were distributed from the Mississippi River to the Pacific Coast prior to the building of the trans-continental railroad and telegraph lines.
8. **A Prairie Emigrant Train Crossing the Plains,** Camping for the night; a quadrille on horseback. Attack by the Indians, who are driven off by scouts and cowboys.
9. **Military Exercises** by Veteran English Cavalrymen. Men from the firing line, who have seen service in all parts of the British Empire, and a detachment of the 10th U.S. Coloured Cavalry.
10. **Exhibition of Riding** by American Girls from the Frontier.
11. **The Horse Thief,** showing how Justice was dealt out in early days on the Frontier.
12. **Mexicans,** from the Land of the Montezumas, will exhibit their skill with the lasso.
13. **Johnny Baker,** Celebrated Young American Marksman.
14. **Custer's Last Fight,** or the Battle of the "Little Big Horn," an historic episode of the final Indian Wars, which occurred in Montana, June 25th, 1876. In this engagement the Sioux Indians annihilated the entire command of 300 men, not one man being left to tell the story. Preceding the battle the Indians are seen in camp, waiting for reinforcements who arrive; war dances ensue; look-outs announce the approach of the U. S. Cavalry; ambush is arranged; troops are surrounded and overwhelmed by superior numbers. With no hope of support, they die fighting to the last man.
15. **A Group of Arabs and Japanese** horsemen in native sports and pastimes.
16. **Cowboy Fun.** Picking objects from the ground, lassoing wild horses, and riding the Bucking Broncho. This is the most severe test of horsemanship known in equestrianism; the spectator must understand that the animals are untamed and the rider is contesting with an unknown quantity.
17. **Cossacks,** from the Caucasus of Russia, in feats of horsemanship.
18. **Veterans** from the 6th U. S. Cavalry, in Military Exercises and Practice Exhibition. NOTE. — The men wear the uniforms adopted by the U. S. Army on the frontier. The horses are from the Western range, and were used for the first time by the Buffalo Bill Wild West, thus bringing their availability to the attention of the Military Market. Previously, the English and U. S. Army adhered to the English and American horse, in distinction to the Spanish-American horse. Their remarkable adaptability for this work is apparent to all.
19. **Attack on the Deadwood Mail Coach By Indians;** Repulse of the Indians by Scouts and Cowboys.
20. **Racing By Indian Boys on Bareback Horses,** showing the basic seat of all perfect riding.
21. **George C. Davis, The Cowboy Cyclist,** in his Wonderful Bicycle-Leap through space, or Cycling through the air, in which he jumps on his bicycle across a chasm of 56ft., covering a distance, in the plunge, of 171ft. Owing to the highly dangerous character of this act, the management cannot guarantee that Mr. George C. Davis will make the jump in very high wind, or heavy rain.
22. **Ranch Life in the West.** A Settler's Cabin attacked by Indians, followed by
23. **A Parting Salute by the Entire Congress of Rough Riders,** led by Col. W. F. Cody, "Buffalo Bill." **Finis**

1905

Two years of touring Continental Europe begins in Paris, France, on April 2, 1905. After a nine week stand, the show was on the road again covering most of France. The Wild West would close the season in Marseilles on November 12 with a farewell performance witnessed by nearly 15,000 people.

This 1905 French program has 77 numbered pages, plus a few advertising pages. The inserted flyer of events is now glued in for good reason. This is commonly called tipped in.

We also find the first appearance of Devlin's Zouaves. This precision drill unit became very popular. Their lightning drills and wall scaling was fun to see. Fortunately, this act and many others were filmed in or around 1907 or 1908, so we can enjoy them and the rest of The Wild West Show to this day.

A fine video cassette of The Wild West Show can be purchased from The Buffalo Bill Historical Center in Cody, Wyoming.

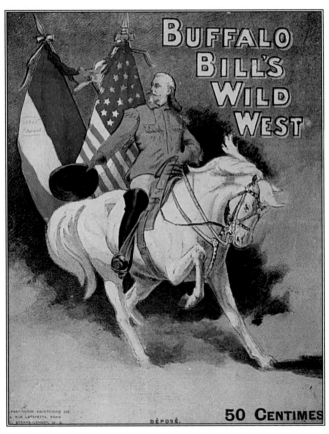

1905 PROGRAM
Size – 7¼" x 9"
Pages – 77 numbered pages, 5 for advertisements
Printed by Partington Advertising Co., 14 Rue Lafayette, Paris, 171 Strand, London, W.C.

Title page for the 1905 French program

1906

1906 PROGRAM

Translation (from the Italian)

1. **Symphony** "The Star-Spangled Banner", a piece of music preformed by the Cowboy Orchestra and directed by William Sweeney, the director of the orchestra.
2. **Big Magazine** (or review), directed by **W.F. Cody** (Buffalo Bill) he presents to the audience his Congress of "Rough Riders of the World." Indians from the Brule Tribe and their chief "Blue Shield"; Indians from the Cheyenne Tribe and their chief "Hard Target"; from the Arrapahoe Tribe and their chief "Black Heart"; the Indian Police and their chief "Lonely Bear"; "Iron Tail", chief warrior; American Cowboys and their chief "Cy Compton"; the American Cavalry; the English Cavalry; Mexicans and their chief "Oropeza"; Arabs; Japanese; young Indians, Indian squaws; Western Girls; The 6th Regiment of the American Cavalry; Colonel W. F. Cody "Buffalo Bill" the last survivor of the great explorers.
3. **Calvary Exercises:** Cowboys, Cossacks, Mexicans, Arabs, and Indians from North America, the most expert riders will give us an idea of all the different ways that those different people get on and ride horses.
4. **A Convoy of Emigrants That Go Across the Plains**; a nocturnal stopping; Far West amusements; quadrille on horseback; the attack of the Red Skins, and the repulse by the Explorers and the Cowboys.
5. **Colonel W.F. Cody** (Buffalo Bill) in his notable exercises of shooting from horseback.
6. **The Pony Express and His Horse Rider.** An interesting reconstruction of the way the dispatch service was, the delivery of letters from Mississippi to the Pacific Ocean, before the construction of the Railway Trans-Continental and the Telegraph lines.
7. **Big Artillery Manuevers** carried out by veteran artillery men from the United States, they include interesting comparative exercises that demonstrate in a very obvious way the superiority of modern cannons rather then the old cannon breech loading system, with a fast (quick) fire.
8. **Calvary Exercises** carried out by English riders from the 10th regiment (Blacks).
9. **The Devlin Zouave**, military life of the U. S., notable for their use of weapons and for the quickness of their military marches, their marches were fast as light. They formed squares and lined up for a battle quickly, they then give a big proof of agility with the way they climbed a high wall without using a ladder.
10. **The Attack of the Deadwood Mail Coach**, by Indians, repulsed by the guides or (Leaders) and the Cowboys.

The 1906 season started where the 1905 season ended in Marseilles, France. The show also wintered in Marseilles. After nine stands in France, the show moved on to Italy in March. Two months in Italy were exceptionally successful. The show would set up in Austria, Hungary, Germany, Luxemburg, and finished in Belgium.

This wonderfully executed program would be the last of the foreign language programs. We know it was printed in Italian and German. It is assumed to have been printed in other languages as well.

James A. Bailey passed away in March of 1906. Another partner was gone, leaving Cody with many more responsibilities. Bailey's widow controlled the Bailey interest.

1906 PROGRAM
Size – 6⅞" x 9¼"
Pages – 80 pages
Published by J. Weiner

11. **Arabs and Japanese**, show their national sports and their favorite exercises.
12. **Brave Equestrian Exercises**, carried out by young riders from the Far West.
13. **Mexicans from the State of Montezuma**, throwers of the lasso and their champion "Vincenzo Oropeza," they are all very fast especially in their way of capturing animals while they are running.
14. **The Last Battle of General Custer or the Battle of "Little Big Horn"** one of the last episodes of the war against the Indians: 25, June, 1876. In this battle the Sioux annihilated General Custer's Army. Big pictures of these scenes, before the battle the Indians wait in the field for reinforcements, the reinforcements arrival is celebrated by War Dances, prelude of their big battles. The Sioux sentinels signal the camp of the approach of the U. S. Cavalry, they then attack Custer's troops. They make their withdrawal impossible, so they all desperately fight but at the end they will all die.
15. **Johnny Baker**, the famous American marksman.
16. **Horse Thieves**. The way they were treated in the past years on the frontier.
17. **Cowboys in their Amusements**; On their horses riding them very fast they bend themselves down to the ground and pick-up different objects. They catch wild horses with their lasso's, they also ride "Bucking Bronchos" untamable horses; these exercises full of audacity (very dangerous too) on wild horses could cause serious accidents.
18. **The 6th Regiment's Veterans of the U.S. Calvary** that are performing a military parade. NB. The men are wearing a uniform that they used to ware in the Far West. The horses they used are being used for the first time by Buffalo Bill's Wild West. These horses have the best qualities of any known horses of today.
19. **Cossacks from the Caucasus** they show their equestrian exercises.
20. **Races Among Young Indians Riding Horses Without a Saddle** which would demonstrate (or show) how much experience they had with horses.
21. **Far West's Life**. The attack on a cabin of a pioneer carried out by the Indians.
    Final Greetings From all the Rough Riders, Directed by Col. W. F. Cody, Buffalo Bill.

1907 & 1908

Finally back home after four long years abroad. This front cover was used for two years. Cody finds himself doing just about everything. For these two years he had no experienced working partner. We find what really interested him with regards to the actual show program — a return to a more traditional American Western group of events. However, the Cossacks were still performing and there was an event that featured Arabs and Japanese riders.

One interesting development was discovered in a letter Cody wrote to Joseph T. McCaddon, just before the season opened in Madison Square Garden. McCaddon was managing the Bailey interests in the show. The Garden had so many new large glass lights that Cody canceled his shooting act while playing in the Garden. He was convinced that all those new large lights would make his shooting number too difficult. He resumed this popular event when the show left the Garden.

The Wild West opened the 1907, 1908, 1909, and 1910 seasons in Madison Square Garden. There is no question, New York City was the Wild West's favorite place to play.

1907 PROGRAM
Size – 7⅜" x 9½"
Pages – 24 pages
Published by Courier Co., Buffalo

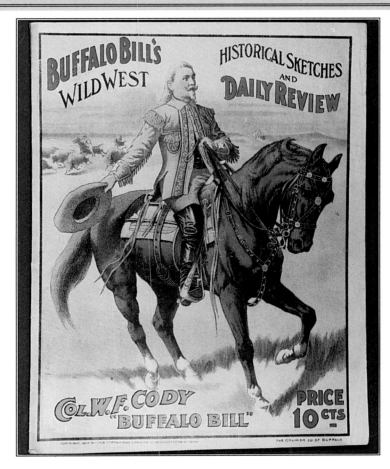

1908 PROGRAM
Cover _ Same as 1907
Size – 7⅜" x 9½"
Pages – 30 pages
Published by Courier Co., Buffalo

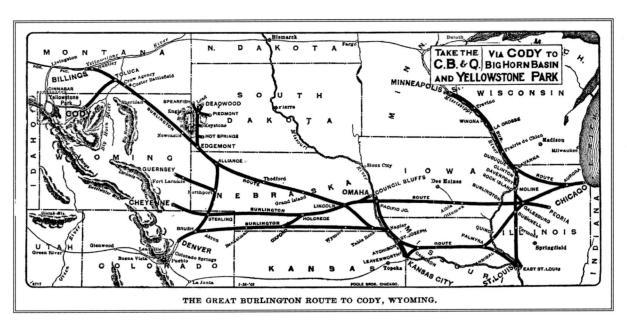

Ad from the 1907 program

1909

Cody and Gordon Lillie, Pawnee Bill, merge shows in 1909. This turned out to be beneficial to both men. Lillie paid dearly for this combination, but he enjoyed profits for four years. Cody was finally free of the Bailey group. Friction had developed after the passing of James Bailey.

This front cover is one of the author's favorites. Its color and layout are striking. The usual sketches on Buffalo Bill, Johnny Baker, cowboys, the Pony Express, wild riding Cossacks, and trained western range horses are included. New entries are a nice introduction biography about Pawnee Bill plus sketches on Rossi's Musical Elephants and the splendors of the Far East.

The passing of the American Indian is an interesting highlight of this 1909 program now called a magazine of wonders and daily reviews.

1909 PROGRAM
Size – 7½" x 9½"
Pages – 28 pages
Published by Courier Co., Buffalo

1910 & 1911

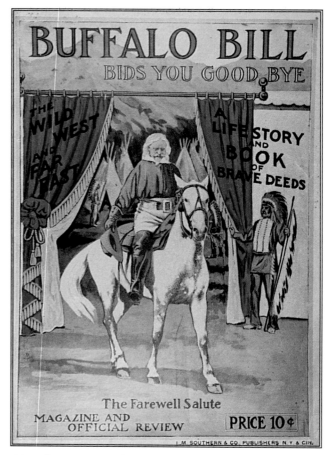

1910 & 1911 PROGRAM #1
Size – 6¾" x 10"
Pages – 28 pages
Published by I.M. Southern & Co., Publishers New York & Cincinatti

The farewell tours that never ended. Starting in 1910 the show proclaimed this would be Cody's "last appearance in your city." Unfortunately for Buffalo Bill, he was so far in debt, that he could not end his show business career.

There were two different front covers used in 1910 and 1911. Both stated "Buffalo Bill bids you good bye." "The Farewell Salute," was also on the front covers. The author believes his intentions were to tour for two years and retire. However, his finances were in turmoil, as they always seemed to be in later years. He had no choice but to carry on.

For these two years, Buffalo Bill and Pawnee Bill made a legitimate effort to play different cities.

BUFFALO BILL'S WILD WEST COMBINED WITH PAWNEE BILL'S GREAT FAR EAST

OFFICIAL PROGRAM OF WILD WEST AND FAR EAST.

NOTE:—A few plain facts due to the spectator: This is the last public personal appearance of Col. W. F. Cody, "Buffalo Bill," in your city. It is rendered notable by the Wild West's alliance with an appropriate feature in Pawnee Bill's Far East in that both adhere to original lines in the genuine character of the people and the

"Keep The Quality Up--Don't Let It Run Down,
Has Built a World's Buisness For HAMILTON-BROWN"

SHERWIN-WILLIAMS PAINTS AND VARNISHES
A RIGHT QUALITY PRODUCT FOR EVERY PURPOSE

- NOTICE -

We have the only store in the city carrying such **PIANOS** as **CHICKERING & SON, KNABE, HARDMAN, ESTEY** and **50** other makes.

WORLDS BEST ANGELUS, ANTITONE and other players
(See ad on other page)

VICTOR AND COLUMBIA TALKING MACHINES $10.00 to $500.00

Standard Music at 5 cents copy, 7 for 25 cents.

CAMPBELL & GETTMAN

HOYT BLOCK - NEW CASTLE, PA. - ON THE DIAMOND

BETTER SEE US

Jamestown, N. Y., June 25, Meadville, Pa., June 27, Newcastle, Pa., June 28.

Title page for the tip-in program for the 1910 and 1911 programs

1910 & 1911 program #2.

This small poster type stamp was affixed to most of the 1910 and 1911 promotional paper.

1912 & 1913

The *Pioneer Scouts*, a book of border life, is the new heading for 1912. The farewell salute is gone. A note at the beginning of this program explains Cody's new role. As long as Father Time permits, Col. Cody will continue in managerial direction and supervision with his partner Major Gordon W. Lillie, "Pawnee Bill."

1912 was a complete season of touring. 1913 was the end for this team of Wild West heroes, because Cody could not cover a loan. The show was closed in Denver, Colorado, on July 23, 1913. The show equipment was sold at auction there and this must have broken Cody's heart.

This front cover was used for both years. The tip in official program of events with advertising, has a very nice Indian logo.

1912 & 1913 PROGRAM
Size – 7¼" x 9½"
Pages – 20 pages
Published by Courier Co.

1912 & 1913 PROGRAM

Overture. "The Star Spangled Banner," by the Cowboy Band. Prof. William Sweeney, Musical Director.

First Episode — **A Grand Review**, wherein the Wild West and Far East join in a display of costumes and color, tribes and types of peoples from both sides of the globe. The Bronze Natives of two hemispheres ride side by side, while many nations contribute men and animals to an interesting possession in Amity of a World's Ethnological Congress, immediately followed by the

Second Episode — **The World's Roughriders.** Introducing equestrian experts from everywhere — Sioux, Cheyenne Indians, Cowboys, Mexicans, Cingalese, Scouts, Guides, Veteran Members of the U. S. Cavalry, a Group of Wild West Girls, Bedouin Arabs, Japanese, and Russian Cossacks.

Third Episode — **Six-Horse Team Work.** The world-conquering six horse dapple gray team, victors in the London and other International Horse Shows, equipped with harness, trappings and wagon as when commended for their deserved triumph by His Imperial Majesty (the late King Edward VII) will be introduced — The Vin-Fiz Company's Prize Winning Blue Ribbon Grays.

The size of the **Unrestricted Arena** gives full scope to the celebrated "Whip" Billy Wales, to illustrate his hypnotic control over these chaffing equine giants in every possible evolution that "magic touch," as a reinsman, permits. Their introduction shows the progressive breeding of a "roadster-action-draft-horse," and a contrast to the once dependent factors, the Mule and the Old ox Teams.

Fourth Episode — **U.S. Artillery Drill.** Showing the old muzzle-loading methods. These guns are relics of the Civil War, and give a lesson in contrasts to the present Rapid-fire breech-loading guns.

Fifth Episode — **A Group of Mexicans** from Old Mexico will illustrate the use of the lasso and expert horsemanship.

Sixth Episode — **An International Military Tournament and Musical Ride,** introducing the cavalry, uniforms, equipment, and drapeau of various countries in concerted maneuvers, with all their National Emblems saluting the White Flag of Peace.

Seventh Episode — **The Stagecoach and Pony Express.** A contrast to the modern Pullman car will be seen, in the then specially invented vehicles for luxury of travel — the Overland Stagecoach, treasure and passenger mode of transportation, which en route, passes its successor as a mail medium — The Pony Express. In both these utilities Col. Cody was actively engaged as driver and rider, when these perilous occupations were most important factors in communication and in which thrilling adventures, risks, and dangers were daily encountered. A faithful portrayal will be presented of the "**Old Concord**" and "**Lone Horseman**" in the Old Overland Trail.

Eighth Episode — **Mr. Johnny Baker.** The American Marksman.

Ninth Episode — **The Far East.** A collection of Oriental peoples have been recruited from around the globe to give contrast in personality, character, costumes, habits, dances and merry-making antics; of feats of Oriental diversions and in a merry melange of Malaysian jollifications.

Cingalese, Dahomians, Siamese, Australian Boomerang Throwers, Hindoo Fakirs, Wonder Workers, Whirling Dervishes, will display the holiday traits and frolics of their homeland. **Ameen Abou Hammed's Troupe of Arabs** will display their dexterity in athletic feats, as will the Japanese and Samalis; the graceful group of **Boris Fridkin's Whirlwind Russian Peasant Dancers** will give an idea of the vim, vigor, and rhythm of the Muscovite "Light Fantastic"; **Max Gruber's Wonderful Elephant Act**, participated in by **A Most Astounding Sextette,** in conjunctive mental and physical action — **The Siamese Elephant "Minnie,"** a thoroughbred stallion, "**Excelsior,**" a sprightly pony, "**Peacock,**" a dog, and **Max Gruber** and **Miss Gruber** execute a variety of different exploits that for their approach to the marvelous — will speak for themselves.

Tenth Episode — **Russian Cossacks.** Wild-riding Cossacks, from the Caucasus of Russia, will present their reckless feats of horsemanship.

Eleventh Episode — **Captain J.S. Melton's Muncie Zouves.** Manual of arms and lightning drill, concluding with an exhibition of wall scaling, illustrating the usefulness of the citizen soldier in case of war.

Twelfth Episode — **The Fox Hunt.** The old cross-country Fox Hunt, with Gerner and Kenny's thoroughbred Hurdle-jumping Prize Winners, following the hounds after Reynard, ending with a High-jumping Contest between the blue ribbon pony "Stayaway" (record 32 feet water jump) and Fred Gerner, the celebrated all-round athlete, and his dog "Bennie."

Thirteenth Episode — **Football on Horseback.** The newest form of equestrian sport, played between groups of Indians and cowboys, under special rules — an exciting contest in saddle skill — a novelty seen with this exhibition for the first time in any arena.

Fourteenth Episode — **Pioneer Events in Frontier Days. Indian Life in Reality. Struggle in Conquering the Continent.** A connected story in animated tableau of the red aborigines of America and the advance guard of the white settlers will be depicted. This will introduce a delegation of real Indians from various Sioux tribes in their primitive conditions, in the chase, garbed in their picturesque native fashions, style of travel, making camp, home life, sports, pastimes, and methods of trailing an enemy by scouts, war dancing, breaking camp, and **on the Warpath.**

The Wagon Train. While the red warriors are following the trail the scene changes and the White Settlers appear with a train of "Prairie Schooners," drawn by the then prevalent style of transportation, the Old Ox and Mule Teams, their saddle ponies, pack horses, burros, and a medley of household and camp equipment, wending their way guardedly across the continent. They go into camp; park the train for defense; picket the stock, happy that no sign of enemies has been discovered by the outriders; enter with joyous spirit into the little merry-makings, frolics, gambols, and conviviality that past immunity from danger has inspired. No dancing floor available, the exuberance of the lads and lassies for that old social treat, find vent in a dashing, yet graceful indulgence in an **Old-Time Quadrille on Horseback.** The wily redskin, skilled in the art of concealment, is on the trail, surveys the conditions without disturbing confidence until, like lightning from a clear sky, he pounces on his prey, resulting in a vivid picture of the most nerve trying adventure of **Frontier Days, The Attack on an Emigrant Train.**

Fifteenth Episode — **Cowboy Fun.** Picking objects from the ground while riding at full speed; throwing the lariat and riding the wild bucking horses.

Sixteenth Episode — **U.S. Calvary Drill.** Veteran members of the Sixth U. S. Calvary in military exercises, athletic sports, and horsemanship, mounted on Western range horses.

Seventeenth Episode — **The Final Salute.** A General Assembly of the Roughriders of the World side by side will bear close inspection, as retiring in a Musical March they give the audience the **Final Friendly Salute.**

1914 & 1915

1914 PROGRAM
Size – 7" x 10"
Pages – 14 pages
Published by F.C. Bonfils & H.H. Tammen
Simulated Autograph

Col. Cody tours with the Sells-Floto Circus. The owners of this show had made that loan to Cody the year before, so now, because of financial problems and money owed, Buffalo Bill found himself the drawing card for another show. These had to be difficult years for Buffalo Bill. He had no real say with regards to running this show plus his health was quickly declining.

The record shows he made appearances at all the touring stops for these two years. He somehow got out of his money problems with the Sells-Floto owners and was finally free after the 1915 season.

These two programs are mainly circus oriented with solid information on Cody and his life.

Vaqueros may have been the finest riders and ropers with the Wild West show.

1915 PROGRAM
Size – 7" x 10"
Pages – 14 pages
Published by F.C. Bonfils & H.H. Tammen

1916

Buffalo Bill's final campaign was with The 101 Ranch Wild West Show. The tipped in program title reads, "Miller and Arlington Wild West Show Company presents Buffalo Bill (Himself) and 101 Ranch and the Military Pageant Preparedness." Keep in mind the country was about to enter World War I.

One very absorbing aspect of this program is the excellent report with photos and map of the Mexican raid on Columbus, New Mexico. This attack took place on March 8, 1916. Event no. 16 of this show was the reenactment of the Battle of Columbus, New Mexico showing Pancho Villa's attack. Men direct from Columbus from the 7th,

12th, 13th, and 14th Cavalry were performing with the show.

The back cover is interesting because Cody advertised the use of his TE Ranch in Ishawooa, Wyoming, for tourists, opening after June 1, 1916. This was about 29 miles southwest of Cody, Wyoming. In an attempt to alleviate his financial problems he opened his beloved ranch to unknown tourists.

It is fitting that the final program mentions Buffalo Bill as an institution. "He belongs to the history of the United States, and no story of our American West would be complete without a record of his participation in it."

Reproduced by permission of the 101 Ranch logo copyright holder Jimmie Gibbs Munroe

1916 PROGRAM
Size – 7¼" x 9½"
Pages – 12 full plus a 4 page tip-in
Published by The Harrison Press, Philadelphia

Spend a Few Weeks in the Mountains with Buffalo Bill

TE RANCH

Ishawooa, Wyoming

COL. W. F. CODY, Owner

Buffalo Bill's Own Home Place Open to Tourists for First Time After June 1st, 1916.

OPEN YEAR AROUND

Fishing within ten minutes walk of the ranch house. Best big game district in the United States, 35 miles from ranch. Good hunting within few hours' ride. Near Yellowstone Park.

A Genuine Western Ranch—Not a Resort

One and two-room cabins for guests.   Also housekeeping cabins.

Address all communications to

F. H. GARLOW, Mgr.   **CODY, WYOMING**

Back cover ad for Cody's own TE Ranch

PHOTOGRAPHY

PLATE 1
Signed, to sister Julia, from W. F. Cody.
Julia was Cody's best lifelong friend.
CDV – 2½" x 4½"
c. 1871

Photography is without a doubt the most popular area of Cody collecting. Buffalo Bill may very well have been the most photographed man of his day. The early images of Cody and his contemporaries form a unique American historical record.

In the 1870s carte-de-visites were very popular. These small photo cards are about 2½" x 4½" in size. Cody first used this form of photography to publicize his career as a stage actor. An early newspaper account mentions Cody handing out these small photo cards to ladies in the audience. There seems to be a reasonable supply of Cody CDVs.

By the mid 1880s the cabinet or studio card was the most popular photo size. These measure about 4½" x 6½" and there is an endless supply of Cody. There is no question that almost all the leading photographers wanted to photograph Buffalo Bill.

There seems to be no end to Cody photos. They came in every imaginable size. In the 1896 Wild West Show program, we find an ad by Stacy offering 100 postage stamp size photographs for $1.00. The example illustrated is Buffalo Bill. Stacy, billed himself as the official photographer for Buffalo Bill's Wild West Show. This was probably true because we find an ample supply of his photo cards in many different sizes. He also liked using Cody's simulated autograph, which has caused some problems with collectors today. Annie Oakley's simulated autograph on her cabinet cards is another concern. Please be careful.

Photographs of Cody's associates are eagerly pursued by collectors and for good reason. The likes of Annie Oakley, Texas Jack Omohundro, Sitting Bull, Buck Taylor, Red Shirt, Lillian Smith, Doc Carver, Johnny Baker, Red Cloud, Pawnee Bill, Wild Bill Hickok, Capt. Jack Crawford, and so many others should spur an interest in any avid western collector. All those wonderful images from the nineteenth century are treasures that should be collected, protected, and preserved. Let us now take a closer look at Buffalo Bill and some of his companions.

W.F. CODY PHOTOGRAPHY

PLATE 2
CDV
By Napoleon Sarony.
680 Broadway, New York.
c. 1873

PLATE 3
CDV
By Napoleon Sarony
680 Broadway, New York
c. 1875

PLATE 5
CDV
No photographer's credit
c. 1875

PLATE 4
CDV
No photographer's credit
c. 1875

PLATE 6
Image size 2¼" x 3¾"
No photographer's credit
c. 1876

PLATE 7
CDV
No photographer's credit
c. 1875

PLATE 8
Cabinet card
6½" x 4¼"
By Mosher, Chicago
c. 1878

PLATE 9
Black and white photograph
9⅝" x 7¾"
By Scott Studio
c. 1885

PLATE 10
Black and white photograph
13¼" x 10⅛"
By Elmer Chickering, Boston
c. 1885

PLATE 11
Sepia-tone
Photograph
12" x 7"
By Max Platz,
Chicago
c. 1880s

SITTING BULL & BUFFALO BILL.

PLATE 12
Cabinet card
By William
Notman & Son,
Montreal
c. 1885

PLATE 13
Cabinet card
By Napolean Sarony,
680 Broadway, New
York
c. 1886

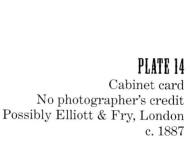

SARONY   NEW YORK

COLONEL W. F. CODY.
"Buffalo Bill."

PLATE 14
Cabinet card
No photographer's credit
Possibly Elliott & Fry, London
c. 1887

PLATE 15
Image size 4" x 5⅝"
By Lauvy,
22 King Street,
Manchester
c. 1888 autographed
by Buffalo Bill

PLATE 16
Black and white
photograph
14⅜" x 9¼"
By Lauvy,
22 King Street,
Manchester
c. 1888

Courtesy Buffalo Bill Historical Center, Cody, Wyoming

Courtesy Buffalo Bill Historical Center, Cody, Wyoming

PLATE 17
Sepia-tone photograph
Size – 12¼" x 8¼"
By Eugene Piron, Paris
Year – circa 1889 , autographed by Buffalo Bill

PLATE 18
Cabinet card
By Brisbois
of Chicago
c. 1893
simulated
autograph
printed on
mount

PLATE 19
Cabinet card
By Newsboy, NY
c. 1893

PLATE 20
Cabinet card
By Prince, New York
& Washington D.C.
c. 1894

PLATE 21
Cabinet card
By Brisbois
of Chicago
c. 1895
simulated
autograph

PLATE 22
Cabinet card
By Newsboy,
New York.
c. 1895

PLATE 23
Cabinet card
By Stacy, Brooklyn
c. 1896

PLATE 24
Cabinet card
By Stacy,
Brooklyn
c. 1896

PLATE 25
Cabinet card
By Stacy,
Brooklyn
c. 1897
autographed
by Buffalo Bill

PLATE 26
Cabinet card
By Stacy,
Brooklyn
c. 1896

PLATE 27
Cabinet card
By Stacy, Brooklyn
c. 1898

PLATE 28
Photo card
5¾" x 4⅛"
Simulated autograph
c. 1898

PLATE 29
Photo card – 5¼" x 3¼"
Simulated autograph
By Stacy, Brooklyn
c. 1899

PLATE 30
Photo card – 5¼" x
3¼"
Simulated autograph
By Stacy
c. 1900

PLATE 32
Black and
white
photograph
9¼" x 7¼"
By Prince
Studio,
31 Union Square
New York
c. 1900
autographed
by Buffalo Bill

PLATE 31
Printed card
4¼" x 6⅜"
Simulated autograph
By The Courier Co.
(a Stacy photo was used)
c. 1900

PLATE 33
Black and white photograph
7⅞" x 6⅞"
By W. Rochard, Bodmin
caption at bottom of photo
"Under the patronage of the
Prince of Wales"
c. 1903

PLATE 35
Black and white
photograph
13⅞" x 10⅞"
By J.O. Hemment
c. 1907

PLATE 34
Sepia-tone photograph
7¾" x 3 ⅝"
By Modiano, Trieste
c 1906

PLATE 36
Black and white
photograph
10¾" x 7¼"
By Marccau,
624 Fifth Avenue,
New York
c. 1912

PLATE 37
Cabinet card
No photographer's
credit
c. 1914

PLATE 38

Black and white photograph
16¾" x 13½"
By C. M. Black,
St. Louis
c. 1916

Courtesy Buffalo Bill Historical Center. Cody, Wyoming

CODY'S COMPANIONS

General Sheridan was the first military man to truly understand the value of Bill Cody. He made Cody chief of scouts for the Fifth Cavalry in 1868. Collecting CDVs of military officers that were a part of Cody's frontier years is both rewarding and challenging.

PLATE 39

General Philip H. Sheridan
CDV
By Hoag & Quick's
Art Palace
100 4th Street
Cincinnati, Ohio
c. 1864

Courtesy Buffalo Bill Historical Center, Cody, Wyoming

PLATE 40

Edward Zane Carroll Judson
Cabinet card
6½" x 4¼"
By Gurney & Son, Fifth Avenue, New York
c. 1875

Edward Zane Carroll Judson, better known by his pen name Ned Buntline, introduced Bill Cody to the American public. First by writing a serial about Buffalo Bill in Street and Smith's *New York Weekly*. This serial started in December of 1869. In December 1872 Buntline talked Cody into appearing on stage and his amazing show business career was underway. Buntline also wrote several dime novels about Cody and was indeed the first to cash in on Buffalo Bill's fame and reputation.

PLATE 41

The Grand Duke Alexis of Russia
CDV
By Gurney & Son
Fifth Avenue
New York City, N.Y.
c. 1871

George Armstrong Custer and Buffalo Bill were the two principle guides during the Grand Duke's royal buffalo hunt in January 1871. The Grand Duke gave Cody gifts of jewelry and a fine fur blanket for his services. These wonderful items can be seen at the Buffalo Bill Historical Center in Cody, Wyoming.

PLATE 42
George Armstrong Custer
CDV
By Brady's National Photographic
Portrait Galleries
No. 352 Pennsylvania Avenue
Washington, D.C.
Broadway & Tenth Street
New York City, N.Y.
c. 1863

Cody guided Custer on the plains at least one time and they also spent time together during the Royal Buffalo Hunt with the Grand Duke from Russia.

Texas Jack was actually John Burwell Omohundro Jr. He was a scout for the Army and a close friend of Bill Cody. He went with Buffalo Bill to Chicago in December 1872 to join Ned Buntline and he became an actor along with Cody. By 1877 Texas Jack started his own stage acting group and unfortunately died on June 28, 1880, being only 33 years old.

PLATE 43
Texas Jack
Cabinet card
By Tipton 8 Co.,
Gettysburg, PA.
c. 1877

PLATE 44
David Franklin
 Powell
Cabinet card
By G. G. Grossfield
Lanesboro, MN.
c. 1879

Dr. Frank Powell was a contract surgeon for the Army during Cody's scouting service. The Sioux named him White Beaver and that name was used in The Wild West Show's programs. He appeared with The Wild West for several years. Powell and Cody were life-long friends as well as business partners.

Dr. W. F. Carver, Champion Rifle Shot of the World,

PLATE 46
Doc Carver
Cabinet
card
c. 1879

William Frank Carver, better known as Doc Carver, was a noted rifle shooting exhibitionist. He was Cody's first Wild West Show partner. Carver would run his own show after he and Cody parted company however he didn't even get close to Cody's success. Doc may have been a nickname given to him by his father.

Courtesy Buffalo Bill Historical Center, Cody, Wyoming

John M. Burke first associated with Cody during the stage acting days of the 1870s. He started with Cody in the first Wild West season of 1883 and would complete the 34 consecutive year run. He was loyal to Cody and was the show's general manager and considered one of the best publicity men of his day.

PLATE 45
John M. Burke
Cabinet card
By Anderson, 785 Broadway, New York
c. 1886

This noted shotgun exhibitionist was with the show in 1883 and actually was a partner in 1884. He patented the first glass target balls in our country and they are nicely designed and marked with the patent date and the Bogardus name.

PLATE 47

Captain Adam Henry Bogardus
& Sons
Cabinet card
By Eisenmann, 229 Bauery,
New York
c. 1890

PLATE 48

John Y. Nelson
Image size 3¾" x 5"
Example trimmed
No photographer's credit
c. 1880s

John Y. Nelson was another scouting companion of Cody's, and was also involved with Buffalo Bill's stage acting group. He and his Indian family were fixtures with The Wild West Show for many years. He is often shown in photos driving the Deadwood stage.

Courtesy Buffalo Bill Historical Center, Cody, Wyoming

PLATE 49

Buck Taylor
Cabinet card
By Anderson,
785 Broadway,
New York
c. 1886

Buck Taylor started with the show in 1883, and may very well have been the first cowboy billed as "King of the Cowboys." Being 6'5" tall and very handsome, he was without a doubt an exceptional example of the American cowboy.

Johnny Baker was like a son to Cody. Only Johnny Baker and John M. Burke completed the 34-year run of The Wild West Show with Buffalo Bill. In 1885 he started performing and became one of the main acts and was always popular. He founded and ran The Buffalo Bill Museum on Lookout Mountain in the mid 1920s. Baker is often referred to as Cody's "adopted son."

PLATE 50
Johnny Baker
Cabinet card
By Place,
337 West Madison St.,
Chicago
c. 1893

Sitting Bull toured with Cody's show in the summer of 1885. In doing so, he settled the question among Indians, if it was proper for them to tour with entertainment shows.

SITTING BULL.

PLATE 51
Sitting Bull
Cabinet card
By D.F. Barry,
West Superior, WI.
c. 1888

Annie Oakley

Annie Oakley can be considered the most famous Western female personality of all time. Annie was an exceptional performer and a lady in the finest meaning of the word.

PLATE 52
Show name – Annie Oakley
Maiden name – Phoebe Ann Moses
Married name – Mrs. Frank Butler
Cabinet card
By J. Wood,
208 Bowery, NY.
c. 1886

Annie made many of her own outfits and most likely was one of the periods best-dressed performers. Simulated autograph.

PLATE 53
Cabinet card
By Brisbois, Mosher Gallery,
125 State Street, Chicago
c. 1893

Sixteen touring seasons with Buffalo Bill's Wild West were done without a formal contract which depicts a special kind of relationship between Annie, husband/manager Frank Butler, and Cody. Please note simulated autograph on the Stacy card identical to the one on the Brisbois card. These simulated autographs were printed right on the mounts.

PLATE 54
Annie Oakley
Cabinet card
By Stacy, 5th Avenue and 9th
Street, Brooklyn, NY.
c. 1894

Courtesy Buffalo Bill Historical Center, Cody, Wyoming

MISS LILLIAN SMITH.
The Celebrated California Rifle Shot.
BUFFALO BILL'S WILD WEST.

PLATE 55
Lillian Smith
Cabinet card
No photographer's credit
c. 1887

The fighting chief of the Sioux nation went to England with the show in 1887 and was introduced to Queen Victoria. Red Shirt represented the Sioux with dignity and grace.

Courtesy Buffalo Bill Historical Center, Cody, Wyoming

RED SHIRT,
The Fighting Chief of the Sioux Nation.

PLATE 56
Red Shirt
Cabinet card
No photographer's credit
c. 1887

Lillian Smith joined the show in 1886 being yet a teenager, but a fine rifle shot. Billed as "The California Huntress and Champion Girl Rifle Shot." She toured in 1886, went to England in 1887, and completed the 1888 season. That seems to be her entire association with Cody's show.

PLATE 57
Larger photo
Original size 8"x 8"
By William Notman & Son,
Montreal, Canada
c. 1885

Standing: Crow Eagle, W.F. Cody, and naturalist W.H. Murray. Seated: interpreter William Halsey, Sitting Bull, and young Johnny Baker. This photo has been trimmed, but is still special.

Orapeza was considered one of the top trick ropers of all time. He was with the show in 1893 and became chief of the Mexicans by 1896, and still listed as the chief in the 1902 route book.

PLATE 58
Vincente Orapeza
Cabinet card
By Stacy, Brooklyn, NY.
c. 1894

PLATE 59
Bronco Bill Irving & Family
Cabinet card
By Anderson, NY.
c. 1890

Courtesy Buffalo Bill Historical Center, Cody, Wyoming

BRONCHO BILL (and Family.)
Cow Boy Interpreter of the Sioux. —Buffalo Bill's Wild West.

Bronco Bill was an interpreter for the Sioux and another "squaw man" like John Nelson.

This famous stage coach was with Cody in 1883 and made it all the way through to the 1913 season. It became a status symbol to ride in the Deadwood stage coach during the performance.

PLATE 60
The Deadwood stage coach
Cabinet card
No photographe's credit
c. 1887

THE FAMOUS DEADWOOD COACH.

ANDERSON.   785 BROADWAY. N.

BENNIE IRVING.
The smallest Cowboy in the World.—*Buffalo Bill's Wild West.*

PLATE 61
Bennie Irving
Cabinet card
By Anderson, NY.
c. 1890

Young Bennie Irving was billed as "The Smallest Cowboy in the World." The pictured saddle is quite interesting.

William Sweeney started with the show in the mid 1880s. By 1892, Sweeney was the leader of the Cowboy Band and remained in that position through the 1913 season.

WM. SWEENEY.

Courtesy Buffalo Bill Historical Center, Cody, Wyoming

PLATE 62
William Sweeney
Cabinet card
By Anderson, NY.
c. 1886

LITTLE BULL.
Chief of the Arapahoes.
BUFFALO BILL'S WILD WEST

Courtesy Buffalo Bill Historical Center, Cody, Wyoming

Another fine example of the American Indians. Just collecting photos of the Indians that toured with Cody would be challenging.

PLATE 63
Little Bull, Chief of the Arapahoes
Cabinet card
No photographer's credit
c. 1887

PLATE 64
Pawnee Bill & May Lillie
Cabinet card
By Swords Bro's, York, PA.
c. 1893

Pawnee Bill and his wife, May Lillie, ran a very successful Wild West Show. Pawnee Bill's Wild West would rank second, just behind Cody's, in terms of longevity and success.

Note pinback on vest. Alfred Heimer was Col. Cody's private car porter. Mrs. Heimer was Cody's personal chef.

PLATE 65
Alfred Heimer
Cabinet card
By G.F. Englund,
342 63rd Street,
Chicago
c. 1902

Ed was born in Salina, Kansas, in 1868 and followed the life of a cowboy from his early youth. He is listed in the 1902 route book and toured with the show in 1903, 1904, and 1905. Note the pinback on his cowboy scarf.

PLATE 66
Ed Phillips
Cabinet card
By A. W. Hohhof,
3510 Wallace Street, Chicago
c. 1902

MISS MAY LILLIE
WITH PAWNEE BILL'S WILD WEST

PLATE 67
May Lillie
Printed image cabinet card
By Carson & Ralston, Philadelphia
c. 1900

May Lillie was an energetic performer
and a fine target and trick shooter.
Pawnee Bill's answer to Annie Oakley.

Cy started with the show in the mid
1890s and was assistant to the chief of
cowboys in 1902. By 1908 he was chief of
the cowboys. Another fine example of
the American cowboy.

PLATE 68
Silas "Cy" Compton
Black and white photograph
9⅛" x 7½"
No photographer's credit
c. 1908

Courtesy Buffalo Bill Historical Center, Cody, Wyoming

ROUTE BOOKS, SHEETS
& SHOW ROUTES

PLATE 69
1896 ROUTE BOOK
4¾" x 7"
Pages – 282
Published by Charles R. Hutchinson
the Treasurer on the J.A. Bailey Staff
Printed by The Courier Co., Buffalo, N.Y.

This route book can also be found with a leather cover. A comprehensive listing of the show personnel and an excellent selection of photo illustrations makes this route book one of the very best available. Interesting daily show entrees through September 27, are also included. Dozens of advertisements help to make this route book fascinating.

1883 — 1916

A thesaurus is sometimes called a "treasure house of words." Route books are the thesaurus of information regarding traveling shows. Pawnee Bill gets the credit for issuing the first Wild West Show route book for his 1893 season. Cody's show put out a remarkable official souvenir route book after the 1896 season with 282 pages and more than 50 photo illustrations. This effort was the show's first and most complete route book. Later editions would contain a map with the route taken during that season.

The overseas tours that started on December 26, 1902, in London would also yield collectors three very nice route books containing maps but the lists of show personnel was eliminated. By 1907 route books were replaced with single sheet or multi-fold out route flyers. These end-of-the-touring-season route flyers come in a variety of sizes and styles.

At the start of each season and during the season, all salaried or show employees were given monthly route sheets to send to their families. Occasionally postcards were utilized for route information. The information contained within route books and on route sheets is essential to any serious collector or researcher. The names and positions of all show personnel are included in the early route books. We would, of course, expect all the performers to be listed and they are, but would not expect to see the names of dishwashers, pastry cooks, or canvasmen. The list of all the different positions is information about the show that assists us to better comprehend the magnitude of this Wild West Show enterprise.

We also find in the 1896, 1899, and 1900 route books brief descriptions of all the show seasons leading up to 1895. Each route book also contains the complete routes for each season beginning in 1895.

The author didn't locate an 1897 or an 1898 route book example, but has hopes someone may have them and would please contact him. It is possible none was ever published. There is no question that these small books, sheets, and flyers are filled with the type of data that would interest any active collector. They are truly treasure houses of show details.

The early route books also include minute descriptions of almost all touring stands. The following example from the 1896 route book is filled with wonderful and interesting information. It will give you the flavor and feel of what was written with each daily entry.

1896 ROUTE BOOK, PIQUA, OHIO

Saturday, July 4. Arrived in town at 5 a.m. Had one-half mile haul to lot, which we found to be in very bad condition, which was caused by the recent rains. Consequently all teams were doubled in going on the lot. Our own Annie Oakley was happy today; her mother, brother, three sisters, and their six children were at the show today. It was the first time they had ever seen the show and they drove 30 miles to get here. Everyone joined with Annie in trying to make things pleasant for them. We all did a little patriotic decorating today. It was especially noticeable in the dining tent; every plate was covered with flags and bunting, every plate bore a flag of our great nation except one, who, not being a native, and not having taken out his naturalization papers was not entitled to it, but nevertheless Brogan is a good fellow. Three rousing cheers were given for the Colonel at the proposal of George Burch, Chief of Cowboys. The Colonel replied with a nice little speech, which contained many good wishes and much good advice. Harry Speigle, the venerable ticket-taker at the side-show door, received an ovation as he came into the dining tent today, this being his 67th birthday and his 42nd year in the show business. Everyone wished him a continuance of good health and prosperity. Harry replied by a neat little speech, which was heartily cheered by the entire company. Taking all in all today was a great Fourth. The street-car system gave out this evening and the patrons of the night show had to walk home. Weather very warm throughout the whole day; a heavy rainstorm at 7 p.m. which continued all the evening.

Business in the afternoon big, in the evening fair. Lot, Driving Park.

Arena, 176 x 345.

OFFICIAL ROUTE

Buffalo Bill's Wild West

AND

Congress of Rough Riders of the World.

Col. W. F. CODY (Buffalo Bill),
President.

NATE SALSBURY,
Vice-Pres. & Mgr.

DATE	PLACE	STATE	RAILROADS	MILES
April 18, Sat.	Philadelphia,	Pa.	N. Y. N. H. & H.	147
" 20, Mon.	"	"	C. of N. J.	
" 21, Tue.	"	"		
" 22, Wed.	"	"	P. & R.	
" 23, Thurs.	"	"		
" 24, Fri.	"	"		
" 25, Sat.	"	"		
SUNDAY.				
" 27, Mon.	Cumberland,	Md.	B. & O.	288
" 28, Tue.	Clarksburg,	W. Va.	"	124
" 29, Wed.	Parkersburg,	"		82
" 30, Thurs.	Chillicothe,	Ohio.	B. & O. S. W.	97
May 1, Fri.	Ironton,	"	C. H. & D.	84
" 2, Sat.	Washington,	"		116
SUNDAY.				
" 4, Mon.	Cincinnati,	"		107
" 5, Tue.	"	"		
" 6, Wed.	Hamilton,	"		25
" 7, Thurs.	Richmond,	Ind.	P. C. C. & St. L.	43
" 8, Fri.	Indianapolis,	"		68
" 9, Sat.	"	"		
SUNDAY.				
" 11, Mon.	Anderson,	"	C. C. C. & St. L.	36
" 12, Tue.	Columbus,	"	P. C. C. & St. L.	127
" 13, Wed.	Louisville,	Ky.		69
" 14, Thurs.	"	"		
" 15, Fri.	Owensboro,	"	L. St. L. & T.	112
" 16, Sat.	Evansville,	Ind.	L. St. L. & T. & L. & N.	42
SUNDAY.				
" 18, Mon.	St. Louis,	Mo.	P. D. & E.	180
" 19, Tue.	"	"		
" 20, Wed.	"	"	L. E. & St. L.	
" 21, Thurs.	"	"		
" 22, Fri.	"	"		
" 23, Sat.	"	"		

1896

PLATE 70

Monthly route sheet
1896 season
Size – 3½" x 5½"

These monthly route sheets were important to show personnel simply because they were able to let their families know where to contact them as the show traveled. Most likely the route for the complete season was not completed until near the end of the season and these partial route sheets were the link to loved ones. The author believes they started with the 1895 season and were used through the 1916 season.

PLATE 71

1899 route book
Size – 3" x 6¼"
Pages – 68 pages
Compiled by George H. Gooch
Published by
The Matthews-Northrup Company
Buffalo, N.Y.

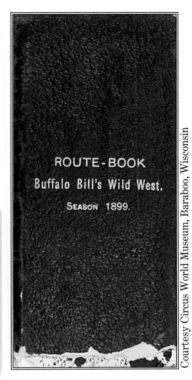

ROUTE-BOOK
Buffalo Bill's Wild West.
SEASON 1899.

Courtesy Circus World Museum, Baraboo, Wisconsin

This route book has a large foldout map with route indicated by a red line. All show personnel are included. Daily entries of the show stands are included through the September 2 date.

Show personnel and daily show entries are indicated through the September 29 date.

PLATE 72

1900 route book
Size – 3" x 6¼"
Pages – 80
Compiled by George H. Gooch
Published by Hudson-Kimberly
Kansas City, MO.

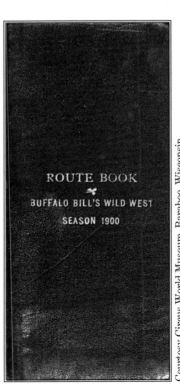

ROUTE BOOK
BUFFALO BILL'S WILD WEST
SEASON 1900

Courtesy Circus World Museum, Baraboo, Wisconsin

FROM OCEAN TO OCEAN.

Souvenir . .

BUFFALO
BILL'S
WILD WEST.

SEASON OF 1902.

Courtesy Buffalo Bill Historical Center, Cody, Wyoming

A complete list of show personnel; large - foldout map of the United States with route indicated. A brief description of the season and the official program of events is also listed. A complete print out of the season's route is included.

PLATE 73
1902 route book
Size – 3½" x 6¼"
Pages – 32
Printed by the Los Angeles
Printing Company
Los Angeles, California USA

PLATE 74
The map of the United
States tour for 1902.

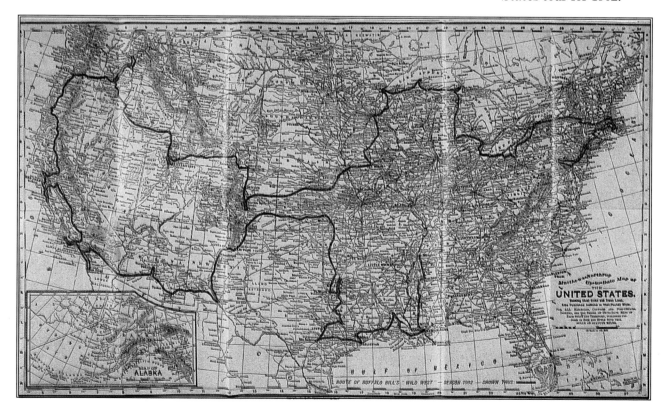

PLATE 75

1902 – 1904 route map
Size – 4⅝" x 6⅞"
Cloth covers
Map folds open to 16" x 24"
Lithographed and printed by Weiners Ltd.
London, England

The 1902 date is misleading because the first show date of this tour was December 26, 1902. The show did not tour Great Britain in 1902. The complete routes for 1903 and 1904 are listed on opposite sides of the map. Here again, we find the simulated autograph of Cody and unfortunately no show personnel are included.

BUFFALO BILL'S WILD WEST, Co.

SEASONS 1903 to 1904.

London Engagement, Dec. 26th, 1902, to April, 1903, Performances........ 172.

	1903	1904		1903	1904
Opening Days Road Season, April	13	25			
Closing Days, ,, October	23	21	No. of Miles Travelled...............	9361	10721
No. of Performances given	333	310			
No. of Performances lost	1	0	No. of Miles drawn by Horses ...	286	349
No. of Repeating stands	—	4			
No. of Stands in England	87	88	No. of Cities with Electric Cars ..	42	56
,, ,, Wales...............	8	15			
,, ,, Scotland	—	29	,, ,, ,, Horse Cars ...	12	6
3 Weeks stands	2	—			
2 ,, ,, ...	1	—	No Transportation	47	70
1 ,, ,, ...	2	3			
4 Day stands................	2	—	No. of Rainy Days	99	81
3 ,, ,, ...	3	2			
2 ,, ,, ...	6	4	No. of Cloudy Days	53	41
1 ,, ,, ...	76	123			
Total No. of Stands	95	132	No. of Clear Days............	42	28

Total No. of Stands in Great Britain...... ..223. Performances........815.

With M. B. BAILEY'S Compliments.

PLATE 76

Route postcard
Year – 1904
Standard size

This interesting postcard, with end of the seasons data, was given out by M.B. Bailey. Mr. Bailey was the electric light department superintendent for the touring Wild West Show. He was instrumental in producing the first and later route books and other route information.

Courtesy Buffalo Bill Historical Center, Cody, Wyoming

PLATE 77
1905 route map
Size – 4⅝" x 6⅞"
Cloth covers
Map folds open to 16" x 24"
Lithographed and printed
by Weiners Ltd., London, England

These route sheets can occasionally be found with notes or short letters on the back. They came in handy for writing home.

PLATE 78
Monthly route sheet
1908 season
Size – 3½" x 6"

OFFICIAL ROUTE

Buffalo Bill's Wild West

ON TOUR 1908

Date		Town	State	Railroad	Miles
June	29	Scranton	Pa.	D. & H.	19
June	30	Binghamton	N. Y.	D. & H.	98
July	1	Oneonta	N. Y.	D. & H.	61
July	2	Schenectady	N. Y.	D. & H.	64
July	3	Holyoke	Mass.	B. & A., B. & M.	128
July	4	Springfield	Mass.	B. & M.	8
July	6	Providence	R. I.	N.Y.,N.H. & H.	106
July	7	Worcester	Mass.	N.Y.,N.H. & H.	44
July	8	Lowell	Mass.	B. & M.	45
July	9	Lawrence	Mass.	B. & M.	14
July	10	Haverhill	Mass.	B. & M.	7
July	11	Biddeford	Me.	B. & M.	67
July	13	Portland	Me.	B. & M.	15
July	14	Waterville	Me.	M. C.	82
July	15	Bangor	Me.	M. C.	55
July	16	Lewiston	Me.	M. C.	103
July	17	Dover	N. H.	M. C., B. & M.	83
July	18	Manchester	N. H.	B. & M.	43
July	20	Concord	N. H.	B. & M.	18
July	21	White River Jc.	Vt.	B. & M.	70
July	22	Montpelier	Vt.	C. V.	63
July	23	Burlington	Vt.	C. V.	25
July	24	Rutland	Vt.	Rut.	67
July	25	Saratoga Spgs.	N. Y.	D. & H.	63
July	27	Utica	N. Y.	D. & H., N.Y.C.	100
July	28	Oswego	N. Y.	N. Y. C.	84
July	29	Syracuse	N. Y.	N. Y. C.	40
July	30	Auburn	N. Y.	N. Y. C.	27
July	31	Rochester	N. Y.	N. Y. C.	77
Aug.	1	Niagara Falls	N. Y.	N. Y. C.	78

Permanent Business Offices:
**Bailey Building, 27 E. 22d Street
NEW YORK CITY, N. Y.**

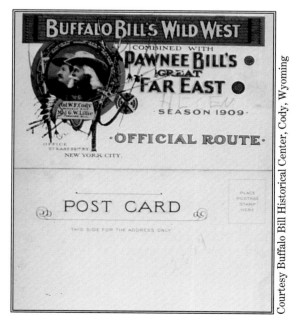

Courtesy Buffalo Bill Historical Center, Cody, Wyoming

The author's favorite route card effort. This postcard folded to close and contained wonderful logo. The opposite side was a monthly route, which could be sent to families and friends.

PLATE 79
1909 route postcard
Standard postcard size

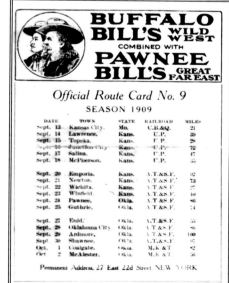

BUFFALO BILL'S WILD WEST
COMBINED WITH
PAWNEE BILL'S GREAT FAR EAST

Official Route Card No. 9
SEASON 1909

DATE		TOWN	STATE	RAILROAD	MILES
Sept.	13	Kansas City.	Mo.	C.B.&Q.	21
Sept.	14	Lawrence.	Kans.	U. P.	39
Sept.	15	Topeka.	Kans.	U. P.	28
Sept.	16	Junction City.	Kans.	U. P.	72
Sept.	17	Salina.	Kans.	U. P.	47
Sept.	18	McPherson.	Kans.	U. P.	45
Sept.	20	Emporia.	Kans.	A.T.&S. F.	82
Sept.	21	Newton.	Kans.	A.T.&S. F.	73
Sept.	22	Wichita.	Kans.	A.T.&S. F.	27
Sept.	23	Winfield.	Kans.	A.T.&S. F.	40
Sept.	24	Pawnee,	Okla.	A.T.&S. F.	46
Sept.	25	Guthrie.	Okla.	A.T.&S. F.	54
Sept.	27	Enid.	Okla.	A.T.&S. F.	55
Sept.	28	Oklahoma City	Okla.	A.T.&S. F.	98
Sept.	29	Ardmore.	Okla.	A.T.&S. F.	100
Sept.	30	Shawnee.	Okla.	A.T.&S. F.	97
Oct.	1	Coalgate.	Okla.	M.K.&T.	82
Oct.	2	McAlester.	Okla.	M.K.&T.	56

Permanent Address, 27 East 22d Street, NEW YORK

Courtesy Buffalo Bill Historical Center, Cody, Wyoming

OFFICIAL ROUTE—1910

BUFFALO BILL'S WILD WEST COMBINED WITH PAWNEE BILL'S GREAT FAR EAST.

No. 7

DATE		TOWN	STATE	R. R.	MILES
Aug.	1	Decatur	Ill.	Wabash	120
	2	Clinton	"	I. C.	22
	3	Mendota	"		98
	4	Rockford	"	C. M. & St. P.	54
	5	Janesville	Wis.		34
	6	Madison	"		41
Aug.	7 }	Milwaukee	Wis.	C. M. & St. P.	82
	8 }	"			
	9	Fon du Lac	"	Soo.	66
	10	Neenah-Menasha	"	"	30
	11	Stevens Point	"	"	63
	12	Chippewa Falls	"	"	108
	14	New Richmond	"	"	66
Aug.	15	St. Paul	Minn.	Soo.	40
	16	Minneapolis	"	N. P.	10
	17	Duluth	"	"	152
	18	Little Falls	"	"	150
	19	Fergus Falls	"	"	104
	20	Crookston	"	G. N.	112
Aug.	22 }	Winnipeg	Man.	G. N.-C. P.	158
	23 }	"			
	24	Grand Forks	N. D.	C. P.-G. N.	152
	25	Fargo	"	G. N.	77
	26	Jamestown	"	N. P.	93
	27	Bismark	"		101

It is interesting to note that even these simple route sheets were given nice touches of artwork. Collecting at least one from each season is a challenge.

PLATE 80

Monthly route
sheet
1910 season
Size – 3½" x 6"

PLATE 81

1910 & 1911 route flyer
Cover (above right)
Back (right)
5¼" x 7¼", closed
14¼" x 21", opened
Printed by
I.M. Southern & Company

One side has a listing of all the show personnel. The other side has the routes for 1910 and 1911 plus the front and back covers. Two show lithographs are shown plus a brief description of the touring difficulties of the two seasons.

Reproduced by permission of Ringling Bros. Barnum & Bailey Combined Shows Inc.

PLATE 82
1914 route flyer
4" x 9", closed
8" x 9", opened

Photo shows flyer open. The other side is the remainder of the 1914 season. The owners of The Sells-Floto Circus also owned Denver's largest newspaper and most likely printed their own paper related material.

PLATE 83
Route sheet
1916 season
3½" x 6"

Reproduced by permission of Jimmie Gibbs Munroe

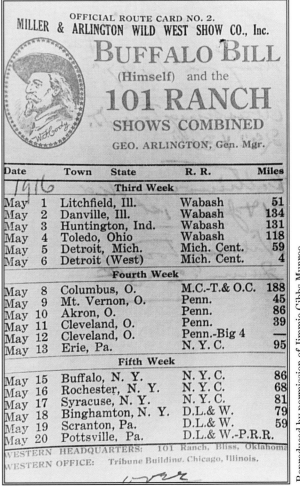

Date	Town	State	R. R.	Miles
		Third Week		
May 1	Litchfield, Ill.		Wabash	51
May 2	Danville, Ill.		Wabash	134
May 3	Huntington, Ind.		Wabash	131
May 4	Toledo, Ohio		Wabash	118
May 5	Detroit, Mich.		Mich. Cent.	59
May 6	Detroit (West)		Mich. Cent.	4
		Fourth Week		
May 8	Columbus, O.		M.C.-T.& O.C.	188
May 9	Mt. Vernon, O.		Penn.	45
May 10	Akron, O.		Penn.	86
May 11	Cleveland, O.		Penn.	39
May 12	Cleveland, O.		Penn.-Big 4	—
May 13	Erie, Pa.		N. Y. C.	95
		Fifth Week		
May 15	Buffalo, N. Y.		N. Y. C.	86
May 16	Rochester, N. Y.		N. Y. C.	68
May 17	Syracuse, N. Y.		N. Y. C.	81
May 18	Binghamton, N. Y.		D.L.& W.	79
May 19	Scranton, Pa.		D.L.& W.	59
May 20	Pottsville, Pa.		D.L.& W.-P.R.R.	

WESTERN HEADQUARTERS: 101 Ranch, Bliss, Oklahoma.
WESTERN OFFICE: Tribune Building, Chicago, Illinois.

Reproduced by permission of Jimmie Gibbs Munroe

The 101 ranch route sheets were for three week segments. This example has a special feature as Buffalo Bill (himself) wrote the continuation of the route on the back.

PLATE 84

Monthly route card
1915 season
4¾" x 6¼"

This Sells-Floto version was printed in two colors and called a route card. Almost all the larger outdoor traveling shows utilized the route sheet or card system.

PLATE 85

Annual route card
1916 season
Size – 7⅞" x 10"
Single sheet, printed on both sides

No printer's credit listed, however, it may have been done by the Harrison Press, Philadelphia, PA.
The back side has the remainder of the 1916 route plus a list of the executive staff for the Miller & Arlington Show. One other interesting note is that during August the show played in Wrigley Field in Chicago, which today is considered by most Chicago Cub fans as a historical landmark.

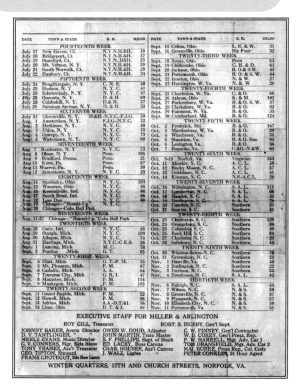

WILD WEST SHOW ROUTES

1883

The Buffalo Bill Wild West Show was organized as an outdoor show in 1883, and opened in Omaha, Nebraska, in May, and traveled through the states of Nebraska, Iowa, Illinois, Kentucky, Indiana, Pennsylvania, New York, Connecticut, Massachusetts, and Rhode Island, giving the performance in fair grounds with the exception of Coney Island, where a temporary stand was erected, and they remained there five weeks. It was at this place that the first horse race was ever given by electric light.

1884 – 1885

Opened in May in St. Louis, Missouri, went through the eastern states and Canada. October 31 took a boat down the Mississippi River bound for New Orleans. The boat was wrecked at Rodney, Mississippi, and everything was lost except horses. Opened in New Orleans Christmas week, and closed April 1, 1885, then worked north through the central and southern states, including Michigan and Wisconsin, and closed October 31 at St. Louis, Missouri.

1886

Opened in St. Louis in May, and then played through to New York, where they opened a season at Erastina, Staten Island, in June, and remained until September 30 then opened a winter season at Madison Square Garden Thanksgiving eve, and closed Washington's Birthday, 1887. During their stay at the Garden they lost sixteen buffaloes from lung trouble.

1887

April first, sailed on the steamer **State of Nebraska** for London, England, where they remained a season of six months, and then went to Manchester, England, for six months, and closed April 30, 1888; then gave one performance at Hull, England, in the afternoon and sailed the same night for New York City on the steamer **Persian Monarch**.

1888

Opened the season at Erastina, Staten Island, on Decoration Day, and remained six weeks; then went to Philadelphia, Baltimore, and Washington, and closed at the State Fair in Richmond, Virginia, October 22.

1889 – 1890

Sailed April 12 on the steamer **Persian Monarch** for Havre, France, where a season of six months was played at Paris. They then toured through France, Spain, Italy, Germany, and Austria, and closed in the City of Strasburg, Alsace Lorraine, October 29, 1890. Some of the troupe returned to the United States, while others remained there.

1891 – 1892

Opened in Stuttgart, April 15, and played through Germany, Belgium, and England; closed at Croyden, England, October 31. Opened again at Glasgow, Scotland, November 15, and remained until April 15, 1892. May 9 opened again in London, and closed October 27, 1892, and sailed on the steamer **Mohawk**, October 29, for New York City.

1893

This was the World's Fair season. There was a grand stand erected at 62nd and 63rd streets and Grace Avenue, Chicago, with a seating capacity of 20,000 people. It was opened April 26, and closed October 31, making 186 days of continuous performance; not one show was missed, and it closed the most successful season known in show history.

1894

Opened at Ambrose Park, Brooklyn, New York, May 12, and closed October 6. One show was missed September 19, on account of heavy rain. No Sunday shows were given, making a run of 126 days.

Buffalo Bill's Wild West Source 1896 Route Book

SEASON 1895   SOURCE 1896 ROUTE BOOK

	APRIL	MAY	JUNE	JULY	AUGUST	SEPTEMBER	OCTOBER	NOVEMBER	
1		Philadelphia, Pa.	New Haven,Conn.	Lowell, Mass.	Malone, N.Y.	SUNDAY	Baltimore, Md.	Atlanta, Ga.	1
2		Philadelphia, Pa.	SUNDAY	Lowell, Mass.	Ogdensburg, N.Y.	Pittsburg, Pa.	Washington, D.C.	Atlanta, Ga.	2
3		Philadelphia, Pa.	Hartford, Conn.	Nashua, N.H.	Watertown, N.Y.	Pittsburg, Pa.	Washington, D.C.	Atlanta, Ga.	3
4		Philadelphia, Pa.	Norwich, Conn.	Concord, N.H.	Syracuse, N.Y.	McKeesport, Pa.	Richmond, Va.	END OF SEASON	4
5		Sunday	Woonsocket, R.I.	Manchester, N.H.	Syracuse, N.Y.	Connellsville, Pa.	Norfolk, Va.		5
6		Pottsville, Pa.	Worcester, Mass.	Lawrence, Mass.	Oswego, N.Y.	Johnstown, Pa.	SUNDAY		6
7		Reading, Pa.	Worcester, Mass.	SUNDAY	Utica, N.Y.	Altoona, Pa.	Wilmington, N.C.		7
8		Easton, Pa.	Fitchburg, Mass.	Haverhill, Mass.	Auburn, N.Y.	SUNDAY	Goldsboro, N.C.		8
9		Allentown, Pa.	SUNDAY	Salem, Mass.	Geneva, N.Y.	Lancaster, Pa.	Raleigh, N.C.		9
10		Wilkes-Barre, Pa.	Boston, Mass.	Gloucester, Mass.	Lockport, N.Y.	York, Pa.	Greensboro, N.C.		10
11		Scranton, Pa.	Boston, Mass.	Lynn, Mass.	SUNDAY	Harrisburg, Pa.	Salisbury, N.C.		11
12		SUNDAY	Boston, Mass.	Portsmouth, N.H.	Rochester, N.Y.	Williamsport, Pa.	Asheville, N.C.		12
13		Carbondale, Pa.	Boston, Mass.	Rochester, N.H.	Olean, N.Y.	SUNDAY	SUNDAY		13
14		Oneonta, N.Y.	Boston, Mass.	SUNDAY	Hornellsville, N.Y.	Ithaca, N.Y.	Charlotte, N.C.		14
15		Schenectady, N.Y.	Boston, Mass.	Biddeford, Me.	Bradford, Pa.	SUNDAY	Columbia, S.C.		15
16		Gloversville, N.Y.	Boston, Mass.	Lewiston, Me.	DuBois, Pa.	Cortland, N.Y.	Charleston, S.C.		16
17		Troy, N.Y.	Boston, Mass.	Waterville, Me.	Warren, Pa.	Norwich, N.Y.	Savannah, Ga.		17
18		Poughkeepsie, N.Y.	Boston, Mass.	Bangor, Me.	SUNDAY	Binghampton, N.Y.	Augusta, Ga.		18
19		SUNDAY	Boston, Mass.	Augusta, Me.	Buffalo, N.Y.	Port Jervis, N.Y.	Macon, Ga.		19
20		Albany, N.Y.	Boston, Mass.	Portland, Me.	Buffalo, N.Y.	Middletown, N.Y.	SUNDAY		20
21		Albany, N.Y.	Boston, Mass.	SUNDAY	Dunkirk, N.Y.	Newburg, N.Y.	Columbus, Ga.		21
22	Philadelphia, Pa.	Pittsfield, Mass.	Boston, Mass.	St. Johnsbury, Vt.	Jamestown, N.Y.	SUNDAY	Montgomery, Ala.		22
23	Philadelphia, Pa.	North Adams, Mass.	SUNDAY	White River Jct.	Meadville, Pa.	Paterson, N.J.	Birmingham, Ala.		23
24	Philadelphia, Pa.	Greenfield, Mass.	Providence, R.I.	Montpelier, Vt.	Erie, Pa.	Orange, N.J.	New Decatur, Ala.		24
25	Philadelphia, Pa.	Holyoke, Mass.	Providence, R.I.	St. Albans, Vt.	SUNDAY	Newark, N.J.	Nashville, Tenn.		25
26	Philadelphia, Pa.	SUNDAY	Newport, R.I.	Burlington, Vt.	Cleveland, O.	Newark, N.J.	Chattanooga, Tenn.		26
27	Philadelphia, Pa.	Springfield, Mass.	Fall River, Mass.	Rutland, Vt.	Youngstown, O.	Trenton, N.J.	SUNDAY		27
28	Philadelphia, Pa.	Waterbury, Conn.	Brockton, Mass.	SUNDAY	Akron, O.	Wilmington, Del.	Atlanta, Ga.		28
29	Philadelphia, Pa.	Danbury, Conn.	New Bedford, Mass.	Saratoga, N.Y.	Canton, O.	SUNDAY	Atlanta, Ga.		29
30	Philadelphia, Pa.	Bridgeport, Conn.	SUNDAY	Glens Falls, N.Y.	E. Liverpool, Pa.	Baltimore, Md.	Atlanta, Ga.		30
31	Philadelphia, Pa.	New Haven, Conn.		Plattsburg, N.Y.	Wheeling, W.V.		Atlanta, Ga.		31

PLATE 86

SEASON 1896   SOURCE 1896 ROUTE BOOK

	APRIL	MAY	JUNE	JULY	AUGUST	SEPTEMBER	OCTOBER	
1		Ironton, O.	Chicago, Ill.	Kokomo, Ind.	Owosso, Mich.	Appleton, Wis.	Muscatine, Ia.	1
2		Washington, O.	Chicago, Ill.	Bluffton, Ind.	Ann Arbor, Mich.	Menominee, Mich.	Ottumwa, Ia.	2
3		Cincinnati, O.	Chicago, Ill.	Marion, Ind.	Ann Arbor, Mich.	Green Bay, Wis.	Oskaloosa, Ia.	3
4		Cincinnati, O.	Chicago, Ill.	Piqua, O.	Adrian, Mich.	Stevens Point,Wis.	Des Moines, Ia.	4
5		Cincinnati, O.	Chicago, Ill.	Dayton, O.	Jackson, Mich.	Centralia, Wis.	Des Moines, Ia.	5
6	Philadelphia, Pa.	Hamilton, O.	Chicago, Ill.	Dayton, O.	Kalamazoo, Mich.	La Crosse, Wis.	Marshalltown, Ia	6
7	Philadelphia, Pa.	Richmond, Ind.	Chicago, Ill.	Springfield, O.	Battle Creek,Mich.	La Crosse, Wis.	Boone, Ia.	7
8	Philadelphia, Pa.	Indianapolis, Ind.	Chicago, Ill.	Kenton, O.	Lansing, Mich.	Winona, Minn.	Carroll, Ia.	8
9	Philadelphia, Pa.	Indianapolis, Ind.	Chicago, Ill.	Lima, O.	Grand Rapids, Mich.	Eau Claire, Wis.	Council Bluffs, I	9
10	Philadelphia, Pa.	Anderson, Ind.	Chicago, Ill.	Marion, O.	Grand Rapids, Mich.	Chippewa Falls, Wis.	Omaha, Neb.	10
11	Philadelphia, Pa.	Anderson, Ind.	Chicago, Ill.	Mansfield, O.	Muskegon, Mich.	Ashland, Wis.	North Platte, Neb	11
12	Philadelphia, Pa.	Columbus, Ind.	Chicago, Ill.	Columbus, O.	Benton Harbor, Mich.	Duluth, Minn.	North Platte, Neb.	12
13	Philadelphia, Pa.	Louisville, Ky.	Chicago, Ill.	Columbus, O.	Goshen, Ind.	Minneapolis, Minn.	Hastings, Neb.	13
14	Philadelphia, Pa.	Louisville, Ky.	Chicago, Ill.	Newark, O.	South Bend, Ind.	Minneapolis, Minn.	Lincoln, Neb.	14
15	Philadelphia, Pa.	Owensboro, Ky.	Kankakee, Ill.	Zanesville, O.	Michigan City, Ind.	Minneapolis, Minn.	Beatrice, Neb.	15
16	Philadelphia, Pa.	Evansville, Ind.	Ottawa, Ill.	Massillon, O.	Joliet, Ill.	St. Paul, Minn.	St. Joseph, Mo.	16
17	Philadelphia, Pa.	St. Louis, Mo.	Rock Island, Ill.	Alliance, O.	Joliet, Ill.	St. Paul, Minn.	Leavenworth, Kas.	17
18	Philadelphia, Pa.	St. Louis, Mo.	Galesburg, Ill.	Steubenville, O.	Streator, Ill.	Mankato, Minn.	Kansas City, Mo.	18
19	Philadelphia, Pa.	St. Louis, Mo.	Burlington, Ia.	Cleveland, O.	Aurora, Ill.	Sheldon, Ia.	Kansas City, Mo.	19
20	Philadelphia, Pa.	St. Louis, Mo.	Quincy, Ill.	Cleveland, O.	Elgin, Ill.	Sioux Falls, S.D.	Kansas City, Mo.	20
21	Philadelphia, Pa.	St. Louis, Mo.	Springfield, Ill.	Cleveland, O.	Dixon, Ill.	Sioux Falls, S.D.	Topeka, Kas.	21
22	Philadelphia, Pa.	St. Louis, Mo.	Springfield, Ill.	Sandusky, O.	Freeport, Ill.	Sioux City, Ia.	Fort Scott, Kas.	22
23	Philadelphia, Pa.	St. Louis, Mo.	Danville, Ill.	Tiffin, O.	Milwaukee, Wis.	Cherokee, Ia.	Sedalia, Mo.	23
24	Philadelphia, Pa.	St. Louis, Mo.	Terre Haute, Ind.	Findlay, O.	Milwaukee, Wis.	Fort Dodge, Ia.	Moberly, Mo.	24
25	Philadelphia, Pa.	Litchfield, Ill.	Crawfordsville,Ind.	Toledo, O.	Milwaukee, Wis.	Mason City, Ia.	SEASON ENDS	25
26	EN ROUTE	Decatur, Ill.	La Fayette, Ind.	Detroit, Mich.	Madison, Wis.	Waterloo, Ia.		26
27	Cumberland, Md.	Lincoln, Ill.	Logansport, Ind.	Detroit, Mich.	Janesville, Wis.	Dubuque, Ia.		27
28	Clarksburg, W.V.	Peoria, Ill.	Ft. Wayne, Ind.	Detroit, Mich.	Rockford, Ill.	Dubuque, Ia.		28
29	Parkersburg, W.V.	Bloomington, Ill.	Ft. Wayne, Ind.	Saginaw, Mich.	Racine, Wis.	Clinton, Ia.		29
30	Chillicothe, O.	Champaign, Ill.	Plymouth, Ind.	Port Huron, Mich.	Sheboygan, Wis.	Cedar Rapids, Ia.		30
31		Chicago, Ill.		Bay City, Mich.	Sheboygan, Wis.			31

PLATE 87

Route layout and design courtesy Circus World Museum, Baraboo, Wisconsin.

SEASON 1897 SOURCE 1899 ROUTE BOOK

	APRIL	MAY	JUNE	JULY	AUGUST	SEPTEMBER	OCTOBER	
1		New York, N. Y.	New Bedford,Mass	Kingston, Ont.	SUNDAY	Chicago, Ill.	St. Louis, Mo.	1
2		SUNDAY	Fall River, Mass	Belleville, Ont.	Easton, Pa.	Chicago, Ill.	St. Louis, Mo.	2
3		New York, N. Y.	Lowell, Mass.	Peterborough,Ont	Allentown, Pa.	Chicago, Ill.	SUNDAY	3
4		New York, N. Y.	Manchester,N. H.	SUNDAY	Reading, Pa.	Chicago, Ill.	Memphis, Tenn.	4
5		New York, N. Y.	Lawrence, Mass.	Toronto, Ont.	Harrisburg, Pa.	SUNDAY	Paducah, Ky.	5
6		New York, N. Y.	SUNDAY	Toronto, Ont.	Williamsport, Pa.	Chicago, Ill.	Union City, Tenn	6
7		New York, N. Y.	Haverhill, Mass.	Barrie,Ont.	Elmira, N. Y.	Chicago, Ill.	Nashville, Tenn.	7
8		New York, N. Y.	Salem, Mass.	Guelph, Ont.	SUNDAY	Chicago, Ill.	Nashville, Tenn.	8
9		SUNDAY	Lynn, Mass.	Stratford, Ont.	Hornellsville,N.Y	Chicago, Ill.	Chattanooga,Tenn	9
10		New York, N. Y.	Fitchburg, Mass.	London, Ont.	Olean, N. Y.	Chicago, Ill.	SUNDAY	10
11		New York, N. Y.	Worcester, Mass.	SUNDAY	Jamestown, N. Y.	Chicago, Ill.	Knoxville, Tenn.	11
12	Brooklyn, N. Y.	New York, N. Y.	Athol, Mass.	Chatham, Ont.	Youngstown, O.	SUNDAY	Bristol, Tenn.	12
13	Brooklyn, N. Y.	New York, N. Y.	SUNDAY	St. Thomas, Ont.	Pittsburg, Pa.	Milwaukee, Wis.	Lynchburg, Va.	13
14	Brooklyn, N. Y.	New York, N. Y.	Rutland, Vt.	Woodstock, Ont.	Pittsburg, Pa.	Janesville, Wis.	Petersburg, Va.	14
15	Brooklyn, N. Y.	New York, N. Y.	Burlington, Vt.	Brantford, Ont.	SUNDAY	Elgin, Ill.	Norfolk, Va.	15
16	Brooklyn, N. Y.	SUNDAY	Montpelier, Vt.	Hamilton, Ont.	Cleveland, O.	Rockford, Ill.	Richmond, Va.	16
17	Brooklyn, N. Y.	Bridgeport, Conn.	St. Albans, Vt.	St.Catherines,On	Toledo, O.	Ottawa, Ill.	END OF SEASON	17
18	SUNDAY	Waterbury, Conn.	Sherbrooke, Que.	SUNDAY	Lima, O.	Joliet, Ill.		18
19	Brooklyn, N. Y.	New Haven, Conn.	St. Hyacinth,Que	Buffalo, N. Y.	Findlay, O.	SUNDAY		19
20	Brooklyn, N. Y.	Hartford, Conn.	SUNDAY	Buffalo, N. Y.	Columbus, O.	Peoria, Ill.		20
21	Brooklyn, N. Y.	Springfield,Mass.	Montreal, Que.	Rochester, N. Y.	Dayton, O.	Bloomington, Ill.		21
22	Brooklyn, N. Y.	Holyoke, Mass.	Montreal, Que.	Syracuse, N. Y.	SUNDAY	Springfield, Ill.		22
23	Brooklyn, N. Y.	SUNDAY	Montreal, Que.	Watertown, N.Y.	Cincinnati, O.	Decatur, Ill.		23
24	Brooklyn, N. Y.	Boston, Mass.	ThreeRivers,Que.	Utica, N.Y.	Cincinnati, O.	Danville, Ill.		24
25	SUNDAY	Boston, Mass.	Quebec, Que.	SUNDAY	Lexington, Ky.	Terre Haute, Ind.		25
26	New York, N. Y.	Boston, Mass.	Quebec, Que.	Gloversville,N.Y	Louisville, Ky.	SUNDAY		26
27	New York, N. Y.	Boston, Mass.	SUNDAY	Troy, N. Y.	Indianapolis,Ind.	St. Louis, Mo.		27
28	New York, N. Y.	Boston, Mass.	Ottawa, Ont.	Albany, N.Y.	Lafayette, Ind.	St. Louis, Mo.		28
29	New York, N. Y.	Boston, Mass.	Ottawa, Ont.	Binghamton,N.Y.	SUNDAY	St. Louis, Mo.		29
30	New York, N. Y.	SUNDAY	Brockville,Ont.	Scranton, N.Y.	Chicago, Ill.	St. Louis, Mo.		30
31		Providence, R.I.		Wilkes-Barre,N.Y	Chicago, Ill.			31

PLATE 88

SEASON 1898 SOURCE 1900 ROUTE BOOK

	MARCH	APRIL	MAY	JUNE	JULY	AUGUST	SEPTEMBER	OCTOBER	
1		New York City, N.Y	SUNDAY	Boston, Mass.	McKeesport, Pa.	Watertown, Wis.	Lincoln, Neb.	Little Rock,Ark.	1
2		New York City, N.Y	Philadelphia, Pa.	Boston, Mass.	Uniontown, Pa.	Oshkosh, Wis.	Grand Island, Neb.	SUNDAY	2
3		SUNDAY	Philadelphia, Pa.	Boston, Mass.	SUNDAY	Wausau, Wis.	North Platte, Neb.	Newport, Ark.	3
4		New York City,N.Y	Philadelphia, Pa.	Boston, Mass.	Wheeling, W. Va.	Eau Claire, Wis.	SUNDAY	PoplarBluff,Mo.	4
5		New York City,N.Y	Philadelphia, Pa.	SUNDAY	Washington, Pa.	Ashland, Wis.	Cheyenne, Wyo.	Cairo, Ill.	5
6		New York City,N.Y	Philadelphia, Pa.	Newburyport,Mass	Butler, Pa.	Duluth, Minn.	Denver, Colo.	Carmi, Ill.	6
7		New York City,N.Y	Philadelphia, Pa.	Gloucester,Mass.	New Castle, Pa.	SUNDAY	Denver, Colo.	Vincennes, Ind.	7
8		New York City,N.Y	SUNDAY	Lynn, Mass.	Oil City, Pa.	Minneapolis,Minn.	ColoradoSprs,Colo	Evansville, Ind.	8
9		New York City,N.Y	Washington, D.C.	Waltham, Mass.	Erie, Pa.	St. Paul, Minn.	Pueblo, Colo.	SUNDAY	9
10		SUNDAY	Washington, D.C.	Keene, N. H.	SUNDAY	Red Wing, Minn.	Trinidad, Colo.	New Albany, Ind.	10
11		New York City,N.Y	Baltimore, Md.	N. Adams, Mass.	Ashtabula, O.	La Crosse, Wis.	SUNDAY	Frankfort, Ind.	11
12		New York City,N.Y	Baltimore, Md.	SUNDAY	Sandusky, O.	Dubuque, Wis.	Hutchinson, Kas.	Covington, Ky.	12
13		New York City,N.Y	Wilmington, Del.	Troy, N. Y.	Monroe, Mich.	Clinton, Ia.	Wichita, Kas.	Maysville, Ky.	13
14		New York City,N.Y	Norristown, Pa.	Albany, N. Y.	Detroit, Mich.	Davenport, Ia.	Winfield, Kas.	Huntington, W.Va	14
15		New York City,N.Y	SUNDAY	Kingston, N. Y.	Flint, Mich.	Kewanee, Ill.	Independence, Kas.	Charleston, W.Va	15
16		New York City,N.Y	Trenton, N. J.	Newburgh, N. Y.	Saginaw, Mich.	Kewanee, Ill.	Ottawa, Kas.	END OF SEASON	16
17		SUNDAY	Bridgeton, N. J.	Paterson, N. J.	SUNDAY	Burlington, Ia.	Emporia, Kas.		17
18		New York City,N.Y	Camden, N. J.	Morristown, N.J.	Manistee, Mich.	Keokuk, Ia.	SUNDAY		18
19		New York City,N.Y	NewBrunswick,N.J.	SUNDAY	TraverseCity,Mic	Jacksonville, Ill	Topeka, Kas.		19
20		New York City,N.Y	Newark, N. J.	Danville, Pa.	BigRapids,Mich.	Hannibal, Mo.	Atchison, Kas.		20
21		New York City,N.Y	Jersey City, N.J.	Shenandoah, Pa.	GrandRapids,Mich	Chillicothe, Mo.	Leavenworth, Kas.		21
22		New York City,N.Y	SUNDAY	Lebanon, Pa.	Kalamazoo, Mich.	Chillicothe, Mo.	Kansas City, Mo.		22
23	ALL NEW YORK DATES	New York City,N.Y	Mt. Vernon, N.Y.	Lancaster, Pa.	S. Bend, Ind.	St. Joseph, Mo.	Sedalia, Mo.		23
24	PLAYED IN MADISON	SUNDAY	Stamford, Conn.	Carlisle, Pa.	SUNDAY	Red Oak, Ia.	Nevada, Mo.		24
25	SQUARE GARDEN.	Brooklyn, N. Y.	Meriden, Conn.	Huntington, Pa.	Chicago, Ill.	Creston, Ia.	SUNDAY		25
26		Brooklyn, N. Y.	Hartford, Conn.	SUNDAY	Chicago, Ill.	Ottumwa, Ia.	Joplin, Mo.		26
27		Brooklyn, N. Y.	Willimantic,Conn.	Altoona, Pa.	Chicago, Ill.	Des Moines, Ia.	Aurora, Mo.		27
28		Brooklyn, N. Y.	Providence, R. I.	Johnstown, Pa.	Chicago, Ill.	SUNDAY	Fayetteville, Ark		28
29	New York City, N.Y.	Brooklyn, N. Y.	SUNDAY	Indiana, Pa.	Chicago, Ill.	Atlantic, Ia.	Ft. Smith, Ark.		29
30	New York City, N.Y.	Brooklyn, N. Y.	Boston, Mass.	E. Liberty, Pa.	Chicago, Ill.	Omaha, Neb.	Russellville, Ark		30
31	New York City, N.Y.		Boston, Mass.		Milwaukee, Wis.	Omaha, Neb.			31

PLATE 89

SEASON 1899   SOURCE 1899 ROUTE BOOK

	APRIL	MAY	JUNE	JULY	AUGUST	SEPTEMBER	OCTOBER	
1		Nashville, Tenn.	Philadelphia, Pa.	Worcester, Mass.	Mansfield, O.	Rochester, Minn.	St. Louis, Mo.	1
2		Bowling Green, Ky.	Philadelphia, Pa	SUNDAY	UpperSandusky,O.	Mankato, Minn.	St. Louis, Mo.	2
3		Louisville, Ky.	Philadelphia, Pa	Salem, Mass.	Lima, O.	SUNDAY	St. Louis, Mo.	3
4		Madison. Ind.	SUNDAY	Lawrence, Mass.	Muncie, Ind.	Watertown, S.D.	St. Louis, Mo.	4
5		Indianapolis,Ind.	Long Branch, N.J	Haverhill, Mass.	Ft. Wayne, Ind.	Huron, S. D.	St. Louis, Mo.	5
6		Richmond, Ind.	Elizabeth, N. J	Dover, N. H.	SUNDAY	Aberdeen, S. D.	St. Louis, Mo.	6
7		SUNDAY	Yonkers, N.Y.	Concord, N. H.	Hillsdale. Mich.	Ortonville, Minn.	St. Louis, Mo.	7
8		Cincinnati, O.	Poughkeepsie,N.Y	Manchester, N.H.	Jackson, Mich.	Fargo, N. D.	SUNDAY	8
9		Cincinnati, O.	Winsted, Conn.	SUNDAY	Lansing, Mich.	Fergus Falls,Minn.	Springfield, Ill	9
10		Dayton, O.	Hartford, Conn.	Lowell, Mass.	Bay City, Mich.	SUNDAY	Decatur, Ill.	10
11		Springfield, O.	SUNDAY	Fitchburg, Mass.	Port Huron, Mich	St. Cloud, Minn.	Terre Haute, Ind	11
12		Columbus, O.	Boston, Mass.	Greenfield, Mass	Detroit, Mich.	Marshall, Minn.	Shelbyville, Ind	12
13		Newark, O.	Boston, Mass.	Saratoga, N.Y.	SUNDAY	Yankton, S. D.	Hamilton, O.	13
14		SUNDAY	Boston, Mass.	Schenectady, N.Y	Toledo, O.	Mitchell, S. D.	Urbana, O.	14
15		Pittsburg, Pa.	Boston, Mass.	Utica, N. Y.	Defiance, O.	Sioux Falls, S.D.	END OF SEASON	15
16		Pittsburg, Pa.	Boston, Mass.	SUNDAY	Peru, Ind.	Sioux City, S. D.		16
17	Baltimore, Md.	Tyrone, Pa.	Boston, Mass.	Syracuse, N.Y.	Lafayette, Ind.	SUNDAY		17
18	Baltimore, Md.	Williamsport, Pa.	SUNDAY	Binghamton, N.Y.	Bloomington,Ill.	Omaha, Neb.		18
19	Washington, D.C.	Wilkes-Barre, Pa.	Brockton, Mass.	Elmira, N. Y.	Peoria, Ill.	Jefferson, Ia.		19
20	Washington, D.C.	Towanda, Pa	NewBedford,Mass.	Rochester, N.Y.	Chicago, Ill.	Webster City, Ia.		20
21	Richmond, Va.	SUNDAY	Newport, R.I.	Buffalo, N.Y.	Chicago, Ill.	Algona, Ia.		21
22	Staunton, Va.	Scranton, Pa.	Fall River,Mass.	Buffalo, N.Y.	Chicago, Ill.	Marshalltown, Ia.		22
23	SUNDAY	Easton, Pa.	NewLondon,Conn.	SUNDAY	Chicago, Ill.	Mason City, Ia.		23
24	Lynchburg, Va.	Allentown, Pa.	Willimantic,Conn	Cleveland, O.	Chicago, Ill.	SUNDAY		24
25	Roanoke, Va.	Pottsville, Pa.	SUNDAY	Akron, O.	Chicago, Ill.	Austin, Minn.		25
26	Bluefield, W.Va.	Reading, Pa.	Bridgeport,Conn.	Canton, O.	Chicago, Ill.	Cresco, Ia.		26
27	Bristol, Tenn.	Chester, Pa.	Waterbury,Conn.	Youngstown, O.	Chicago, Ill.	Monticello, Ia.		27
28	Knoxville, Tenn.	SUNDAY	New Haven,Conn.	BeaverFalls,Pa.	Milwaukee, Wis.	Cedar Rapids, Ia.		28
29	Chattanooga,Tenn	Philadelphia, Pa.	Holyoke, Mass.	Steubenville, O.	Fond du Lac, Wis	Centerville, Ia.		29
30	SUNDAY	Philadelphia, Pa.	Springfield,Mass	SUNDAY	Madison, Wis.	Kirksville, Mo.		30
31		Philadelphia, Pa.		Coshocton, O.	Winona, Wis.			31

PLATE 90

SEASON 1900   SOURCE 1900 ROUTE BOOK

	APRIL	MAY	JUNE	JULY	AUGUST	SEPTEMBER	OCTOBER	NOVEMBER	
1		New York, N. Y.	Springfield,Mass.	SUNDAY	Iona, Mich.	Chicago, Ill.	Topeka, Kas.	Greenville, Miss.	1
2		New York, N. Y.	Worcester, Mass.	Rome, N. Y.	GrandRapids,Mich	SUNDAY	Lawrence, Kas.	Clarksdale, Miss.	2
3		New York, N. Y.	SUNDAY	Watertown, N. Y.	Kalamazoo,Mich.	Davenport, Ia.	Emporia, Kas.	Memphis, Tenn.	3
4		New York, N. Y.	Providence, R.I.	Syracuse, N. Y.	SouthBend,Ind.	Iowa City, Ia.	Pittsburg, Kas.	END OF SEASON	4
5		New York, N. Y.	So.Fram'ham,Mass	Auburn, N. Y.	SUNDAY	Burlington, Ia.	Joplin, Mo.		5
6		SUNDAY	Lynn, Mass.	Ithaca, N. Y.	Racine, Wis.	Washington, Ia.	Springfield, Mo.		6
7		Brooklyn, N. Y.	Portsmouth,N.H.	Rochester, N. Y.	Manitowoc, Wis.	Oskaloosa, Ia.	SUNDAY		7
8		Brooklyn, N. Y.	Biddeford, Me.	SUNDAY	Green Bay, Wis.	Des Moines, Ia.	OklahomaCity,O.T		8
9		Brooklyn, N. Y.	Lewiston, Me.	Bradford, Pa.	Rhinelander, Wis	SUNDAY	Gainesville, Tex		9
10		Brooklyn, N. Y.	SUNDAY	Meadville, Pa.	Ashland, Wisc.	Omaha, Neb.	Ft. Worth, Tex.		10
11		Brooklyn, N. Y.	Bangor, Me.	Warren, Pa.	Duluth, Minn.	Lincoln, Neb.	Dallas, Tex.		11
12		Brooklyn, N. Y.	Dover, Me.	Cleveland, O.	SUNDAY	York, Neb.	Greenville, Tex.		12
13		SUNDAY	Augusta, Me.	Marion, O.	Minneapolis,Minn	Nebr. City, Neb.	Paris, Tex.		13
14		Philadelphia, Pa.	Portland, Me.	Columbus, O.	St. Paul, Minn.	Clarinda, Ia.	SUNDAY		14
15		Philadelphia, Pa.	Rochester, N.H.	SUNDAY	Owatonna, Minn.	Chariton, Ia.	Sherman, Tex.		15
16		Philadelphia, Pa.	Nashua, N.H.	Mt. Vernon, O.	CharlesCity,Ia.	SUNDAY	Corsicana, Tex.		16
17		Philadelphia, Pa.	SUNDAY	Zanesville, O.	Independence,Ia.	Ottumwa, Ia.	Waco, Tex.		17
18		Philadelphia, Pa.	Boston, Mass.	Marietta, O.	Dubuque, Ia.	Keokuk, Ia.	Temple, Tex.		18
19		Philadelphia, Pa.	Boston, Mass.	Athens, O.	SUNDAY	Quincy, Ill.	Austin, Tex.		19
20		SUNDAY	Boston, Mass.	Portsmouth, O.	Prairie duChein,W	Louisiana, Mo.	San Antonio,Tex.		20
21		Harrisburg, Pa.	Boston, Mass.	Hillsboro, O.	Sparta, Wis.	Mexico, Mo.	SUNDAY		21
22		Lancaster, Pa.	Boston, Mass.	SUNDAY	PortageCity,Wis.	Marshall, Mo.	Houston, Tex.		22
23	New York, N.Y.	Wilmington, Del.	Boston, Mass.	Chillicothe, O.	Beloit, Wis.	SUNDAY	Beaumont, Tex.		23
24	New York, N. Y.	Trenton, N.J.		Xenia, O.	Freeport, Ill.	Kansas City, Mo.	Lafayette, La.		24
25	New York, N. Y.	Newark, N. J.	Hartford, Conn.	Greenville, O.	Aurora, Ill.	St. Joseph, Mo.	New Orleans, La.		25
26	New York, N. Y.	Paterson, N. J.	New Haven, Conn.	Bryan, O.	Chicago, Ill.	Marysville, Kas.	New Orleans, La.		26
27	New York, N. Y.	SUNDAY	S. Norwalk, Conn	Adrian, Mich.	Chicago, Ill.	Salina, Kas.	New Orleans, La.		27
28	New York, N. Y.	Kingston, N.Y.	Danbury, Conn.	Ypsilanti,Mich.	Chicago, Ill.	Jct. City, Kas.	New Orleans, La.		28
29	SUNDAY	Albany, N.Y.	Pittsfield,Mass.	SUNDAY	Chicago, Ill.	Concordia, Ia.	Baton Rouge, La.		29
30	New York, N.Y.	Troy, N.Y.	Hudson, N. Y.	Pontiac, Mich.	Chicago, Ill.	SUNDAY	Natchez, Miss.		30
31		N. Adams, Mass.		Saginaw, Mich.	Chicago, Ill.		Vicksburg, Miss.		31

PLATE 91

SEASON 1901   SOURCE 1901 ROUTE SHEET

#	APRIL	MAY	JUNE	JULY	AUGUST	SEPTEMBER	OCTOBER
1		Hinton, W. Va.	Lewistown, Pa.	Toledo, O.	Waterloo. Ia.	SUNDAY	Murphysboro, Il.
2	New York City, N.Y	Charleston, W. Va.	SUNDAY	Detroit, Mi.	Iowa Fall, Ia.	Buffalo, N.Y.	Centralia, Il.
3	New York City, N.Y	Ironton, O.	Pottsville, Pa.	Port Huron, Mi.	Emmetsburg, Ia	Buffalo, N.Y.	Paducah, Ky.
4	New York City, N.Y	Circleville, O.	Reading, Pa.	Bay City, Mi.	SUNDAY	Buffalo, N.Y.	Hopkinsville, Ky.
5	New York City, N.Y	Cincinnati, O.	Allentown, Pa.	Alma, Mi.	Sioux City, Ia.	Buffalo, N.Y.	Fulton, Ky.
6	New York City, N.Y	Cincinnati, O.	Easton, Pa.	Greenville, Mi.	Council Bluffs,Ia	Buffalo, N.Y.	SUNDAY
7	SUNDAY	Cincinnati, O.	Scranton, Pa.	SUNDAY	Carroll, Ia.	Buffalo, N.Y.	Jackson, Tn.
8	New York City, N.Y	Lexington, Ky.	Scranton, Pa.	Lansing, Mi.	Boone, Ia.	SUNDAY	Paris, Tn.
9	New York City, N.Y	Louisville, Ky.	SUNDAY	Battle Creek, Mi.	Marshalltown, Ia.	Du Bois, Pa.	Nashville, Tn.
10	New York City, N.Y	Owensboro, Ky.	Binghampton, N.Y.	Jackson, Mi.	Newton, Ia.	Butler, Pa.	Tullahoma, Tn.
11	New York City, N.Y	Evansville, Ind.	Oneonta, N.Y.	Auburn, Ind.	SUNDAY	Connellsville, Pa.	Huntsville, Tn.
12	New York City, N.Y	St. Louis, Mo.	Schenectady, N.Y.	Fort Wayne, Ind.	Knoxville, Ia.	Clarksburg, W. Va.	Columbia, Tn.
13	New York City, N.Y	St. Louis, Mo.	Utica, N.Y.	Warsaw, Ind.	Sibourney, Ia.	Parkersburg. W. Va.	SUNDAY
14	SUNDAY	St. Louis, Mo.	Cortland, N.Y.	SUNDAY	Fairfield, Ia.	Jackson, O.	Chattanooga, Tn.
15	New York City, N.Y	St. Louis, Mo.	Elmira, N.Y.	Chicago, Il.	Rock Island, Il.	SUNDAY	Gadsden, Al.
16	New York City, N.Y	St. Louis, Mo.	SUNDAY	Chicago, Il.	Galesburg, Il.	Lawrenceburg, Ind.	Birmingham, Al.
17	New York City, N.Y	St. Louis, Mo.	Hornellsville, N.Y.	Chicago, Il.	Peoria. Il.	Anderson, Ind.	Selma, Al.
18	New York City, N.Y	St. Louis, Mo.	Olean, N.Y.	Chicago, Il.	SUNDAY	Elkhart, Ind	Montgomery, Al.
19	New York City, N.Y	SUNDAY	Oil City, Pa.	Chicago, Il.	Watseka, Il.	Marion, Ind.	Opelika, Al.
20	New York City, N.Y	Terre Haute, Ind.	Youngstown, O.	Chicago, Il.	Logansport, Il	North Vernon, Ind.	SUNDAY
21	SUNDAY	Indianapolis, Ind.	Erie, Pa.	SUNDAY	Lafayette, Ind.	Bedford, Ind.	Atlanta, Ga.
22	Baltimore, Ma.	Richmond, Ind.	Painsville, O.	Milwaukee, Wi.	Portland, Ind.	SUNDAY	Macon, Ga.
23	Baltimore, Ma.	Dayton, O.	SUNDAY	Janesville, Wi.	Fremont, O.	Washington, Ind.	Augusta, Ga.
24	Washington D. C.	Springfield, O.	Cleveland, O.	Madison, Wi.	Elyria, O.	Olney, Il.	Savannah, Ga.
25	Washington D. C.	Newark, O.	Akron, O.	Monroe, Wi.	SUNDAY	Mattoon, Il.	Charleston, S.C.
26	Richmond, Va.	SUNDAY	Canton, O.	Rockford, Il.	Buffalo, N.Y.	Havana, Il.	Columbia, S.C.
27	Norfolk, Va.	Wheeling, W. Va.	Wooster, O.	Dixon, Il.	Buffalo, N.Y.	Springfield, Il.	SUNDAY
28	SUNDAY	Pittsburg, Pa.	Bucyrus, O.	SUNDAY	Buffalo, N.Y.	Pontiac, Il.	Charlette, N.C.
29	Lynchburg, Va.	Pittsburg, Pa.	Delaware, O.	Clinton, Ia.	Buffalo, N.Y.	SUNDAY	Danville, Va.
30	Clifton Forge, Va.	Johnstown, Pa.	SUNDAY	Cedar Rapids, Ia.	Buffalo, N.Y.	Belleville, Il.	END OF SEASON
31		Altoona, Pa.		West Union, Ia.	Buffalo, N.Y.		

PLATE 92

SEASON 1902   SOURCE 1902 ROUTE BOOK

#	APRIL	MAY	JUNE	JULY	AUGUST	SEPTEMBER	OCTOBER	NOVEMBER
1		New York, N. Y.	SUNDAY	Rochester, N. Y.	Lincoln, Neb.	Redding, Cal.	Deming, N. M.	New Orleans, La.
2		New York, N. Y.	Bridgeport, Conn.	Batavia, N. Y.	Fairbury, Neb.	Marysville, Cal.	El Paso, Tex.	New Orleans, La.
3		New York, N. Y.	New Haven, Conn.	Jamestown, N. Y.	SUNDAY	Sacramento, Cal.	Albuquerque, NM	McComb, Miss.
4		SUNDAY	Waterbury, Conn.	Meadeville, Pa.	Pueblo, Colo.	Santa Rosa, Cal.	Las Vegas, N. M.	Jackson, Miss.
5		Brooklyn, N. Y.	New Britain, Conn.	New Castle, Pa.	Col. Springs, Col	Vallejo, Cal.	SUNDAY	Yazoo City, Miss.
6		Brooklyn, N. Y.	Hartford, Conn.	SUNDAY	Denver, Colo.	Oakland, Cal.	Hutchinson, Kan.	Greenwood, Miss.
7		Brooklyn, N. Y.	Norwich, Conn.	Cleveland, Ohio	Denver, Colo.	San Francisco, Cal.	Wichita, Kans.	Holly Springs, MI
8		Brooklyn, N. Y.	SUNDAY	Sandusky, Ohio	Greeley, Colo.	San Francisco, Cal.	Guthrie, Okla.	Memphis, Tenn.
9		Brooklyn, N. Y.	Providence, R. I.	Adrian, Mich.	Cheyenne, Wyo.	San Francisco, CA.	Gainsville, Tex.	SEASON ENDS.
10		Brooklyn, N. Y.	Woonsocket, R.I.	Detroit, Mich.	SUNDAY	San Francisco, CA.	Ft. Worth, Tex.	
11		SUNDAY	Taunton, Mass.	Owosso, Mich.	Evanston, Wyo.	San Francisco, CA.	Dallas, Tex.	
12		Philadelphia, Pa.	New Bedford, Ma.	Grand Rapids, Mi	Ogden, Utah	San Francisco, CA.	SUNDAY	
13		Philadelphia, Pa.	Newport, R. I.	SUNDAY	Salt Lake, Utah	San Francisco, CA.	Denison, Tex.	
14		Philadelphia, Pa.	Fall River, Mass.	Petoskey, Mich.	Salt Lake, Utah	San Francisco, CA.	McKinney, Tex.	
15		Philadelphia, Pa.	SUNDAY	So. St. Marie, Mi	Logan, Utah	Salinas, Cal.	Waxahachie, Tex.	
16		Philadelphia, Pa.	Boston, Mass.	Marquette, Mich.	Pocatello, Idaho	San Jose, Cal.	Corsicana, Tex.	
17		Philadelphia, Pa.	Boston, Mass.	Ishpeming, Mich.	SUNDAY	Stocton, Cal.	Waco, Tex.	
18		SUNDAY	Boston, Mass.	Hancock, Mich.	Boise, Idaho	Merced, Cal.	Bryan, Tex.	
19		Harrisburg, Pa.	Boston, Mass.	Calumet, Mich.	Baker City, Ore.	Fresno, Cal.	SUNDAY	
20		Lancaster, Pa.	Boston, Mass.	SUNDAY	Pendleton, Ore.	Bakersfield, Cal.	Austin, Tex.	
21	New York, N. Y.	Wilmington, Del.	Boston, Mass.	Ironwood, Mich.	Walla Walla, Wash	SUNDAY	San Antonio, Tex	
22	New York, N. Y.	Trenton, N. J.	SUNDAY	Superior, Wis.	Colfax, Wash.	Santa Barbara, CA.	Columbus, Tex.	
23	New York, N. Y.	New Brunsw'k N. J.	Worcester, Mass.	Duluth, Minn.	Spokane, Wash.	Los Angeles, Cal.	Galveston, Tex.	
24	New York, N. Y.	Newark, N. J.	Springfield, Mass	Rice Lake, Wis.	SUNDAY	Los Angeles, Cal.	Houston, Tex.	
25	New York, N. Y.	SUNDAY	Pittsfield, Mass	St. Paul, Minn.	The Dalles, Ore.	San Deigo, Cal.	Beaumont, Tex.	
26	New York, N. Y.	New York, N. Y.	Albany, N. Y.	Minneapolis, Minn	Portland, Ore.	Santa Anna, Cal.	SUNDAY	
27	SUNDAY	New York, N. Y.	Troy, N. Y.	SUNDAY	Portland, Ore.	San Bernardino, CA.	Lake Charles, La	
28	New York, N. Y.	New York, N. Y.	Amsterdam, N. Y.	Ft. Dodge, Ia.	Salem, Ore.	Yuma, Ariz.	Alexandria, La.	
29	New York, N. Y.	New York, N. Y.	SUNDAY	Des Moines, Ia.	Eugene, Ore.	Phoenix, Ariz.	Opelousas, La.	
30	New York, N. Y.	New York, N. Y.	Syracuse, N. Y.	Atlantic, Ia.	Roseburg, Ore.	Tucson, Ariz.	New Iberia, La.	
31		New York, N. Y.		Omaha, Neb.	SUNDAY		New Orleans, La.	

PLATE 93

SEASON 1903   SOURCE 1902-03-04 ROUTE MAP

	DEC. '02 – JAN. FEB. MARCH	APRIL	MAY	JUNE	JULY	AUGUST	SEPTEMBER	OCTOBER	
1		London	Manchester	Birmingham	Gloucester	Plymouth	Luton	Leeds	1
2	1ST DATE	London	Manchester	Birmingham	Hereford	SUNDAY	Leyton	Leeds	2
3	DECEMBER 26, 1902	London	SUNDAY	Birmingham	Abergavenny,Wales	Tauton	Southend	Leeds	3
4	LONDON.	London	Liverpool	Birmingham	Aberdare, Wales	Weymouth	Colchester	SUNDAY	4
5			Liverpool	Birmingham	SUNDAY	Bournemouth	Bury St. Edmunds	Bradford	5
6	THE SHOW		Liverpool	Birmingham	Cardiff, Wales	Salisbury	SUNDAY	Bradford	6
7	WOULD PLAY		Liverpool	Birmingham	Cardiff, Wales	Southhampton	Ipswich	Keighley	7
8	LONDON THROUGH		Liverpool	Birmingham	Cardiff, Wales	Southhampton	Lowestoft	Halifax	8
9	APRIL 4TH.		Liverpool	Birmingham	Cardiff, Wales	SUNDAY	Great Yarmouth	Wakefield	9
10			Liverpool	Birmingham	Cardiff, Wales	Portsmouth	Norwich	Doncaster	10
11			Liverpool	Birmingham	Cardiff, Wales	Portsmouth	King's Lynn	SUNDAY	11
12			Liverpool	Birmingham	SUNDAY	Portsmouth	Wisbech	Sheffield	12
13		Manchester	Liverpool	Birmingham	Llanelly, Wales	SUNDAY	Sheffield		13
14		Manchester	Liverpool	SUNDAY	Swansea, Wales	Brighton	Petersborough	Sheffield	14
15		Manchester	Liverpool	Worcester	Swansea, Wales	Brighton	Ely	Sheffield	15
16		Manchester	Liverpool	Kidderminster	Newport	SUNDAY	Bedford	Chesterfield	16
17		Manchester	Liverpool	Dudley	Bath	Guildford	Northampton	Newark	17
18		Manchester	Liverpool	Wolverhampton	Weston-superMare	Tunbridge Wells	Wellingsborough	SUNDAY	18
19		Manchester	Liverpool	Stafford	SUNDAY	Eastbourne	Kettering	Nottingham	19
20		Manchester	Liverpool	Coventry	Bristol	Hastings	SUNDAY	Nottingham	20
21		Manchester	Liverpool	SUNDAY	Bristol	Ashford	Liecester	Loughborough	21
22		Manchester	Liverpool	Rugby	Bristol	Folkestone	Liecester	Derby	22
23		Manchester	Liverpool	Leamington	Bristol	SUNDAY	Spalding	Burton	23
24		Manchester	SUNDAY	Banbury	Westbury	Ramsgate	Boston	SEASON ENDS.	24
25		Manchester	Warrington	Oxford	Yeovil	Margate	Grantham		25
26		Manchester	Birkenhead	Reading	SUNDAY	Canterbury	Lincoln		26
27		Manchester	Rhyl, Wales	Reading	Barnstaple	Maidstone	SUNDAY		27
28		Manchester	Bangor, Wales	SUNDAY	Exeter	Chatham	Leeds		28
29		Manchester	Ruabon, Wales	Swindon	Newton Abbott	Croydon	Leeds		29
30		Manchester	Shrewsbury	Cheltenham	Plymouth	SUNDAY	Leeds		30
31			SUNDAY		Plymouth	Watford			31

PLATE 94

SEASON 1904   SOURCE 1902-03-04 ROUTE MAP

	APRIL	MAY	JUNE	JULY	AUGUST	SEPTEMBER	OCTOBER	
1		SUNDAY	Truo, E.	Hull, E.	Glasgow, S.	Elgin, S.	St. Helens, E.	1
2		Llandudno, W.	Bodmin, E.	Hull, E.	Glasgow, S.	Inverness, S.	SUNDAY	2
3		Holyhead, W.	Plymouth, E.	SUNDAY	Glasgow, S.	Inverness, S.	Leigh (Lancs.) E.	3
4		Carnarvon, W.	Taunton, E.	York, E.	Glasgow, S.	SUNDAY	Bolton, E.	4
5		Portmadoc, W.	SUNDAY	Scarborough, E.	Glasgow, S.	Perth, S.	Bury, E.	5
6		Dolgelly, W.	Dorchester, E.	Darlington, E.	Glasgow, S.	Stirling, S.	Rochdale, E.	6
7		Aberystwyth, W.	Poole, E.	Stockt'n-on-tees.E.	SUNDAY	Palsley, S.	Oldham, E.	7
8		SUNDAY	Southampton, E.	Middles Borough, E.	Edinburgh, S.	Greenock, S.	Burnley, E.	8
9		Chester, E.	Winchester, E.	West Hartlepool, E.	Edinburgh, S.	Saltcoats, S.	SUNDAY	9
10		Wrexham, E.	Newbury, E.	SUNDAY	Edinburgh, S.	Kilmarnock, S.	Skipton, E.	10
11		Oswestry, W.	Nigh Wycombe, E.	Newcastle-on-tyne,E.	Edinburgh, S.	SUNDAY	Harrogate, E.	11
12		Builth Wells, W.	SUNDAY	Newcastle-on-tyne,E.	Edinburgh, S.	Ayr, S.	Castleford, E.	12
13		Carmarthen, W.	Windsor, E.	Newcastle-on-tyne,E.	Edinburgh, S.	Strarear, S.	Barnsley, E.	13
14		Pembroke Dock, W.	Aldershot, E.	Newcastle-on-tyne,E.	SUNDAY	Dumfries, S.	Hudderfield, E.	14
15		SUNDAY	Horsham, E.	Newcastle-on-tyne,E.	Falkirk, S.	Carlisle, E.	Ashton-under-lyneE.	15
16		Llanelly, W.	Lewes Sussex, E.	Newcastle-on-tyne,E.	Dunfermline, S.	Penrith, E.	SUNDAY	16
17		Neath, W.	Redhill, Surrey, E.	SUNDAY	Kirkcaldy, S.	Maryport. E.	Glossop, E.	17
18		Bridgend, W.	Wimbledon, E.	Sunderland, E.	Dundee, S.	SUNDAY	Stockport, E.	18
19		Barry Dock, W.	SUNDAY	Sunderland, E.	Dundee, S.	Workington, E.	Northwich, E.	19
20		Cardiff, W.	Chelmsford, E.	Durham, E.	Dundee, S.	Whitehaven, E.	Macclesfield, E.	20
21		Cardiff, W.	Ilford, E.	South Shields, E.	SUNDAY	Barrow-in-furnessE.	Hanley, E.	21
22		SUNDAY	St. Albans, E.	Hexham, E.	Arbroath, S.	Kendal, E.	END OF SEASON	22
23		Stroud, E.	Hitchin, E.	North Shields, E.	Forfar, S.	Lancaster, E.		23
24		Trowbridge, E.	Cambridge, E.	SUNDAY	Montrose, S.	Blackpool, E.		24
25	Stoke-On-Trent, E.	Wells, Somerset,E.	Ilkeson, E.	Ber'ick-on-twe'd,E.	Aberdeen, S.	SUNDAY		25
26	Nuneaton, E.	Bridgewater, E.	SUNDAY	Hawick, E.	Aberdeen, S.	Preston, E.		26
27	Walsall, E.	Exmouth, E.	Mansfield, E.	Galashiels, S.	Aberdeen, S.	Blackburn, E.		27
28	Stourbridge, E.	Torquay, E.	Rotherham, E.	Motherwell, S.	SUNDAY	Chorley, E.		28
29	Wellingt'n Salop. E.	SUNDAY	Gainsborough, E.	Coatbridge, S.	Peterhead, S.	Wigan, E.		29
30	Crewe, E.	Penzance, E.	Great Grimsby, E.	Dumbarton, S.	Fraserburgh, S.	Southport, E.		30
31		Cambourne, E.		SUNDAY	Huntly, S.			31

PLATE 95

SEASON 1905　　　SOURCE 1905 ROUTE MAP

	– MAY	JUNE	JULY	AUGUST	SEPTEMBER	OCTOBER	NOVEMBER	
1		Paris	Lille	Besancon	Poitiers	Bordeaux	Marseilles	1
2	PARIS	Paris	Lille	Lons-Le-Saunier	Angoulême	Dax	Marseilles	2
3	"	Paris	Lille	Bourg	Saintes	Bayonne	Marseilles	3
4	"	Paris	Lille	Lyon	Rochefort	Pau	Marseilles	4
5	"	Chartres	Valenciennes	Lyon	La Rochelle	Tarbes	Marseilles	5
6	"	Alencon	Maubeuge	Lyon	Niort	Mont-de-Marsan	Marseilles	6
7	"	Flers	Cambeuge	Lyon	La-Roche s Yon	Agen	Marseilles	7
8	"	Saint-Lo	Saint-Quentin	Lyon	Saint-Nazaire	Villeneuve-s-Lot	Marseilles	8
9	"	Cherbourg	Compiegne	Lyon	Vannes	Bergerac	Marseilles	9
10	"	Caen	Laon	Lyon	Lorient	Brive	Marseilles	10
11	"	Caen	Reims	Lyon	Quimper	Cahors	Marseilles	11
12	"	Lisieux	Reims	Lyon	Brest	Montauban	Marseilles	12
13	"	Evreux	Reims	Lyon	Saint-Brievc	Toulouse	END OF SEASON	13
14	"	Elbeuf	Mezieres-Charleville	Macon	Saint-Malo	Toulouse		14
15	"	Rouen	Sedan	Chalon-S-Saône	Ren nes	Toulouse		15
16	"	Rouen	Verdun	Le Creusot	Laval	Albi		16
17	"	Le-Havre	Charlons-s-Marne	Nevers	Le Mans	Castres		17
18	"	Le-Havre	Bar-Le-Due	Moulins	Tours	Carcassonne		18
19	"	Dieppe	Nancy	Roanne	Châteavroux	Narbonne		19
20	"	Abbeville	Nancy	Vichy	Limoges	Perpignan		20
21	"	Amiens	Lunéville	Riom	Pêrigveix	Béziers		21
22	"	Amiens	Saint-Die	Montlucon	Bordeaux	Béziers		22
23	"	Arras	Epinal	Bourges	Bordeaux	Cette		23
24	"	Douai	Belfort	Orleans	Bordeaux	Montpellier		24
25	"	Dunkerque	Vesoul	Orleans	Bordeaux	Montpellier		25
26	"	Calais	Chaumont	Naumur	Bordeaux	Alais		26
27	"	Boulogne	Troyes	Angers	Bordeaux	Nimes		27
28	"	Armentieres	Sens		Bordeaux	Nimes		28
29	"	Roubaix	Auxerre	Cholet	Bordeaux	Avignon		29
30	"	Roubaix	Dijon	Thovars	Bordeaux	Aries		30
31	"		Dijon	Châtellerault	Bordeaux	Aix		31

PLATE 96

SEASON 1906　　　SOURCE 1906 ROUTE MAP

	MARCH	APRIL	MAY	JUNE	JULY	AUGUST	SEPTEMBER	
1		Ferinze, Italy	Milano, Italy	Vienna, Austria	Debreczen, Hung.	Przemysl, Galicia	Metz,Germany	1
2		Firenze, Italy	Milano, Italy	Vienma, Austria	Bekescsaaba, Hung.	Rzeszow, Galicia	Metz, Germany	2
3		Firenze, Italy	Milano, Italy	Vienna, Austria	Szentes, Hung.	Tarnow, Galicia	Luxemburg,Luxember	3
4	Marseille, France	Pisa, Italy	Milano, Italy	Vienna, Austria	Szeged, Hungary	Krakau, Galicia	Trier, Germany	4
5	Marseille, France	Parma, Italy	Milano, Italy	Vienna, Austria	Nagykilkanda,Hung	Krakau, Galicia	Coblenz, Germany	5
6	Toulon, France	Modena, Italy	Milano, Italy	Vienna, Austria	NagyBecskerke,Hu.	Biala, Austria	Bonn, Germany	6
7	Toulon, France	Modena, Italy	Bergamo, Italy	Vienna, Austria	Pancsova, Hungary	Teschen, Austria	Duren, Germany	7
8	Draguinan, France	Bologna, Italy	Brescia, Italy	Vienna, Austria	Versecz, Hungary	MahrOstrau, Aust.	MGladbach,Germany	8
9	Nice, France	Forli, Italy	Vicenza, Italy	Vienna, Austria	Temesvar, Hung.	Troppau, Austria	MGladbach, Germany	9
10	Nice, France	Ancona, Italy	Treviso, Italy	Vienna, Austria	Arad, Hungary	Prerau, Austria	Verviers, Belgium	10
11	Nice, France	Rimini, Italy	Udine, Italy	Vienna, Austria	Arad, Hungary	Brunn, Austria	Namur, Belgium	11
12	Nice, France	Ravenna, Italy	Gorz, Austria	Vienna, Austria	GyulaFehervar,Hu.	Brunn, Austria	Chareroi, Belgium	12
13	EN ROUTE	Frearara, Italy	Trieste, Austria	Vienna, Austria	NagySzeben, Hung.	LgLau, Austria	Mons, Belgium	13
14	Genoa, Italy	Padova, Italy	Trieste, Austria	Vienna, Austria	Brasso, Hungary	Reinhenberg, Aust.	Brussels,Belgium	14
15	Genoa, Italy	Verona, Italy	Trieste, Austria	En Route	Brasso, Hungary	Zittau, Germany	Brussels,Belgium	15
16	Genoa, Italy	Verona, Italy	Laibach, Austria	Budapest, Hung.	Segesvar, Hungary	Bautzen, Germany	Brussels,Belgium	16
17	Spezia, Italy	Mantova, Italy	Agram, Kroatia	Budapest, Hung.	MarosVararnely,Hu.	Dresden, Germany	Brussels,Belgium	17
18	Livorno, Italy	Cremona, Italy	Agram, Kroatia	Budapest, Hung.	Kolosvar, Hungary	Dresden, Germany	Antwerp, Belgium	18
19	Livorno, Italy	Piacenza, Italy	Marburg, Austria	Budapest, Hung.	Kolosvar, Hungary	Dresden, Germany	Antwerp, Belgium	19
20	Livorno, Italy	Pavia, Italy	Klagenfurt, Aust.	Budapest, Hung.	Nagyvarad, Hung.	Dresden, Germany	Ghent, Belgium	20
21	EN ROUTE	Alessandrie, It.	Graz, Austria	Budapest, Hung.	SzatmarNemeti,Hu.	Chemnitz, Germany	Ghent, Belgium	21
22	Rome, Italy	Torino, Italy	Graz, Austria	Budapest, Hung.	MaramarosSziget,H.	Chemnitz, Germany	SEASON ENDS	22
23	Rome, Italy	Torino, Italy	Leoben, Austria	Budapest, Hung.	Kolomea,Galicia	Zwickan, Germany		23
24	Rome, Italy	Torino, Italy	Linz, Austria	Budapest, Hung.	Czernowitz,Buckow	Plauen, Germany		24
25	Rome, Italy	Torino, Italy	En Route	Miskolez,Hung.	Czernowitz,Buckow	Gera, Reuss		25
26	Rome, Italy	Torino, Italy	Vienna, Austria	Hassa, Hungary	Stanislau, Galicia	Weimar,S. Weimar		26
27	Rome, Italy	Asti, Italy	Vienna, Austria	Ungyar, Hungary	Taraopol,Galicia	Eisenach, Germany		27
28	Rome, Italy	Novara, Italy	Vienna, Austria	Munkacs, Hungary	Lemberg, Galicia	Fulda, Prussia		28
29	Terni, Italy	Como, Italy	Vienna, Austria	Nyiregyhaza, Hun	Lemberg, Galicia	Hanau,HasseDarmst.		29
30	Perggia, Italy	Milano, It..ly	Vienna, Austria	Debreczen, Hung.	Lemberg, Galicia	Worms, Germany		30
31	Arezzo, Italy		Vienna, Austria		Lemberg, Galicia	Saarbrucken,Pruss.		31

PLATE 97

SEASON 1907   SOURCE 1907 ROUTE SHEET

	APRIL	MAY	JUNE	JULY	AUGUST	SEPTEMBER	OCTOBER	NOVEMBER	
1		New York, N. Y.	Washington, D. C.	Worcester, Mass.	Chicago, Ill.	SUNDAY	Clarksville, Tenn.		1
2		New York, N. Y.	SUNDAY	Norwich, Conn.	Chicago, Ill.	Cincinnati, O.	Nashville, Tenn.		2
3		New York, N. Y.	Philadelphia, Pa.	Woonsocket, R. I.	Chicago, Ill.	Chillicothe, O.	Huntsville, Ala.		3
4		New York, N. Y.	Philadelphia, Pa.	Fitchburg, Mass.	SUNDAY	Columbus, O.	Chattanooga, Tenn.		4
5		New York, N. Y.	Philadelphia, Pa.	Greenfield, Mass.	Aurora, Ill.	Newark, O.	Rome, Ga.		5
6		New York, N. Y.	Philadelphia, Pa.	North Adams, Mass.	Ottawa, Ill.	Wheeling, W. Va.	SUNDAY		6
7		New York, N. Y.	Philadelphia, Pa.	SUNDAY	Kewanee, Ill.	Washington, Pa.	Atlanta, Ga.		7
8		New York, N. Y.	Philadelphia, Pa.	Troy, N. Y.	Peoria, Ill.	SUNDAY	Opelika, Ala.		8
9		New York, N. Y.	SUNDAY	Utica, N. Y.	Lincoln, Ill.	McKeesport, Pa.	Montgomery, Ala.		9
10		New York, N. Y.	Newark, N. J.	Watertown, N. Y.	Springfield, Ill.	Uniontown, Pa.	Dothan, Ala.		10
11		New York, N. Y.	Jersey City, N. J.	Syracuse, N. Y.	SUNDAY	Connellsville, Pa.	Valdosta, Ga.		11
12		SUNDAY	Newburg, N. Y.	Rochester, N. Y.	Bloomington, Ill.	Cumberland, Md.	Jacksonville, Fla		12
13		Brooklyn, N. Y.	Kingston, N. Y.	Buffalo, N. Y.	Kankakee, Ill.	Hagerstown, Md.	SUNDAY		13
14		Brooklyn, N. Y.	Albany, N. Y.	SUNDAY	Champaign, Ill.	Martinsburg, W.Va.	Savannah, Ga.		14
15		Brooklyn, N. Y.	Pittsfield, Mass.	Erie, Pa.	Decatur, Ill.	SUNDAY	Charleston, S. C.		15
16		Brooklyn, N. Y.	SUNDAY	Ashtabula, O.	Olney, Ill.	Grafton, W. Va.	Florence, S. C.		16
17		Brooklyn, N. Y.	Boston, Mass.	Cleveland, O.	Evansville, Ind.	Clarksburg, W. Va.	Wilmington, N. C.		17
18		Brooklyn, N. Y.	Boston, Mass.	Sandusky, O.	SUNDAY	Parkersburg, W. Va.	Goldsboro, N. C.		18
19		SUNDAY	Boston, Mass.	Toledo, O.	Terre Haute, Ind.	Marietta, O.	Richmond, Va.		19
20		Bridgeport, Conn.	Boston, Mass.	Ft. Wayne, Ind.	Danville, Ill.	Athens, O.	SEASON ENDS.		20
21		New Haven, Conn.	Boston, Mass.	SUNDAY	Lafayette, Ind.	Charleston, W. Va.			21
22		Hartford, Conn.	Boston, Mass.	Chicago, Ill.	Logansport, Ind.	SUNDAY			22
23	New York, N. Y.	SUNDAY	Providence, R. I.	Chicago, Ill.	Marion, Ind.	Portsmouth, O.			23
24	New York, N. Y.	Waterbury, Conn.	Providence, R. I.	Chicago, Ill.	Anderson, Ind.	Huntington, W. Va.			24
25	New York, N. Y.	Poughkeepsie, N. Y.	Newport, R. I.	Chicago, Ill.	SUNDAY	Ashland, Ky.			25
26	New York, N. Y.	SUNDAY	Fall River, Mass.	Chicago, Ill.	Indianapolis, Ind.	Mt. Sterling, Ky.			26
27	New York, N. Y.	Paterson, N. J.	New Bedford, Mass.	Chicago, Ill.	Muncie, Ind.	Lexington, Ky.			27
28	New York, N. Y.	Trenton, N. J.	Brockton, Mass.	Chicago, Ill.	Springfield, O.	Louisville, Ky.			28
29	New York, N. Y.	Baltimore, Md.	Taunton, Mass.	Chicago, Ill.	Dayton, O.	SUNDAY			29
30	New York, N. Y.	Baltimore, Md.	SUNDAY	Chicago, Ill.	Richmond, Ind.	Princeton, Ky.			30
31		Washington, D. C.		Chicago, Ill.	Hamilton, O.				31

PLATE 98

SEASON 1908   SOURCE 1908 ROUTE SHEET

	APRIL	MAY	JUNE	JULY	AUGUST	SEPTEMBER	OCTOBER	NOVEMBER	
1		New York, N. Y.	Cleveland, O.	Oneonta, N. Y.	Niagra Falls, N. Y.	Denver, Col.	Sacramento, Cal.	SUNDAY	1
2		New York, N. Y.	Mansfield, O.	Schenectady, N. Y.	SUNDAY	Colorado Springs, C	Stockton, Cal.	Dallas, Tex.	2
3		New York, N. Y.	Marion, O.	Holyoke, Mass.	Detroit, Mich.	Pueblo, Col.	San Jose, Cal.	Corsicana, Tex.	3
4		New York, N. Y.	Lima, O.	Springfield, Mass	Port Huron, Mich.	Canon City, Col.	Oakland, Cal.	Waco, Tex.	4
5		New York, N. Y.	Muncie, Ind.	SUNDAY	Saginaw, Mich.	Leadville, Col.	Oakland, Cal.	Temple, Tex.	5
6		New York, N. Y.	Kokomo, Ind.	Providence, R. I.	Flint, Mich.	SUNDAY	San Francisco, Cal	SUNDAY	6
7		New York, N. Y.	SUNDAY	Worcester, Mass.	Lansing, Mich.	Grand Junction, Col	San Francisco, Cal	San Antonio, Tex.	7
8		New York, N. Y.	St. Louis, Mo.	Lowell, Mass.	Jackson, Mich.	Provo, Ut.	San Francisco, Cal	SUNDAY	8
9		New York, N. Y.	St. Louis, Mo.	Lawrence, Mass.	SUNDAY	Salt Lake City, Ut.	San Francisco, Cal	Houston, Tex.	9
10		SUNDAY	St. Louis, Mo.	Haverhill, Mass.	Grand Rapids, Mich	Ogden, Ut.	San Francisco, Cal	Beaumont, Tex.	10
11		Philadelphia, Pa.	St. Louis, Mo.	Biddeford, Me.	Kalamazoo, Mich	Idaho Falls, Ida.	San Francisco, Cal	Crowley, La.	11
12		Philadelphia, Pa.	St. Louis, Mo.	SUNDAY	Battle Creek, Mich	Butte, Mont.	Salinas, Cal.	Franklin, La.	12
13		Philadelphia, Pa.	St. Louis, Mo.	Portland, Me.	South Bend, Ind.	SUNDAY	San Luis Obispo, C	New Orleans, La.	13
14		Philadelphia, Pa.	SUNDAY	Waterville, Me.	Joliet, Ill.	Spokane, Wash.	Santa Barbara, Cal	New Orleans, La.	14
15		Philadelphia, Pa.	Indianapolis, Ind	Bangor, Me.	Elgin, Ill.	Colfax, Wash.	Los Angeles, Cal	New Orleans, La.	15
16		Philadelphia, Pa.	Piqua, O.	Lewiston, Me.	SUNDAY	Walla Walla, Wash.	Los Angeles, Cal	SUNDAY	16
17		SUNDAY	Coshocton, O.	Dover, N. H.	Milwaukee, Wis.	N. Yakima, Wash.	San Bernardino, C	Vicksburg, Miss.	17
18		Washington, D. C.	Beaver Falls, Pa.	Manchester, N. H.	Madison, Wis.	Seattle, Wash.	SUNDAY	Memphis, Tenn.	18
19		Washington, D. C.	Pittsburg, Pa.	SUNDAY	La Crosse, Wis.	Seattle, Wash.	Phoenix, Ariz.	SEASON ENDS.	19
20		Baltimore, Md.	Pittsburg, Pa.	Concord, N. H.	Eau Claire, Wis.	SUNDAY	Tucson, Ariz.		20
21	New York, N. Y.	SUNDAY	White River Jct. Vt	Superior, Wis.	Bellingham, Wash.	Bisbee, Ariz.		21
22	New York, N. Y.	York, Pa.	Du Bois, Pa.	Montpelier, Vt.	Duluth, Minn.	Everett, Wash.	Douglas, Ariz		22
23	New York, N. Y.	Lancaster, Pa.	Williamsport, Pa.	Burlington, Vt.	SUNDAY	Tacoma, Wash.	Deming, N. M.		23
24	New York, N. Y.	SUNDAY	Harrisburg, Pa.	Rutland, Vt.	Minneapolis, Minn.	Chehalis, Wash.	El Paso, Tex.		24
25	New York, N. Y.	Johnstown, Pa.	Reading, Pa.	Saratoga Springs,	St. Paul, Minn.	Portland, Ore.	SUNDAY		25
26	New York, N. Y.	Butler, Pa.	Pottsville, Pa.	SUNDAY	St. James, Minn.	Portland, Ore.	Abilene, Tex.		26
27	New York, N. Y.	Oil City, Pa.	Wilkes Barre, Pa.	Utica, N. Y.	Sioux City, Ia.	SUNDAY	Ft. Worth, Tex.		27
28	New York, N. Y.	Youngstown, O.	SUNDAY	Oswego, N. Y.	Omaha, Neb.	Medford, Ore.	Terrell, Tex.		28
29	New York, N. Y.	Canton, O.	Scranton, Pa.	Syracuse, N. Y.	Grand Island, Neb.	Red Bluff, Cal.	Greenville, Tex.		29
30	New York, N. Y.	Akron, O.	Binghamton, N. Y.	Auburn, N. Y.	SUNDAY	Marysville, Cal.	Paris, Tex.		30
31		SUNDAY		Rochester, N. Y.	Denver, Col.		Sherman, Tex.		31

PLATE 99

SEASON 1909   SOURCE 1909 ROUTE SHEET

	APRIL	MAY	JUNE	JULY	AUGUST	SEPTEMBER	OCTOBER	NOVEMBER	
1		New York, N. Y.	Washington, D. C.	London, Ont.	SUNDAY	Hastings, Neb.	Coalgate, Okla.	Wilmington, N. C.	1
2		New York, N. Y.	Baltimore, Md.	St. Thomas, Ont.	Terre Haute, Ind.	Kearney, Neb.	McAlester, Okla.	Wilson, N. C.	2
3		New York, N. Y.	Baltimore, Md.	Chatham, Ont.	Champaign, Ill.	Columbus, Neb.	SUNDAY	Tarboro, N. C.	3
4		New York, N. Y.	Wilmington, Del.	SUNDAY	Mattoon, Ill.	Fremont, Neb.	Muskogee, Okla.	Suffolk, Va.	4
5		New York, N. Y.		Detroit, Mich.	Springfield, Ill.	SUNDAY	Tulsa, Okla.	Norfolk, Va.	5
6		New York, N. Y.	SUNDAY	Toledo, O.	Jacksonville, Ill.	Omaha, Neb.	Bartlesville, Okla	Richmond, Va.	6
7		New York, N. Y.	Trenton, N. J.	Ft. Wayne, Ind.	Keokuk, Ia.	Red Oak, Ia.	Parsons, Kan.	SEASON ENDS.	7
8		New York, N. Y.	Long Branch, N. J	Warsaw, Ind.	SUNDAY	Shenandoah, Ia.	Joplin, Mo.		8
9		New York, N. Y.	New Brunswick,N.J	Valparaiso, Ind.	Burlington, Ia.	Maryville, Mo.	Springfield, Mo.		9
10		New York, N. Y.	Elizabeth, N. J.	Hammond, Ind.	Muscatine, Ia.	St. Joseph, Mo.	SUNDAY		10
11		New York, N. Y.	Newark, N. J.	SUNDAY	Cedar Rapids, Ia.	Leavenworth, Kan.	Memphis, Tenn.		11
12		New York, N. Y.	Jersey City, N.J.	Chicago, Ill.	Davenport, Ia.	SUNDAY	Aberdeen, Miss.		12
13		New York, N. Y.	SUNDAY	Chicago, Ill.	Washington, Ia.	Kansas City, Mo.	Birmingham, Ala.		13
14		New York, N. Y.	Paterson, N. J.	Chicago, Ill.	Oskaloosa, Ia.	Lawrence, Kan.	Decatur, Ala.		14
15		New York, N. Y.	Newburg, N. Y.	Chicago, Ill.	SUNDAY	Topeka, Kan.	Columbia, Tenn.		15
16		SUNDAY	Kingston, N. Y.	Chicago, Ill.	Des Moines, Ia.	Junction City, Kan	Nashville, Tenn.		16
17		Brooklyn, N. Y.	Albany, N. Y.	Chicago, Ill.	Marshalltown, Ia.	Salina, Kan.	SUNDAY		17
18		Brooklyn, N. Y.	Glens Falls, N. Y.	SUNDAY	Waterloo, Ia.	McPherson, Kan.	Chattanooga, Tenn		18
19		Brooklyn, N. Y.	Plattsburg, N. Y.	Kenosha, Wis.	New Hampton, Ia.	SUNDAY	Marietta, Ga.		19
20		Brooklyn, N. Y.	SUNDAY	Beloit, Wis.	Rochester, Minn.	EMPORIA, KAN	Atlanta, Ga.		20
21		Brooklyn, N. Y.	Montreal, Que.	Freeport, Ill.	Faribault, Minn.		Macon, Ga.		21
22		Brooklyn, N. Y.	Montreal, Que.	Clinton, Ia.	SUNDAY		Cordele, Ga.		22
23		SUNDAY	Ottawa, Ont.	Maquoketa, Ia.	Mankato, Minn.		Fitzgerald, Ga.		23
24		Philadelphia, Pa.	Brookville, Ont.	Sterling, Ill.	Worthington, Minn.	Pawnee, Okla.	SUNDAY		24
25		Philadelphia, Pa.	Kingston, Ont.	SUNDAY		Guthrie, Okla	Jacksonville, Fla		25
26		Philadelphia, Pa.	Belleville, Ont.	Peoria, Ill.	Sioux Falls, S. D.	SUNDAY	Waycross, Ga.		26
27	New York, N. Y.	Philadelphia, Pa.	SUNDAY	Bloomington, Ill.	Sioux City, Ia.	Enid, Okla.	Savannah, Ga.		27
28	New York, N. Y.	Philadelphia, Pa.	Toronto, Ont.	Pontiac, Ill.	Council Bluffs, Ia	Oklahoma City,Okla	Charleston, S. C.		28
29	New York, N. Y.	Philadelphia, Pa.	Hamilton, Ont.	Kankakee, Ill.	SUNDAY	Ardmore, Okla.	Sumter, S. C.		29
30	New York, N. Y.	SUNDAY	Brantford, Ont.	Danville, Ill.	Lincoln, Neb.	Shawnee, Okla.	Fayetteville, N.C		30
31			Washington, D. C.	Crawfordsville,Ill	York, Neb.		SUNDAY		31

PLATE 100

SEASON 1910   SOURCE 1910 ROUTE SHEET

	APRIL	MAY	JUNE	JULY	AUGUST	SEPTEMBER	OCTOBER	NOVEMBER	
1		New York City, NY	Wheeling, W. Va.	Mt. Vernon, Ohio	Decatur, Ill.	Helena, Mont.	Oakland, Calif.	San Antonio, Tex.	1
2		New York City, NY	Parkersburg, W.V	Washington, Ohio	Clinton, Ill.	Butte, Mont.	Oakland, Calif.	Victoria, Tex.	2
3		New York City, NY	Chillicothe, O.	Cincinnati, Ohio	Mendota, Ill.	Missoula, Mont.	Santa Cruz, Calif	Galveston, Tex.	3
4		New York City, NY	Columbus, Ohio	Cincinnati, Ohio	Rockford, Ill.	SUNDAY	Watsonville, Cal.	Houston, Tex.	4
5		New York City, NY	SUNDAY	Dayton, Ohio	Janesville, Wis.	Spokane, Wash.	San Francisco, C.	Brenham, Tex.	5
6		New York City, NY	Cleveland, Ohio	Springfield, Ohio	Madison, Wis.	Ritzville, Wash.	San Francisco, C.	SUNDAY	6
7		New York City, NY	Cleveland, Ohio	Bellefontaine, O.	Milwaukee, Wis.	N. Yakima, Wash.	San Francisco, C.	Austin, Tex.	7
8		New York City, NY	Erie, Pa.	Findlay, Ohio	Milwaukee, Wis.	Seattle, Wash.	San Francisco, C.	Temple, Tex.	8
9		New York City, NY	Dunkirk, N. Y.	Lima, Ohio	Fond du Lac, Wis.	Seattle, Wash.	San Francisco, C.	Waco, Tex.	9
10		New York City, NY	Buffalo, N. Y.	SUNDAY	Neenah-Menasha, W	Seattle, Wash.	San Jose, Calif.	Corsicana, Tex.	10
11		New York City, NY	Buffalo, N. Y.	Adrian, Mich.	Stevens Point, W.	SUNDAY	Stockton, Calif.	Dallas, Tex.	11
12		New York City, NY	SUNDAY	Ypsilanti, Mich.	Chippewa Falls, W	Vancouver, B. C.	Fresno, Calif.	Fort Worth, Tex.	12
13		New York City, NY	Rochester, N. Y.	Detroit, Mich.	New Richmond, Wis	Vancouver, B. C.	Visalia, Calif.	SUNDAY	13
14		New York City, NY	Geneva, N. Y.	Jackson, Mich.	SUNDAY	Bellingham, Wash.	Bakersfield, Cal.	Sherman, Tex.	14
15		SUNDAY	Auburn, N. Y.	Battle Creek, Mi.	St. Paul, Minn.	Everett, Wash.	Santa Barbara, C.	Paris, Tex.	15
16		Trenton, N. J.	Syracuse, N. Y.	Kalamazoo, Mich.	Minneapolis, Minn.	Tacoma, Wash.	SUNDAY	SUNDAY	16
17		Coatesville, Pa.	Utica, N. Y.	SUNDAY	Duluth, Minn.	Centralia, Wash.	Los Angeles, Cal	Camden, Ark.	17
18		Harrisburg, Pa.	Norwich, N. Y.	Grand Rapids, Mi.	Little Falls, Min	SUNDAY	Los Angeles, Cal	Pine Bluff, Ark.	18
19		Reading, Pa.	SUNDAY	Lansing, Mich.	Fergus Falls, Min	Portland, Ore.	San Diego, Cal.	Little Rock, Ark.	19
20		Allentown, Pa.	Binghampton, NY	Flint, Mich.	Crookston, Minn.	Portland, Ore.	Santa Ana, Cal.		20
21		Easton, Pa.	Corning, N. Y.	Bay City, Mich.	Salem, Ore.	Riverside, Cal.	SEASON ENDS	21
22		SUNDAY	Hornell, N. Y.	Saginaw, Mich.	Winnipeg, Man.	Eugene, Ore.	San Bernardino, C		22
23		Scranton, Pa.	Olean, N. Y.	Big Rapids, Mich.	Winnipeg, Man.	Roseburg, Ore.	Yuma, Ariz.		23
24		Wilkesbarre, Pa.	Bradford, Pa.	SUNDAY	Grand Forks, N. D	Medford, Ore.	Phoenix, Ariz.		24
25		Sunbury, Pa.	Jamestown, N. Y.	Muskegon, Mich.	Fargo, N. D.	SUNDAY	Tucson, Ariz.		25
26	New York City NY	Williamsport, Pa.	SUNDAY	Benton Harbor, M.	Jamestown, N. D.	Redding, Calif.	Bisbee, Ariz.		26
27	New York City NY	Tyrone, Pa.	Meadville, Pa.	Goshen, Indiana	Bismarck, N. D.	Chico, Calif.	Douglas, Ariz.		27
28	New York City NY	Johnstown, Pa.	New Castle, Pa.	South Bend, Ind.	Dickinson, N. D.	Sacramento, Calif	Deming, N. Mex.		28
29	New York City NY	SUNDAY	Youngstown, Ohio	Logansport, Ind.	Miles City, Mont.	Santa Rosa, Calif	El Paso, Texas		29
30	New York City NY	Pittsburg, Pa.	Akron, Ohio	Lafayette, Ind.	Billings, Mont.	Vallejo, Calif.	SUNDAY		30
31		Pittsburg, Pa.		SUNDAY	Great Falls, Mont		Del Rio, Texas		31

PLATE 101

SEASON 1911   SOURCE 1910 & 1911 ROUTE FLYER

	APRIL	MAY	JUNE	JULY	AUGUST	SEPTEMBER	OCTOBER	NOVEMBER	
1		Chester, Pa.	Bangor, Me.	Greensburg, Pa.	Burlington, Ia.	Emporia, Kan.	SUNDAY	Richmond, Va.	1
2		Camden, N. J.	Waterville, Me.	SUNDAY	Moline, Ill.	Topeka, Kan.	St. Louis, Mo.	SEASON ENDS.	2
3		Trenton, N. J.	Lewiston, Me.	Allagheny, N. Y.	Davenport, Ia.	Kansas City, Mo.	St. Louis, Mo.		3
4		Newark, N. J.	SUNDAY	Beaver Falls, Pa.	Clinton, Ia.	Kansas City, Mo.	St. Louis, Mo.		4
5		Jersey City, N. J.	Portland, Me.	Canton, O.	Cedar Rapids, Ia.	Harrisonville, Mo.	St. Louis, Mo.		5
6		Newburg, N. Y.	Dover, N. H.	Mansfield, O.	SUNDAY	Nevada, Mo.	St. Louis, Mo.		6
7		SUNDAY	Haverhill, Mass.	Toledo, O.	Ottumwa, Ia.	Joplin, Mo.	St. Louis, Mo.		7
8		Kingston, N. Y.	Lawrence, Mass.	Ft. Wayne, Ind.	Des Moines, Ia.	Pittsburg, Kan.	SUNDAY		8
9		Albany, N. Y.	Manchester, N. H.	SUNDAY	Marshalltown, Ia.	Ft. Scott, Kan.	Belleville, Ill.		9
10		Poughkeepsie, N.Y	Nashua, N. H.	Muncie, Ind.	Waterloo, Ia.	SUNDAY	Murphysboro, Ill		10
11		Winsted, Conn.	SUNDAY	Indianapolis, Ind	Ft. Dodge, Ia.	Iola, Kan.	Cairo, Ill.		11
12		Hartford, Conn.	Concord, N. H.	Terre Haute, Ind.	Council Bluffs, Ia	Ottawa, Kan.	Dyersburg, Tenn.		12
13		Springfield, Mass.	White River, Jct.	Danville, Ill.	SUNDAY	Leavenworth, Kan.	Memphis, Tenn.		13
14		SUNDAY	Montpelier, Vt.	Watseka, Ill.	Omaha, Neb.	St. Joseph, Mo.	Tupelo, Miss.		14
15		Boston, Mass.	Burlington, Vt.	Chicago, Ill.	Lincoln, Neb.	Atchison, Kan.	SUNDAY		15
16		Boston, Mass.	Rutland, Vt.	Chicago, Ill.	York, Neb.	Falls City, Neb.	Birmingham, Ala.		16
17	Washington, D. C.	Boston, Mass.	Saratoga, N. Y.	Chicago, Ill.	Hastings, Neb.	SUNDAY	Columbus, Ga.		17
18	Washington, D. C.	Boston, Mass.	SUNDAY	Chicago, Ill.	Grand Island, Neb	Nebraska City, Neb	Macon, Ga.		18
19	Baltimore, Md.	Boston, Mass.	Troy, N. Y.	Chicago, Ill.	North Platte, Neb	Clarinda, Ia.	Atlanta, Ga.		19
20	Baltimore, Md.	Boston, Mass.	Schenectady, N.Y.	Chicago, Ill.	SUNDAY	Red Oak, Ia.	Rome, Ga.		20
21	Wilmington, Del.	SUNDAY	Little Falls, N.Y	Chicago, Ill.	Sterling, Col.	Creston, Ia.	Chattanooga, Tenn.		21
22	Lancaster, Pa.	Worcester, Mass.	Watertown, N. Y.	Chicago, Ill.	Greeley, Col.	Maryville, Mo.	SUNDAY		22
23	SUNDAY	Fitchburg, Mass.	Oswego, N. Y.	Chicago, Ill.	Denver, Col.	Chillicothe, Mo.	Knoxville, Tenn.		23
24	Philadelphia, Pa.	Lowell, Mass.	Cortland, N. Y.	Aurora, Ill.	Denver, Col.	Carrollton, Mo.	Morristown, Tenn.		24
25	Philadelphia, Pa.	Lynn, Mass.	SUNDAY	Galesburg, Ill.	Col. Springs, Col.	Moberly, Mo.	Bristol, Tenn.		25
26	Philadelphia, Pa.	Salem, Mass.	Ithaca, N. Y.	Peoria, Ill.	Pueblo, Col.	Kirksville, Mo.	Pulaski, Va.		26
27	Philadelphia, Pa.	Newburyport, Mass.	Wellsboro, Pa.	Springfield, Ill.	SUNDAY	Macon, Mo.	Roanoke, Va.		27
28	Philadelphia, Pa.	SUNDAY	Lock Haven, Pa.	Jacksonville, Ill	Garden City, Kan.	Hannibal, Mo.	Lynchburg, Va.		28
29	Philadelphia, Pa.	Portsmouth, N. H.	Altoona, Pa.	Quincy, Ill.	Great Bend, Kan.	Louisiana, Mo.	SUNDAY		29
30	SUNDAY	Biddeford, Me.		SUNDAY	Hutchinson, Kan.		Norfolk, Va.		30
31		Augusta, Me.		Keokuk, Ia.	Wichita, Kan.		Petersburg, Va.		31

PLATE 102

SEASON 1912   SOURCE 1912 ROUTE SHEET

	APRIL	MAY	JUNE	JULY	AUGUST	SEPTEMBER	OCTOBER	
1		Brooklyn, N. Y.	Jamestown, N. Y.	Wheeling, W. Va.	La Crosse, Wis.	SUNDAY	Beaumont, Tex.	1
2		Brooklyn, N. Y.	SUNDAY	Canal Dover, O.	Winona, Minn.	Iowa Falls, Ia.	Crowley, La.	2
3		Brooklyn, N. Y.	Warren, Pa.	Akron, O.	Eau Claire, Wis.	Webster City, Ia.	Opelousas, La.	3
4		Brooklyn, N. Y.	Titusville, Pa.	Cleveland, O.	SUNDAY	Cherokee, Ia.	Baton Rouge, La.	4
5		SUNDAY	Oil City, Pa.	Sandusky, O.	Minneapolis, Minn	Sheldon, Ia.	New Orleans, La.	5
6		Mt. Vernon, N. Y.	Kittanning, Pa.	Fremont, O.	St. Paul, Minn.	Sioux Falls, S. D.	New Orleans, La.	6
7		S. Norwalk, Conn.	Butler, Pa.	SUNDAY	Superior, Wis.	Sioux City, Ia.	Hattiesburg, Miss.	7
8		Bridgeport, Conn.	Charleroi, Pa.	Detroit, Mich.	Duluth, Minn.	SUNDAY	Mobile, Ala.	8
9		New Haven, Conn.	SUNDAY	Port Huron, Mich.	Ashland, Wis.	Norfolk, Neb.	Meridian, Miss.	9
10		New London, Conn.	Connellsville, Pa	Flint, Mich.	Ironwood, Mich.	Fremont, Neb.	Columbus, Miss.	10
11		New Bedford, Conn.	Uniontown, Pa.	Saginaw, Mich.	SUNDAY	Columbus, Neb.	Tuscaloosa, Ala.	11
12		SUNDAY	Morgantown, W. Va	Owosso, Mich.	Iron Mountain, Mich	Seward, Neb.	Montgomery, Ala.	12
13		Providence, R. I.	Fairmont, W. Va.	Lansing, Mich.	Hancock, Mich.	Beatrice, Neb.	SUNDAY	13
14		Norwich, Conn.	Clarksburg, W.Va.	SUNDAY	Calumet, Mich.	Marysville, Kan.	Dothan, Ala.	14
15		Willimantic, Conn.	Parkersburg, W.Va	Jackson, Mich.	Ishpeming, Mich.	SUNDAY	Thomasville, Ga.	15
16		Middletown, Conn.	SUNDAY	Grand Rapids, Mich.	Escanaba, Mich.	Abiline, Kan.	Valdosta, Ga.	16
17		Meriden, Conn.	Charleston, W. Va.	Kalamazoo, Mich.	Menominee, Mich.	Eldorado, Kan.	Lake City, Fla.	17
18		Danbury, Conn.	Huntington, W. Va	Elkhart, Ind.	SUNDAY	Arkansas City, Kan.	Gainesville, Fla.	18
19		SUNDAY	Ashland, Ky.	La Porte, Ind.	Green Bay, Wis.	Oklahoma City, Okla	Ocala, Fla.	19
20	Harrisburg, Pa.	Albany, N. Y.	Ironton, O.	Chicago, Ill.	Oshkosh, Wis.	El Reno, Okla.	SUNDAY	20
21	SUNDAY	Amsterdam, N. Y.	Portsmouth, O.	Chicago, Ill.	Appleton, Wis.	Chickasha, Okla.	Tampa, Fla.	21
22	Reading, Pa.	Gloversville, N. Y	Hillsboro, O.	Joliet, Ill.	Manitowoc, Wis.	SUNDAY	Orlando, Fla.	22
23	Allentown, Pa.	Utica, N. Y.	SUNDAY	Rock Island, Ill.	Sheboygan, Wis.	Ft. Worth, Tex.	Palatka, Fla.	23
24	Wilkes Barre, Pa.	Syracuse, N. Y.	Cincinnati, O.	Muscatine, Ia.	Milwaukee, Wis.	Dallas, Tex.	Jacksonville, Fla	24
25	Scranton, Pa.	Lyons, N. Y.	Hamilton, O.	Iowa City, Ia.	Milwaukee, Wis.	Waco, Tex.	Brunswick, Ga.	25
26	Middletown, N. Y.	SUNDAY	Dayton, O.	Oelwein, Ia.	Waukegan, Ill.	Taylor, Tex.	Savannah, Ga.	26
27	Paterson, N. J.	Rochester, N. Y.	Springfield, O.	Decorah, Ia.	Elgin, Ill.	Austin, Tex.	SUNDAY	27
28	SUNDAY	Batavia, N. Y.	Columbus, O.	SUNDAY	Freeport, Ill.	San Antonio, Tex.	Augusta, Ga.	28
29	Brooklyn, N. Y.	Lockport, N. Y.	Zanesville, O.	Charles City, Ia.	Dubuque, Ia.	SUNDAY	Sumter, S. C.	29
30	Brooklyn, N. Y.	Buffalo, N. Y.	SUNDAY	Austin, Minn.	Manchester, Ia.	Houston, Tex.	Columbia, S. C.	30
31		Dunkirk, N. Y.		Spring Valley, Minn	Cedar Falls, Ia.		SEASON ENDS.	31

PLATE 103

SEASON 1913   SOURCE 1913 MONTHLY ROUTE SHEETS.

	APRIL	MAY	JUNE	JULY	
1		New York, N. Y.	SUNDAY	Chicago, Ill.	1
2		New York, N. Y.	Lynchburg, Va.	Chicago, Ill.	2
3	Philadelphia, Pa.	New York, N. Y.	Roanoke, Va.	Chicago, Ill.	3
4	Philadelphia, Pa.	New York, N. Y.	Wytheville, Va.	Chicago, Ill.	4
5	Philadelphia, Pa.	New York, N. Y.	Bristol, Tenn.	Chicago, Ill.	5
6	Philadelphia, Pa.	New York, N. Y.	Knoxville, Tenn.	Chicago, Ill.	6
7	Philadelphia, Pa.	New York, N. Y.	Chattanooga, Tenn	Ottawa, Ill.	7
8	Philadelphia, Pa.	New York, N. Y.	SUNDAY	Moline, Ill.	8
9	Philadelphia, Pa.	New York, N. Y.	Atlanta, Ga.	Davenport, Ia.	9
10	Philadelphia, Pa.	New York, N. Y.	Anniston, Ala.	Fairfield, Ia.	10
11	Philadelphia, Pa.	SUNDAY	Birmingham, Ala.	Oskaloosa, Ia.	11
12	Philadelphia, Pa.	Jersey City, N. J.	Sheffield, Ala.	Des Moines, Ia.	12
13	Philadelphia, Pa.	Newark, N. J.	Corinth, Miss.	SUNDAY	13
14	Philadelphia, Pa.	Trenton, N. J.	Jackson, Tenn.	Council Bluffs, Ia.	14
15	Philadelphia, Pa.	Wilmington, Del.	SUNDAY	Omaha, Neb.	15
16	Philadelphia, Pa.	Lancaster, Pa.	Memphis, Tenn.	Lincoln, Neb.	16
17	Philadelphia, Pa.	York, Pa.	Fulton, Ky.	York, Neb.	17
18	Philadelphia, Pa.	SUNDAY	Paducah, Ky.	Hastings, Neb.	18
19	Philadelphia, Pa.	Baltimore, Md.	Evansville, Ind.	Kearney, Neb.	19
20	SUNDAY	Baltimore, Md.	Owensboro, Ky.	Julesburg, Col.	20
21		Washington, D. C.	Louisville, Ky.	Denver, Col.	21
22	New York, N. Y.	Washington, D. C.	SUNDAY	Denver, Col.	22
23	New York, N. Y.	Fredericksburg, Va.	Indianapolis, Ind	SEASON ENDS.	23
24	New York, N. Y.	Richmond, Va.	Terre Haute, Ind.		24
25	New York, N. Y.	SUNDAY	Danville, Ill.		25
26	New York, N. Y.	Norfolk, Va.	Lafayette, Ind.		26
27	New York, N. Y.	Henderson, N. C.	Kankakee, Ill.		27
28	New York, N. Y.	Raleigh, N. C.	Chicago, Ill.		28
29	New York, N. Y.	Durham, N. C.	Chicago, Ill.		29
30	New York, N. Y.	Winston Salem, N.C	Chicago, Ill.		30
31		Danville, Va.			31

PLATE 104

SEASON 1914   SOURCE 1914 ROUTE FLYER

	MARCH	APRIL	MAY	JUNE	JULY	AUGUST	SEPTEMBER	OCTOBER	
1		Tucson, Ariz.	Berkeley, Cal.	N. Yakima, Wash.	Sioux City, Ia.	Spokane, Wash.	Kalamazoo, Mich.	Pittsburg, Kan.	1
2		Phoenix, Ariz.	Modesto, Cal.	Walla Walla, Wash.	Yankton, S. D.	SUNDAY	Battle Creek, Mich	Independence, Kan.	2
3		Yuma, Ariz.	SUNDAY	Pendleton, Ore.	Mitchell, S. D.	Missoula, Mont.	Jackson, Mich.	Winfield, Kan.	3
4		Redlands, Cal.	Hanford, Cal.	Baker City, Ore.	Sioux Falls, S.D.	Butte, Mont.	Lansing, Mich.	SUNDAY	4
5		SUNDAY	Fresno, Cal.	Fayette, Ida.	SUNDAY	Helena, Mont.	Saginaw, Mich.	Oklahoma City, O.	5
6		San Diego, Cal.	Stockton, Cal.	Boise, Ida.	Minneapolis, Minn	Great Falls, Mont	SUNDAY	Ardmore, Okla.	6
7		Santa Ana, Cal.	Sacramento, Cal.	SUNDAY	Minneapolis, Minn	Lewistown, Mont.	Detroit, Mich.	Gainesville, Tex.	7
8		Riverside, Cal.	Chico, Cal.	Twin Falls, Ida.	St. Paul, Minn.	Billings, Mont.	Toledo, O.	Denison, Tex.	8
9		Pomona, Cal.	Redding, Cal.	Pocatello, Ida.	St. Cloud, Minn.	SUNDAY	Cleveland, O.	Durant, Okla.	9
10		Long Beach, Cal.	Montague, Cal.	Logan, Utah	Fargo, N. D.	Sheridan, Wyo.	Cleveland, O.	Denton, Tex.	10
11		Pasadena, Cal.	Medford, Ore.	Salt Lake City, U	Grand Forks, N.D.	Edgemont, S. D.	Akron, O.	SUNDAY	11
12		Venice, Cal.	Roseburg, Ore.	Ogden, Utah	SUNDAY	Alliance, Neb.	Canton, O.	Dallas, Tex.	12
13		Los Angeles, Cal.	Eugene, Ore.	Rock Springs, Wyo.	St. Boniface, Man	Grand Island, Neb	SUNDAY	Corsicana, Tex.	13
14		Los Angeles, Cal.	Salem, Ore.	SUNDAY	St. Boniface, Man	Columbus, Neb.	Columbus, O.	Ft. Worth, Tex.	14
15		Los Angeles, Cal.	Albany, Ore.	Greeley, Col.	Brandon, Man.	Beatrice, Neb.	Springfield, O.	Wichita Falls, Tex	15
16		Santa Barbara, Cal	McMinnville, Ore.	Denver, Col.	Weyburn, Sask.	SUNDAY	Dayton, O.	SEASON ENDS.	16
17		San Luis Obispo, C	SUNDAY	Denver, Col.	Moose Jaw, Sask.	St. Joseph, Mo.	Hamilton, O.		17
18		Santa Cruz, Cal.	Portland, Ore.	Colorado Springs,	Regina, Sask.	Creston, Ia.	Richmond, Ind.		18
19		Richmond, Cal.	Portland, Ore.	Pueblo, Col.	SUNDAY	Des Moines, Ia.	Muncie, Ind.		19
20		Oakland, Cal.	Centralia, Wash.	La Junta, Col.	Saskatoon, Sask.	Iowa City, Ia.	SUNDAY		20
21		Oakland, Cal.	Aberdeen, Wash.	SUNDAY	N. Brattleford, S.	Cedar Rapids, Ia.	Indianapolis, Ind.		21
22		San Francisco, Cal	Tacoma, Wash.	Hutchinson, Kan.	Edmonton, Alta.	Dubuque, Ia.	Terre Haute, Ind.		22
23		San Francisco, Cal	Sedro Wooley, Wash	Wichita, Kan.	Edmonton, Alta.	SUNDAY	Danville, Ill.		23
24		San Francisco, Cal	SUNDAY	Emporia, Kan.	Calgary, Alta.	Milwaukee, Wis.	Bloomington, Ill.		24
25		San Francisco, Cal	Vancouver, B. C.	Topeka, Kan.	Calgary, Alta.	Oshkosh, Wis.	Jacksonville, Ill		25
26		San Francisco, Cal	Bellingham, Wash.	Kansas City, Kan.	SUNDAY	Racine, Wis.	Hannibal, Mo.		26
27		San Jose, Cal.	Everett, Wash.	Kansas City, Kan.	Medicine Hat, Alta	Waukegan, Ill.	SUNDAY		27
28	Albuquerque, N. M.	Vallejo, Cal.	Seattle, Wash.	SUNDAY	Lethbridge, Alta.	Gary, Ind.	Moberly, Mo.		28
29	SUNDAY	Petaluma, Cal.	Seattle, Wash.	Lincoln, Neb.	Fernie, B. C.	Elkhart, Ind.	Sedalia, Mo.		29
30	El Paso, Texas	Santa Rosa, Cal.	Seattle, Wash.	Omaha, Neb.	Kalispel, Mont.	SUNDAY	Fort Scott, Kan.		30
31	Douglas, Arizona		Gle Elum, Wash.		Sand Point, Ida.	Grand Rapids, Mich			31

PLATE 105

Reproduced by permission of Ringling Bros. – Barnum & Bailey Combined Shows Inc.

SEASON 1915   SOURCE 1915 ROUTE FLYER

	APRIL	MAY	JUNE	JULY	AUGUST	SEPTEMBER	OCTOBER	NOVEMBER	
1		San Jose, Cal.	Seattle, Wash.	York, Neb.	SUNDAY	Columbus, Kan.	Elk City, Okla.	Laredo, Tex.	1
2		San Francisco, Cal	Seattle, Wash.	Hastings, Neb.	Ottawa, Ill.	Chanute, Kan.	Amarillo, Tex.	Pearsall, Tex.	2
3		San Francisco, Cal	Everett, Wash.	Fairbury, Neb.	Streator, Ill.	Lawrence, Kan.	SUNDAY	San Antonio, Tex.	3
4		San Francisco, Cal	Cle Elum, Wash.	SUNDAY	Princeton, Ill.	Ottawa, Kan.	Roswell, N. M.	Del Rio, Tex.	4
5		San Francisco, Cal	N. Yakima, Wash.	Kansas City, Mo.	Galesburg, Ill.	SUNDAY	Clovis, N. M.	Enroute	5
6		San Francisco, Cal	SUNDAY	St. Joseph, Mo.	Keokuk, Ia.	Wichita, Kan.	Lubbock, Tex.	El Paso, Tex.	6
7		Santa Cruz, Cal.	Lewiston, Ida.	Shenandoah, Ia.	Ft. Madison, Ia.	McPherson, Kan.	Sweetwater, Tex.	SUNDAY	7
8		Berkley, Cal.	Moscow, Ida.	SUNDAY	SUNDAY	Pratt, Kan.	Brownwood, Tex.	Albuquerque, N. M	8
9		Richmond, Cal.	Walla Walla, Wash	Fremont, Neb.	Oskaloosa, Ia.	Dodge City, Kan.	San Angelo, Tex.	SEASON ENDS.	9
10		Oakland, Cal.	Pendleton, Ore.	Norfolk, Neb.	Washington, Ia.	Larned, Kan.	SUNDAY		10
11		Oakland, Cal.	Baker City, Ore.	SUNDAY	Ottumwa, Ia.	Newton, Kan.	Ballenger, Tex.		11
12		Oakland, Cal.	Boise, Ida.	Mankato, Minn.	Kirksville, Mo.	SUNDAY	Dublin, Tex.		12
13	San Bernardino, Cal	Santa Rosa, Cal.	SUNDAY	Fairbault, Minn.	Columbia, Mo.	Salina, Kan.	Stamford, Tex.		13
14	Riverside, Cal.	Sacramento, Cal.	Twin Falls, Ida.	Austin, Minn.	Moberly, Mo.	Manhattan, Kan.	Alslene, Tex.		14
15	Santa Ana, Cal.	Chico, Cal.	Pocatello, Ida.	La Crosse, Wis.	Clinton, Mo.	Clay Center, Kan.	Weatherford, Tex.		15
16	San Diego, Cal.	Montague, Cal.	Logan, Utah	Grand Rapids, Wis.	Clinton, Mo.	Holton, Kan.	Cleburne, Tex.		16
17	San Diego, Cal.	Medford, Ore.	Salt Lake City, Ut	Wausau, Wis.	Sedalia, Mo.	Kansas City, Mo.	SUNDAY		17
18	SUNDAY	Roseburg, Ore.	Ogden, Ut.	SUNDAY	Jefferson City, Mo	Independence, Mo.	Ft. Worth, Tex.		18
19	Los Angeles, Cal.	Eugene, Ore.	Rock Springs, Wyo	Green Bay, Wis.	Marshall, Mo.	SUNDAY	Terrell, Tex.		19
20	Los Angeles, Cal.	Salem, Ore.	SUNDAY	Appleton, Wis.	Lexington, Mo.	Ft. Scott, Kan.	Ennis, Tex.		20
21	Los Angeles, Cal.	McMinnville, Ore.	Denver, Col.	Sheboygan, Wis.	Warrenburg, Mo.	Independence, Kan.	Corsicana		21
22	Long Beach, Cal.	Astoria, Ore.	Denver, Col.	Kenosha, Wis.	SUNDAY	Ponca City, Kan.	Bryan, Tex.		22
23	Pasadena, Cal.	SUNDAY	Boulder, Col.	Elgin, Ill.	Nevada, Mo.	Perry, Okla.	Brenham, Tex.		23
24	Santa Barbara, Cal	Portland, Ore.	Greeley, Col.	Chicago, Ill.	Webb City, Mo.	Cushing, Okla.	SUNDAY		24
25	SUNDAY	Portland, Ore.	Ft. Collins, Col.	Chicago, Ill.	Aurora, Mo.	Enid, Okla.	Galveston, Tex.		25
26	Bakersfield, Cal.	Centralia, Wash.	Cheyenne, Wyo.	Hammond, Ind.	Springfield, Mo.	SUNDAY	Houston, Tex.		26
27	Hanford, Cal.	Aberdeen, Wash.	SUNDAY	Dowagiac, Mich.	Carthage, Mo.	Anadarko, Okla.	Yoakum, Tex.		27
28	Fresno, Cal.	Tacoma, Wash.	N. Platte, Neb.	Battle Creek, Mich	Vinita, Okla.	Mangum, Okla.	Beeville, Tex.		28
29	Modesto, Cal.	Bellingham, Wash.	Kearney, Neb.	Kalamazoo, Mich.	Muskogee, Okla.	Frederick, Okla.	Victoria, Tex.		29
30	Stockton, Cal.	SUNDAY	Columbus, Neb.	Benton Harbor, Mich	Muskogee, Okla.	Frederick, Okla.	Corpus Christi, T.		30
31		Seattle, Wash.		Joliet, Ill.	Parsons, Kan.		SUNDAY		31

PLATE 106

BUFFALO BILL (HIMSELF) AND 101 RANCH WILD WEST COMBINED
******* **** ********* *** *** ***** **** **** *******

SEASON 1916   SOURCE 1916 ROUTE SHEET

	APRIL	MAY	JUNE	JULY	AUGUST	SEPTEMBER	OCTOBER	NOVEMBER	
1		Litchfield, Ill.	Baltimore, Md.	Quincy, Mass.	Amsterdam, N. Y.	Lansing, Mich.	SUNDAY	Danville, Va.	1
2		Danville, Ill.	Wilmington, Del.	SUNDAY	Herkimer, N. Y.	Pontiac, Mich.	Frederick, Md.	Burlington, N. C.	2
3		Huntington, Ind.	Wilmington, Del.	New Bedford, Mass	Utica, N. Y.	SUNDAY	Martinsburg, W. Va	Durham, N. C.	3
4		Toledo, O.	SUNDAY	Fall River, Mass.	Oswego, N. Y.	Flint, Mich.	Winchester, Va.	Henderson, N. C.	4
5		Detroit, Mich.	Newburg, N. Y.	Newport, R. I.	Watertown, N. Y.	Mt. Pleasant, Mich	Staunton, Va.	SUNDAY	5
6		Detroit, Mich.	Albany, N. Y.	Pawtucket, R. I.	SUNDAY	Cadillac, Mich.	Lexington, Va.	Wilson, N. C.	6
7		SUNDAY	N. Adams, Mass.	Providence, R. I.	Rochester, N. Y.	Traverse City, Mich	Roanoke, Va.	Scotland Neck, N. C.	7
8		Columbus, O.	Springfield, Mass	Providence, R. I.	Olean, N. Y.	Manistee, Mich.	SUNDAY	Greenville, N. C.	8
9		Mt. Vernon, O.	Worcester, Mass.	SUNDAY	Bradford, Pa.	Muskegon, Mich.	Norfolk, Va.	Plymouth, N. C.	9
10		Akron, O.	Webster, Mass.	Norwich, Conn.	Kane, Pa.	Grand Rapids, Mich	Portsmouth, Va.	Elizabeth City, N C	10
11		Cleveland, O.	SUNDAY	New London, Conn.	Warren, Pa.	Dundee, Mich.	Ahoskie, Va.	Portsmouth, Va.	11
12		Cleveland, O.	Boston, Mass.	New Britain, Conn	Jamestown, N. Y.	Adrian, Mich.	Rocky Mount, N. C.	SEASON ENDS.	12
13		Erie, Pa.	Boston, Mass.	Hartford, Conn.	SUNDAY	Lima, O.	Goldsboro, N. C.		13
14		SUNDAY	Boston, Mass.	Waterbury, Conn.	Sandusky, O.	Celina, O.	Kinston, N. C.		14
15		Buffalo, N. Y.	Boston, Mass.	Meriden, Conn.	Wauseon, O.	Lima, O.	SUNDAY		15
16		Rochester, N. Y.	Boston, Mass.	SUNDAY	Kendallville, Ind	Greenville, O.	Wilmington, N. C.		16
17		Syracuse, N. Y.	Boston, Mass.	New Haven, Conn.	South Bend, Ind.	SUNDAY	Lumberton, N. C.		17
18		Binghamton, N. Y.	SUNDAY	Bridgeport, Conn.	Open Date.	Xenia, O.	Hamlet, N. C.		18
19		Scranton, Pa.	Lowell, Mass.	Stanford, Conn.	Chicago, Ill.	Chillicothe, O.	Darlington, S. C.		19
20	Ponca City, Okla.	Pottsville, Pa.	Lawrence, Mass.	Mt. Vernon, N. Y.	Chicago, Ill.	Jackson, O.	Camden, S. C.		20
21	Oklahoma City, Okla	SUNDAY	Haverhill, Mass.	S. Norwalk, Conn.	Chicago, Ill.	Portsmouth, O.	Sumter, S. C.		21
22	Tulsa, Okla.	Philadelphia, Pa.	Salem, Mass.	Danbury, Conn.	Chicago, Ill.	Ironton, O.	SUNDAY		22
23	SUNDAY	Philadelphia, Pa.	Lynn, Mass.	SUNDAY	Chicago, Ill.	Huntington, W. Va.	Charleston, S. C.		23
24	Pittsburg, Kan.	Philadelphia, Pa.	Biddeford, Me.	Poughkeepsie, N. Y	Chicago, Ill.	SUNDAY	Orangeburg, S. C.		24
25	Sedalia, Mo.	Philadelphia, Pa.	Hudson, N. Y.	Chicago, Ill.	Charleston, W. Va.	Columbia, S. C.		25
26	Jefferson City, Mo	Philadelphia, Pa.	Portland, Me.	Schenectady, N. Y.	Chicago, Ill.	Athens, O.	Rock Hill, S. C.		26
27	St. Louis, Mo.	Philadelphia, Pa.	Manchester, N. H.	Oneonta, N. Y.	Chicago, Ill.	Parkersburg, W. Va	Charlotte, N. C.		27
28	St. Louis, Mo.	SUNDAY	Concord, N. H.	Cobleskill, N. Y.	Gary, Ind.	Clarksburg, W. Va.	Salisbury, N. C.		28
29	St. Louis, Mo.	Washington, D. C.	Nashua, N. H.	Saratoga Springs.	Sturgis, Mich.	Fairmont, W. Va.	SUNDAY		29
30	St. Louis, Mo.	Washington, D. C.	Brockton, Mass.	SUNDAY	Allegan, Mich.	Cumberland, Md.	Winston Salem, N C		30
31		Baltimore, Md.		Goversville, N. Y.	Hastings, Mich.		Greensboro, N. C.		31

PLATE 107

Reproduced by permission of Jimmie Gibbs Munroe

WILD WEST HERALDS & ADVANCE COURIERS

PLATE 108
Four section herald – 1893
Printed by Blakely Printing, Chicago
7" x 7" closed
14" x 14" opened

When opened one side has a picturesque map of The World's Fair Grounds, and the location of Buffalo Bill's Wild West Show Grounds adjacent to the Fair. The famous western artist, Frederic Remington, writes a strong endorsement for the show, while another section proclaims the return of the show to America after being abroad for four years. The last section explains how to reach the show grounds and why the show should be seen by all.

Heralds of many different sizes and styles were used by the show for many years. They are basically paper printed efforts to advertise the coming of The Wild West Show. The examples included here are representative of the many ways the public was informed of the coming of Buffalo Bill.

When circus manager, James A. Bailey ,joined The Wild West staff in 1895, many changes took place. A rather exciting new method of advertising was introduced. The advance courier was first used in a special booklet form. The green color with bright gold lettering on the 1895 courier was an attractive combination of colors and an excellent start for these wonderful booklets. These couriers were given to businesses that would exhibit posters of The Wild West Show and sell advance tickets. At times the couriers were placed in mail boxes along the route in advance of the show. This was a rather extravagant practice, but Cody always did things in a "big" way. These couriers performed the same service as the "coming attractions" do at today's movie theaters. There is no question they helped to create interest in the show. They are filled with pictures and fantastic descriptions of the show and its performers. There are even philosophical type statements in most couriers. One interesting statement reads how education and amusement go hand in hand. Another engaging heading reads how amusement, like education and religion, is a real need of human beings.

In 1898 the attractive buffalo head die cut courier was used. These die cut couriers are unique and are eagerly pursued by collectors. A number of these were used in 1899 to use up the remaining stock.

The *Rough Rider* tabloid style courier was introduced in 1899. This publication became the standard courier. It was used at least through the 1912 season. One very interesting aspect of the *Rough Rider* issue for 1902 is the fact that it has colored front and back covers. The author would like to hear from readers who might have any other *Rough Rider* issues that have colored covers.

The Indian head die cut was used in 1907 and 1908. This courier is one of the most desirable Cody collectibles. The 1908 Indian head has the same 1907 date on the front cover, however the year can be identified by checking the city and date printed inside against the 1907 or 1908 route sheets. This same procedure can be used on the 1898 and 1899 Buffalo head couriers.

When the two Bills' show began (with Pawnee Bill) in 1909, a wonderful new die cut was introduced to celebrate this union. This courier utilized full-color pictures of some of the show's lithographs. The 1910 version of this courier included Cody's farewell proclamation. Some different full-color pictures were also used in the 1910 courier.

All couriers were marked with the town or city, day, and date, example; "Elgin, Thursday, August 20th." These dates appear on the front covers or inside on the first page. All advance couriers are also dated either on the front cover or inside.

There are many myths pertaining to Buffalo Bill. In recent years a myth has developed about the Buffalo Bill die cut Wild West couriers. On too many occasions the word rare has been used to describe these couriers. The many examples that are available today proves that items which incorporate a special uniqueness will be saved in significant numbers. Some of the Wild West show programs that do not have the actual list of events printed inside, may also be classified as couriers. The author believes they served a dual purpose, acting as couriers and programs. The 1883 and 1884 programs are two examples that surely were also utilized as couriers.

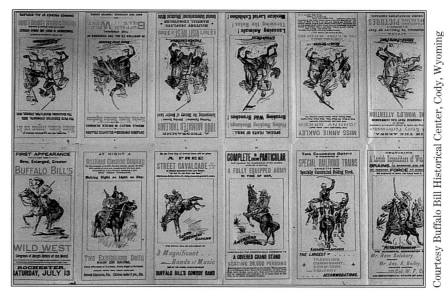

PLATE 109

Multi foldout herald – 1895
No printer's information
Most likely Blakely Co., Chicago
3⅜" x 7⅛" closed
14¼" x 20½" opened

Fully opened, one side has an interesting illustration of the show grounds in all its glory, with surrounding advertising. The opposite side has 12 sections each showing a different Rough Rider.

The 1895 season produced the first circus influenced tabloid sized courier. "The Frontier Express and Buffalo Bill's Pictorial Courier" was the new title. The courier company of Buffalo, New York, did the printing and it measured 17¾" x 22¾". Eight pages of entertaining text and many illustrations set the pattern for future editions. A fine example entered the author's collection too late to photograph for this project.

PLATE 110

Herald 1895
Printed both sides
Size – 10" x 28" approximate

There are two credits on this wonderful herald. The Courier Company of Buffalo New York and The Springer Litho. Co. New York with the date of 1895. The opposite side of this herald has an open area where train schedules and rates were posted. Some railroads offered special excursion rates to and from the show.

PLATE 111

Advance courier – 1896
Printed by Courier Lithographic Co.,
Buffalo, N.Y.
Size – 9"
Pages – 8

Courtesy Circus World Museum, Baraboo, Wisconsin

Courtesy Circus World Museum, Baraboo, Wisconsin

PLATE 112
Advance courier – 1895
Printed by Courier
Lithographic Co.,
Buffalo, N.Y.
Size – 6" x 9¼"
Pages – 8

PLATE 113
Advance courier –
1897
Printed by Courier
Lithographic Co.,
Buffalo, N.Y.
Size – 9" x 12"
Pages – 8

This tabloid size courier has many
fine illustrations. The usual text
superlatives are utilized. This
example unfortunately was folded
twice and a youngster colored a
few figures. A better issue could
not be obtained.

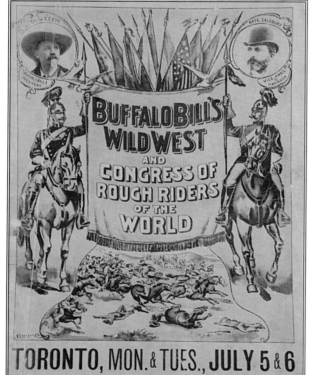

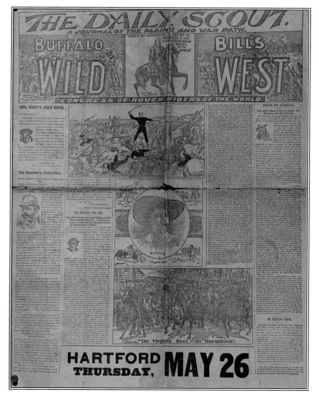

PLATE 114
The Daily Scout advance courier – 1898
Printed by The Courier Co.,
Buffalo, N.Y.
Size – 18" x 22¾"
Pages – 8 numbered

96

PLATE 115
Advance courier
1898 and some used in 1899
Printed by Courier Lithographic Co.,
Buffalo, N.Y.
Copyright by J. A. Rudole, 1898
Size – 8" x 9½"
Pages – 32 numbered

This unique design was also used for a
Grand Army of the Republic program,
for the 1901 Pan American Exposition
in Buffalo, New York, and it was also
utilized by Pawnee Bill as a souvenir of
his buffalo ranch in Pawnee, Oklahoma.

Courtesy Buffalo Bill Historical Center, Cody, Wyoming

The *Roughrider* was printed on quality paper
and its illustrations are nicely executed.
Inside is terrific information about the show
and performers. A liberal use of illustrations
is the real asset of these wonderful couriers.
The back page is general advertising. J. & H.
Mayer, 1123 Broadway, New York City, were
the agents used to secure advertisers. They
also performed the same service for Cody's
Wild West programs.

PLATE 116
Advance courier
Large tabloid size
The Roughrider, 1899
Vol. 1, first edition
Printed by The Courier Co.,
Buffalo, N.Y.
Size – 10⅞" x 16"
Pages – 16 numbered

PLATE 117
Herald – 1901
Printed both sides
Size – 7½" x 27½" approximate

Black and red ink was used on this very common style herald. Each side of these double printed heralds are different. They, of course, were intended for the use in store front windows.

THIS IS
"JUST A FLYER"
Scattered broadcast, to notify the general public that the
BIG NEW SHOW
TO WHICH ALL RAILWAYS
WILL RUN SPECIAL LOW RATE
EXCURSIONS
TO
BUFFALO BILL'S
WILD WEST
AND CONGRESS OF
ROUGH RIDERS
OF THE WORLD
AN EXHIBITION THAT KNOWS NO RIVAL AND STANDS ALONE ON THE VERY PINNACLE OF FAME.
The World's Warriors
IN MILITARY ARRAY,
TEACHING IN LIVING, CHEERFUL,
OBJECT LESSONS
...THAT WHICH NATIONS MOST ADMIRE...
Heroic Deeds and Manly Sport
THIS SEASON AUGMENTED BY
ENOUGH NEW FEATURES
TO MAKE
AN ENTIRELY NEW SHOW
AND STILL
THE PRICES REMAIN THE SAME.
REMEMBER THIS IS NOT A CIRCUS
No Close "Stuffy" Tents, No Cheap Masquerading Mummies
EVERYTHING REALISM ITSELF.
All in the Open Air!
Under the Blue Dome of Heaven!
AND IT WILL EXHIBIT IN
JANESVILLE
TUESDAY
JULY 23
JUST AS ADVERTISED, WITH
COL. W. F. CODY
BUFFALO BILL
IN THE SADDLE.
Two Exhibitions Daily, Rain or Shine
AFTERNOON AT 2 O'CLOCK; EVENING AT 8 O'CLOCK
DOORS OPEN ONE HOUR EARLIER
IE TICKET ADMITS TO ALL
Children Under 9 Years, Half Price.
ID THE RATES. REMEMBER THE DAY.

Courtesy Circus World Museum, Baraboo, Wisconsin

PLATE 118
Advance courier
Large tabloid size
The Roughrider
1901
Printed by
The Courier Co.,
Buffalo, N.Y.
Size – 10⅞" x 16"
Pages – 16 numbered

THE ROUGHRIDER
VOL. III. 4TH EDITION.   SEASON OF 1901.   CIRCULATION, 500,000.

COL. W. F. CODY (BUFFALO BILL).
THE WORLD-FAMOUS SCOUT, GUIDE AND HERO OF THE PLAINS
WHOSE "ROUGH RIDERS" HAVE RIDDEN FROM THE RIO GRANDE TO THE DANUBE.
AT MADISON SQUARE GARDEN, TWO WEEKS AND FIVE DAYS, COMMENCING TUESDAY, APRIL 2.

Courtesy Buffalo Bill Historical Center, Cody, Wyoming

Note – Cody would start many seasons at Madison Square Garden in New York to get an earlier start on the new season.

The color front and back covers of the 1902 *Roughrider* leads one to believe there may be other issues with color covers.

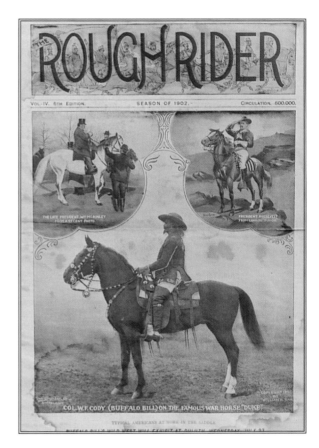

PLATE 119
Advance courier
The Roughrider
Cover, inside cover, and back
Printed by The Courier
Company, Buffalo, New York
Year – 1902

PLATE 120

The Wild West Illustrated
advance courier
Printed by the
Courier Company,
Buffalo, New York
Year – 1902
Size – 17" x 22¾"
Pages – 4 numbered

The 1901, 1902, and 1903 issues of *The Wild West Illustrated* have the same front cover layout. The text is different, with a good mix inside and on the back page, of information and illustration.

PLATE 121

Roughriders,
advance courier
Printed in Italy
Year – 1906
Size – 11" x 14"
approximately

The 1905 French edition of *Roughriders* has the same front cover. Note that the title was put in the plural format. Surely other *Roughriders* were printed using different European languages.

PLATE 122

Endorsement herald, printed on one side
Year – 1903
Size – 25" x 39½"

A unique concept utilizing 31 different newspaper accounts of the opening of Cody's show at the Olympia arena on December 26, 1902. The columns are dated December 27, 1902, and December 28, 1902. This interesting style of endorsement advertising had a positive effect on the British public. No doubt these were posted all around London and the countryside.

PLATE 123
Heralds
Year – 1906
Printed both sides
Size – 6⁵⁄₁₆" x 29⁵⁄₈"

The herald on the left is in Polish. Another example is in Italian. The 1906 touring season included many European countries and all the different languages are represented on these interesting heralds.

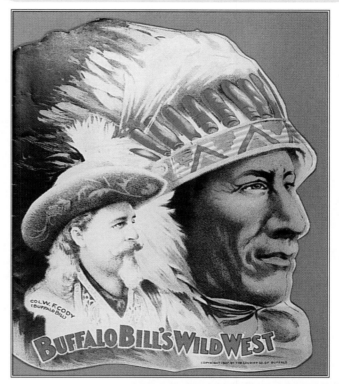

PLATE 124
Advance courier
1907 & 1908
Indian head diecut
Copyrighted & printed by
The Courier Co., Buffalo, N.Y.
Size – 7¾" x 9"
Pages – 32 numbered

This diecut Indian head courier is one of the most sought after Cody collectibles. The design and color are outstanding. Even the back cover is special. These are not rare. However, when one appears on the open market it disappears quickly.

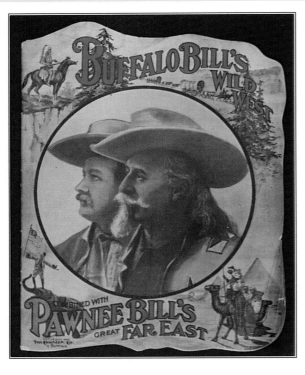

PLATE 125
Advance courier
1909 & 1910
Buffalo Bill's
Wild West &
Pawnee Bill's
Great Far East
Printed by
The Courier Co.,
Buffalo, N.Y.
Copyrighted 1909
Size – 7¼" x 9½"
Pages – 31 numbered

This interesting new die cut design celebrated the union of these two western heroes. The 1909 version proclaims the positive purpose of this merger. The 1910 edition includes Buffalo Bill's farewell proclamation. Both couriers contain full-color illustrations, which makes these extra special.

PLATE 126
The Overland Trail
advance courier
Front and back
printed by
Russell &
Morgan Print,
Cincinnati &
New York
Year – 1913
Size –
17⅛" x 23¾"
Pages – 4

PLATE 127
Heralds
Postcard style
Year –1913
Printed both sides
Size – 7" x 32" approximately

The attractive concept exemplifies the creativity of the early publicists. The message reads:
"Dear Friend,
'Buffalo Bill' is to exhibit at: Covention Hall, Broad Street and Allegheny Avenue, Philadelphia,
2 weeks and 3 days, starting Thursday night, April 3rd.
Please mail this to your best friend.
The Colonel"

LITHOGRAPHS

PLATE 128

W.F. Carver Wild West
Printed by W.J. Morgan & Company,
Cleveland, Ohio
Year – 1885
Size – 28" x 42" approximately

W.F. (Doc) Carver lithographs are
scarce. This example may be considered rare. A value will not be
included in the price guide by
request of the contributor.

Nineteenth and early twentieth century lithographs are among the most visually exciting collectibles available today. Circus collectors past and present are responsible for preserving the majority of these magnificent works of art. One wonders why it took the collectors so long to embrace this art form. Everyone should have the good fortune to view an early circus and Wild West lithograph collection. It is truly an awesome experience. The Circus World Museum in Baraboo, Wisconsin, has the world's largest poster collection dealing mainly with circus and Wild West Show material. The Buffalo Bill Historical Center in Cody, Wyoming, also has a fine collection of Cody lithos. Collectors today have available a fine reference book on Buffalo Bill posters. *100 Posters of Buffalo Bill's Wild West* by Jack Rennert was published in 1976. Soft cover and cloth or hard cover editions were printed. The large format with great images and a most articulate text adds up to a most valuable reference.

No one seems to know exactly how many different Buffalo Bill posters were produced. Perhaps between 300 and 400 different examples may exist. The majority of lithographs were printed in what is called the one-sheet size. There are size variations of the one sheet however, most measure 28" by 42". By adding the one sheet unit size together with another and multiple sheets, a wide variety of sizes were made available. Cody lithographs can be found in a dozen or more different sizes. The half-sheet, one-sheet, and two-sheet posters are the popular sizes collectors seek. The three-sheet is also popular, however, anything larger becomes difficult to handle or display. These larger sizes are best suited for museums.

One very interesting aspect about lithograph collectors is the fact that most except and encourage the restoration of early lithographs. The art of fine restoration is something to behold. Seeing before and after restoration lithographs is actually amazing. The cost of restoring lithographs is expensive, however, like many other collectors, the author is convinced it is a worthy investment. Should you encounter an early damaged lithograph, take heart because it can be brought back to life.

Related ephemera associated with bill posting is also available. Informative bill posting contracts and lithograph tickets are occasionally found. Store owners were given free admission for allowing posters to be displayed in their store front windows. Finding photos of store fronts with Wild West Show lithographs in the windows is another interesting aspect of collecting Buffalo Bill.

The information on early heralds is extremely important to the research-orientated collector. For example, it is interesting to find out Cody had his own military band performing in a street parade before each daily show. Professor Rampone was the leader of this superb orchestra of string and brass, playing classical selections. Colonel Prentiss Ingraham wrote this play for Cody and put more ink to paper for and about Buffalo Bill than any of his contemporary counterparts in the dime novel world.

PLATE 129
Herald lithograph
Printed by Calhoun Printing Company,
Hartford, Connecticut
Year – 1879
Size – 10" x 30" approximately

Cut No. 123—TEXAS JACK—Three Sheet Cut In 4 Colors, $45 per hundred.

PLATE 130
Texas Jack
Buffalo Bill
Wild Bill
Circa 1873 – 1876
Size – 3-sheet

Cut No. 124—BUFFALO BILL—Three Sheet Cut in 4 Colors, $45 per hundred.

Cut No. 125—WILD BILL—Three Sheet Cut in 4 Colors, $45 per hundred.

Three terrific lithographs that many collectors will be viewing for the first time. Jackson Brothers of Philadelphia had salesmen out with proof books of stock posters offered to minstrel shows, circuses, and theaters in 1876. Surely these first appeared in 1873 during the tour of Cody's acting group which included Texas Jack and Wild Bill. We learn from the litho caption the size and price per hundred. The three sheet presentations in the vertical plane are basically lifesize. Close examination of the proof cuts here unfortunately turned up no lithographer's logos. It is unclear at this time if the Jackson Brothers of Philadelphia were the lithographers or just provided proof books and salesmen.

The proof book caption under each lithograph gives cut number, name of subject, followed by – Three sheet in four colors $45 per hundred.

PLATE 131

Hon. W. F. Cody – Buffalo Bill
Printed by W. J. Morgan
& Company, Ohio
Circa – 1883
Size – 13⅝" x 37⅞"

This litho was most likely used for stage appearences and later for the Wild West Exhibition.

Courtesy Circus World Museum, Baraboo, Wisconsin

The Hoen Company of Baltimore, Maryland, reissued this one sheet in 1894 but added Congress Rough Riders of the World at the top and an American on the bottom.

PLATE 132

Buffalo Bill's Wild West
Printed by Forbes Lithographic
Company, Boston
Year – 1886
Size – 28" x 40"

PLATE 133
Lillian Francis Smith,
The California Girl
Printed by Calhoun
Printing Company,
Hartford, Conn.
Circa – late 1880s
Size – 3 sheets

PLATE 134
General Nelson A.
Miles and Buffalo
Bill
Printed by A. Hoen
& Company, Balti-
more, MD
Year – 1892
Size – 19¼" x 28¾"

GENERAL NELSON A. MILES AND "BUFFALO BILL"

Courtesy Buffalo Bill Historical Center, Cody, Wyoming

Lillian Smith was a headliner
with Cody's show in 1886,
1887, and 1888. She performed
with a variety of shows after
touring with Cody, however,
was forever in the shadow of
Annie Oakley and May Lillie.
She was an intrepid veteran
Wild West Show trouper.

Courtesy Circus World Museum, Baraboo, Wisconsin

PLATE 135
Buffalo Bill's Wild
West and Congress of
Routh Riders Russian
Cossacks
Printed by A. Hoen &
Company,
Baltimore, MD
Year – 1893
Size – ½ sheet

PLATE 136

Pawnee Bill's Historical Wild West
Printed by Avil Litho. Company,
Philadelphia, PA
Circa – 1888 – 1893
Size – one sheet

This poster is rare and believed to be one of the first used by Pawnee Bill. It is obvious that Pawnee Bill understood the meaning of quality artwork.

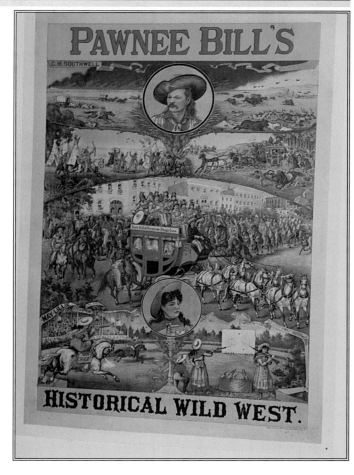

This Avil effort has one of the finest images of Pawnee Bill ever produced. The bottom reads "Pawnee Bill And His Colony Of 4200 Original Oklahoma Boomers as they actually appeared, when they entered the territory of Oklahoma on April 22, 1889. See the original prairie schooners and outfit that carried Pawnee Bill and his council in on that eventful day."

PLATE 137

Pawnee Bill's Historical Wild West
Printed by Avil Litho. Company,
Philadelphia, PA
Circa 1890 – 1893
Size – one sheet

PLATE 138
Pawnee Bill's Historic Wild West
May Lillie
Printed by Strobridge Lithographic
Company, Cincinnati, Ohio
Year – 1894 – 96
Size – 28" x 42"

Pawnee Bill's wife, May Lillie, was a solid performer. The lithographic presentation of May Lillie bares a close resemblance to one of Annie Oakley.

PLATE 139
Buffalo Bill's Wild West &
Congress of Rough Riders
of the World
Printed by A. Hoen & Company,
Baltimore, Maryland
Year – 1895
Size – 28½" x 42"

PLATE 140
Buffalo Bill's Wild West
Printed by Courier Lithographic
Company, Buffalo, New York
Year – 1896
Size – 28" x 42"

A series of this interesting busy design was printed. A Native American, a Russian Cossack, a South American Gaucho, and an Arab were also featured.

PLATE 141
I Am Coming
Printed by Bien & Company, Litho,
New York
Year – 1898
Size – 28" x 42"
Date banner – 6½" x 40"

Printed just above the Bien & Company name is "Copyrighted 1898 By." Map making was the principle product of Bien & Company. Apparently they made lithographs for Cody only for the 1898 season. The show date banner nails down the place and time. Here again, the route sheets are invaluable. Giving us the year and state in this case. The Bien copyrighted design is one of the best produced for the show. Other lithographers copied this idea, however, none seem to measure up to this original beauty.

PLATE 142
Buffalo Bill's Wild West and Congress of Rough Riders of the World
Printed by A. Hoen & Company, Baltimore, Maryland
Year – 1898
Size – 28" x 39¾"
Date banner – 6½" x 40"

The Virginia Reel on horseback is depicted. This dance number was used for many years in the show and one wonders if that is Annie Oakley with Cody.

PLATE 143
Col. W.F. Cody, "Buffalo Bill"
Printed by Strobridge Litho Company, Cincinnati, Ohio
Year – 1907
Size – one sheet

The 1907 and 1908 Wild West Show programs utilized this image for the front covers. Indeed, several program front cover designs were also printed in the larger poster format.

PLATE 144
Buffalo Bill's Wild West Pioneer and Exhibition
Printed by The Strobridge Litho Company, Cincinnati & New York
Circa 1907
Size – 28⅛" x 38¼"

PLATE 145

Buffalo Bill's Wild West & Rough
Riders
Miss Lillian Shaffer
Printed by The Strobridge
Litho Company
Circa – 1907
Size – three sheet

Miss Lillian Shaffer was billed as the
only lady in the world successfully
riding bucking broncos. The poster is
outstanding but was she that relaxed
during the actual ride? Many would
select this litho as the finest cowgirl
presentation of the period.

About the time this poster was produced, film makers were recording
Cody's show and we are indeed fortunate that the filming occurred. A
decent portion of Johnny Baker's
shooting act has been preserved and
it is exciting to see.

PLATE 146

Buffalo Bill's Wild West
Johnny Baker, The Expert Marksman
Printed by The Strobridge Litho Com-
pany, Cincinnati & New York
Circa – 1908
Size – three sheet

PLATE 147

Buffalo Bill's Wild West combined
with Pawnee Bill's Great Far East
Printed by Strobridge Litho.,
Cincinnati, Ohio
Year – 1909
Size – one sheet

Here we have another terrific design also used for the 1909 Two Bill's Wild West Show program

PLATE 149

Buffalo Bill's Wild West – Pawnee Bill's Far East
Printed by Russell–Morgan Printing Company,
Cincinnati, Ohio
Circa 1910
Size – 13¼" x 39½"

PLATE 148

Buffalo Bill's Wild West combined
with Pawnee Bill's Great Far East
Miss May Lillie
Printed by Strobridge Litho.
Company, Cincinnati, Ohio
Year – 1909
Size – two sheet

May Lillie's shooting act was discontinued when the two Bill's Show began in 1909.

Courtesy Buffalo Bill Historical Center, Cody, Wyoming

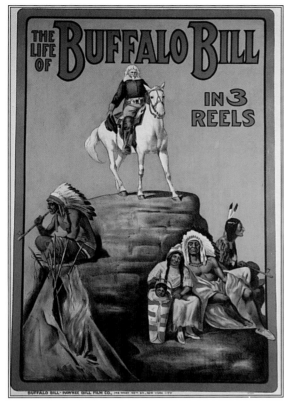

PLATE 151
Iron Tail, Last of the Great Chiefs
Printed by U.S. Lithograph Company, Russell-Morgan print
Year – 1912
Size – 27⅝" x 40"

PLATE 150
The Life of Buffalo Bill in Three Reels
Printed by unknown
Year – 1910
Size – one sheet

This one sheet lithograph is marked "Buffalo Bill - Pawnee Bill Film Co.," 145 West 45th Street, New York City. At least three different one sheet posters were utilized to advertise this three reeler. Copies of "The Life Of Buffalo Bill" are available on video tape.

The American bison is an excellent symbol of our Wild West heritage.

PLATE 152
Buffalo Bill's Wild West, Pawnee Bill's Far East
Printed by Russell - Morgan Print
Year –1913
Size – one sheet

PLATE 153
"Preparedness"
Printed by Strobridge Litho Company,
Cincinnati, Ohio
Year – 1916
Size – one sheet

The 101 Ranch Show with Buffalo Bill was a good mix. The military theme was a sign of the times as the country was about to enter World War I. The letter was from Major General Hugh Scott, chief of staff, granting furloughs for selected soldiers to tour with show for six months.

Here is perhaps the final image of Cody to appear on a poster during his lifetime. Iron Tail is on Cody's right and on his left it appears to be Lillian Shaffer, two well-known performers.

PLATE 154
Buffalo Bill "Himself" and the 101 Ranch Show Combined
Printed by The Strobridge Litho Company,
Cincinnati, Ohio
Year – 1916
Size –19½" x 29¾"

Advance advertising was indeed one of the shows most important duties. In fact the success and longevity of Cody's show can be attributed to its extraordinary advance advertising policy. Few traveling outdoor shows could match Buffalo Bill's bill posting or newspaper advertisements. This ticket order for posting two lithographs in windows was basically free advertising space for the show. Giving two free admissions for this courtesy didn't actually cost the show. If the holders of these free admissions brought family or friends extra money was realized by the show. The sophisticated advertising techniques utilized by management is a topic that needs serious research.

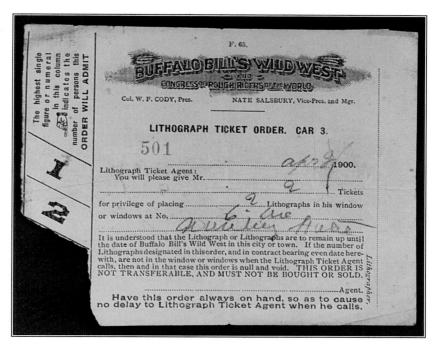

PLATE 155
Lithograph ticket order car 3
April 1900
Size – 3¾" x 4¾"

PLATE 156
City bill
poster contract
Aug. 11, 1909
Size – 5⅜" x 8½"

Bill or lithograph posting companies were to be found in all cities and many smaller towns during Cody's show years. This contract tells us that from September 6, 1909, to September 20, 1909, the actual show date, that 800 sheets were to be posted in and around Emporia, Kansas, for seven cents a sheet. The 800 sheets information is written on the back with locations to be satisfactory to the car managers. This contract form was from 1908 and here again we have the show utilizing the previous season's remaining stock. At the very top of this contract it reads "Agents are forbidden to give or promise any free tickets." Note, notation at upper left hand corner, apparently Cody wasn't the only one giving out too many free tickets.

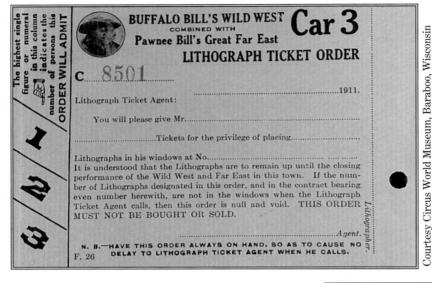

BUFFALO BILL'S WILD WEST
COMBINED WITH
Pawnee Bill's Great Far East **Car 3**
LITHOGRAPH TICKET ORDER

C 8501

....1911.

Lithograph Ticket Agent: ....

You will please give Mr..

..................................Tickets for the privilege of placing...........................

Lithographs in his windows at No.................................. ....
It is understood that the Lithographs are to remain up until the closing
performance of the Wild West and Far East in this town. If the number of Lithographs designated in this order, and in the contract bearing
even number herewith, are not in the windows when the Lithograph
Ticket Agent calls, then this order is null and void. THIS ORDER
MUST NOT BE BOUGHT OR SOLD.

....*Agent.*

N. B.—HAVE THIS ORDER ALWAYS ON HAND, SO AS TO CAUSE NO
F. 26   DELAY TO LITHOGRAPH TICKET AGENT WHEN HE CALLS.

The highest single figure or numeral in this column indicates the number of persons this ORDER WILL ADMIT

1
2
3

Lithographer.

Courtesy Circus World Museum, Baraboo, Wisconsin

The two Bill's Show continued to use this beneficial method of advertising. The back logo design is wonderful.

PLATE 157
Lithograph ticket order
car 3
Year – 1911
Size – 3¾" x 5"
approximately

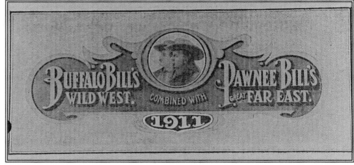

W.R.FRANTZ.

Here is an excellent example of what is waiting out there for collectors to discover. Close examination of the photo shows six lithographs in the upper portions of the windows. Five different posters were utilized in three different sizes to accommodate the space. The date banners indicate Warren, June 3. The route sheets tell the photo was taken in Warren, Pennsylvania, in 1912.

PLATE 158
Store front photo

PLATE 159
Buffalo Land
By W. E. Webb of Topeka, Kansas
Published by
Cincinnati & Chicago,
E. Hannaford & Company
San Francisco, F. Dewing
& Co.
Year – 1872
Pages – 503 pages

This book is about a semi-scientific expedition in mainly the western half of Kansas in 1869. It recounts the authentic discoveries, adventures, and mishaps of a scientific and sporting party in the Wild West. Also, containing graphic descriptions of the country, the Redman (savage and civilized), plus hunting the buffalo, antelope, elk, and wild turkey replete with information, wit, and humor.

This book is profusely illustrated from actual photographs and original drawings by Henry Worrall. *Buffalo Land* is included in this reference book because it most likely is the first hard cover publication mentioning Buffalo Bill. He was the guide and is written about in a complimentary way, with some very interesting descriptions of Cody and his guiding techniques, and includes a very nice illustration of both Buffalo Bill and Wild Bill. This book is an excellent example of early Cody material.

Books can be considered treasures of any civilized society. How fortunate that many improvements in the printing processes were achieved by the mid nineteenth century. By the 1880s books were selling at prices the average person could afford. At the turn of the century books had become affordable for just about everyone. This relates to more books being printed and explains why there are so many fine examples available today.

There is an abundant supply of Cody books covering nearly every aspect of his life. Most have attractive covers and at least some interesting and accurate information. Unfortunately, most period books on Cody include stories that just are not true. Some of these were actually started by Cody. Other authors were equal to that task and added more fiction regarding Cody's life. Nonetheless, his books are very collectible. To better appreciate these period books one has to research the present day assortment of Buffalo Bill material. We have had the good fortune of having authors like Henry Blackman Sell, Victor Weybright, the very special Don Russell, and Nellie Snyder Yost to help with this maze of Cody confusion.

Researching Cody's life is a fascinating and rewarding experience. Using books is an excellent way to start that process. At the end of this chapter will be a recommended list of books for reading about this nineteenth century superstar.

PLATE 160

Life of Buffalo Bill
By W.F. Cody
Published by Frank E. Bliss,
Hartford, Connecticut
Year – 1879
Pages – 365

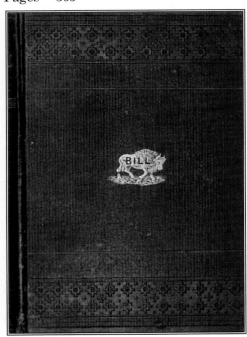

There is good news and bad news about this autobiography. The good news is that it was written at a time not too distant from Cody's frontier experiences. The bad news is that artistic license was alive and well in the 1870s. Cody himself wrote things that just were not true. How was he to know that so many writers would continue copying his stories. Regardless, this work is a valuable reference. Much of this book is true and accurate. All Cody material from the 1870s is special. This book is no exception. A collector should try to obtain one as soon as possible, as they are becoming scarce.

PLATE 161
The Poet Scout
By Captain J.W. Crawford
Published by H. Keller & Company,
San Francisco, California
Year – 1879
Pages – 208

John Wallace Crawford called himself "Captain Jack, The Poet Scout." He was born on March 4, 1847, in Donegal, Ireland, and immigrated to America in 1860. He fought for the Union side in the Civil War and scouted on the plains in the 1870s and became friendly with Cody. This was his first published book and it is basically his collection of poetry.

HEROES OF THE PLAINS

The Lives and Wonderful Adventures of

BUFFALO BILL,
WILD BILL,
TEXAS JACK,
KIT CARSON,
CALIFORNIA JOE,
CAPT. PAYNE,
CAPT. JACK,

Hunters and Guides,

Also other Celebrated Indian Fighters and Scouts, including a **True and Thrilling History** of Gen. Custer's Famous "**LAST FIGHT**" on the Little Big Horn with Sitting Bull.

A SPLENDID BOOK OF

548 large, closely-printed pages, containing **100 Illustrations,**

BUFFALO BILL.

Address the CINCINNATI PUBLISHING CO., 174 West Fourth Street, CINCINNATI, OHIO.

Embracing **16 Full-paged Lithograph Colored Plates,** by distinguished artists, printed in

Five BRILLIANT Colors

Surpassing anything of the kind ever attempted in book illustrations.

500,000 Copies

WILL BE SOLD.

Agents sell from **20** to **30** Copies per Day.

AGENTS WANTED

Subscription Price:

Handsomely bound in Cloth, Gold Side Stamp, - - **$2.00.**

The territory is going rapidly, so don't delay a **MOMENT,** but send **50 CENTS** for **OUTFIT** and **GO TO WORK.** Circulars free.

PLATE 162

Heroes of the Plains
By J.W. Buel
Published by
The Historical Publishing
Co., St. Louis, Missouri
Year – 1881
Pages – 548, 1st edition

This early effort of a multiple biography format is entertaining. A healthy mix of fact and fiction is typically found in these period books. The use of 16 color plates surely helped with sales. The public responded by purchasing this book for many years. A wide variety of styles and sizes will be encountered. The two 1881 first editions the author examined were both leather bound. The 1881 advertisement for agents wanted has great information plus the Buffalo Bill illustration.

PLATE 163

Heroes of the Plains
By J.W. Buel
Published by N.D.
Thompson & Company,
New York & St. Louis
Year – 1882
Pages – 548

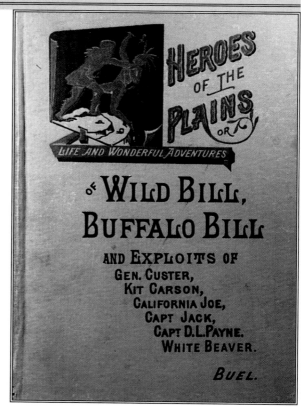

PLATE 164

Heroes of the Plains
by J.W. Buel
Published by West
Philadelphia Publishing Co.
Year – 1891
Pages – 612

A fine new front cover design was introduced in 1882. The color plates are also included and makes these books worth finding.

This 1891 version includes extra sketches on Sitting Bull and "White Beaver" who was Dr. D. Frank Powell, a friend of Cody's. A different attractive color frontispiece was used, however no other color plates are included.

PLATE 165

Famous Frontiersmen, Pioneers and Scouts
By E.G. Catterole
Published by M. A. Donohue & Co., Chicago & New York
No Date
Pages – 544

Another book with general biographies of many western characters. Seen are rather obscure individuals and that makes this book interesting. The first issue was in 1883. These books are not year dated for some reason. This example is a new and enlarged edition circa 1890.

We can date the first issue by reading the last paragraph of the Buffalo Bill biography. "This year, 1883, Buffalo Bill and Dr. Carver have formed a combination on a more extensive plan than ever before attempted. The plan is to visit all large places with a herd of buffalo, a large band of Indians, and other accessories, and give exhibitions of various characters, in fairgrounds or on race courses. As this volume goes to press, the season has not commenced and we are obliged to leave Buffalo Bill in the midst of active preparations for a grander exhibition of western life, than was ever before given the people east of the Mississippi. Barnum must look well to his laurels, or the 'Scout of the Plains' will eclipse him as showman."

PLATE 166

The Rifle Queen Annie Oakley of the Wild West Exhibition
Author Anonymous
Published by The General Publishing Company,
280 Strand W.C. London
Year – 1887
Pages – 64 numbered

This paper-covered short book is very interesting. A color front cover with inside advertising was added as the original black and white cover is page one. Three pages of advertising were utilized by the publisher to hawk their other one penny and two penny weeklies. One page was about the Buffalo Bill Wild West series of two penny books. Twelve titles are listed and each book contained 128 pages and each had colored wrappers. It is interesting to note that the Buffalo Bill books of 128 pages cost two cents while *The Rifle Queen* of only 64 pages cost three cents. The writer actually attempted to write a factual account of Annie Oakley's life. However, the dime novel mentality does invade the text. A preface page is included plus a "Kind Words" page of complimentary comments by Cody, Nate Salsbury, Doc Carver, Capt. Bogardus, and several London newspapers. *The London Evening News* of May 10, 1887, wrote "The most interesting item on Buffalo Bill's program was the splendid marksmanship, Miss Oakley being far and away the best."

PLATE 166A
Original black and white front cover

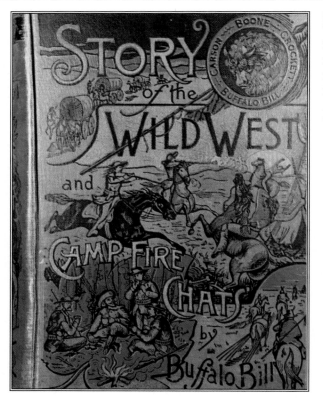

PLATE 167

Story of the Wild West and Campfire Chats
By Buffalo Bill (Hon. W.F. Cody)
Published by Historical Publishing Company,
Philadelphia, Pennsylvania
Year – 1888
Pages – 766

This is considered the most attractive and appealing Cody period book. The covers are of a fine quality and nicely done. A color frontispiece was used with an equally interesting title page. There are also 250 original illustrations made especially for this book. An impressive volume with its real worth being the addition of Buffalo Bill's conquests in England from the 1887 season.

There are several variations of the book as it was also published in Chicago and Boston. A salesman's sample book is also available and, of course, interesting. A magnificent large tabloid style advertising paper was also utilized to help sell this book.

PLATE 167A
Tabloid size
advertising
flyer front

PLATE 167B
Flyer back
cover

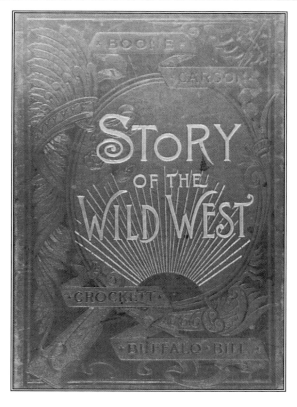

PLATE 168

Story of the Wild West
The prospectus or salesman's sample
of Cody's 1888 book
Published by R.S. Peale & Co., Chicago, Illinois
Year – 1888

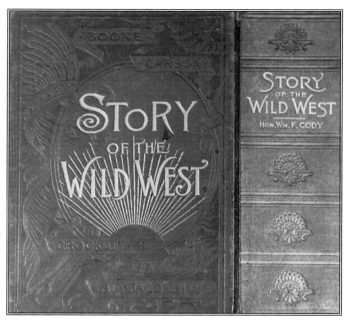

PLATE 168A
Front cover opened

Salesman's sample books are fascinating and eagerly pursued by collectors. The front cover is done in the full morocco treatment and would cost $4.00. The back inside cover shows the fine silk cloth binding in gold and colors, and would cost $3.00. Also, available was a half morocco with gold stamps at a cost of $3.50. Inside is found selected text and illustrations to help create interest and potential buyers. Included inside, are small tipped-in explanations about different aspects of this work. The author would highly recommend acquiring this interesting Cody related example.

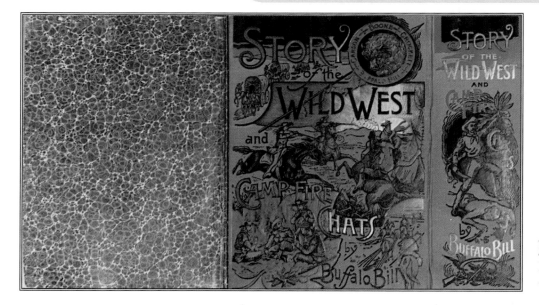

PLATE 168B
Back inside
cover opened

PLATE 169
Out West
No maker's identifying information
c. 1890

This 6" by 9" accordion style view book of 30 pages was most likely made by The Ward Brothers of Columbus, Ohio. They were manufacturers and importers of souvenir albums of American cities and sceneries. It contains wonderful cuts of cowboys, Indians, western cities, and of course, Buffalo Bill.

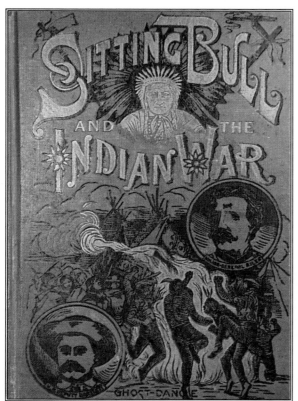

PLATE 170
Sitting Bull and The Indian War
By W. Fletcher Johnson
Published by Edgewood Publishing Co.
Copyrighted 1891 by H.W. Stringer
Pages – 587

PLATE 171
Camp Fire Sparks
By Jack Crawford
Published by Charles H. Kerr & Company,
175 Monroe Street, Chicago
Year – 1893
Pages – 48
soft cover

A decent effort by a capable author. We learn a good deal about Sitting Bull, the Sioux nation, his tragic death, and the Wounded Knee affair. The book is profusely illustrated and many are very nice including two of Buffalo Bill. A worth while book to own.

The Charles H. Kerr Publishing Company was incorporated in 1893 as a socialist publishing house. Was Jack Crawford the Poet Scout a socialist, or was the association strictly business? A very interesting subject to explore. This book is all poetry and Captain Jack should receive credit for helping to popularize the art of "historical" poems.

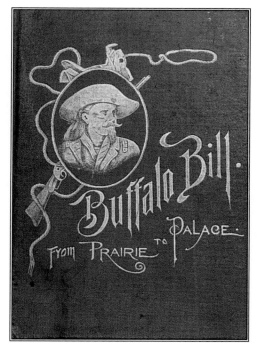

PLATE 172
Buffalo Bill from Prairie to Palace
By John M. Burke
Published by
Rand, McNally & Co.,
Chicago & New York
Year – 1893
Pages – 275

PLATE 172A
Paperback example

Interestingly, this book was printed in hard cover and paper back formats. These were sold at the Chicago 1893 season. John M. Burke was the shows general manager plus one of the best publicity men that ever plied that trade. The highlights of this book are the wonderful description of the 1887 London season plus the articulate account of the first four-year tour of Europe and Great Britain.

This is an important Cody collectible simply because it was written by a man from the inner circle. Only Cody, John M. Burke, and Johnny Baker completed the Wild West Show experience from 1883 through 1916.

A fascinating book that is well written. Most of the photo illustrations used are excellent. Alexander Majors was a key player during the frontier years. He was a principal owner of the Russell, Majors and Waddell Freighting Company. They supplied the western military forts. They also organized and ran the Pony Express in which Cody participated.

Solid information about the early freighting days and believable evidence of Cody's association with this firm. A must book, however not easy to find.

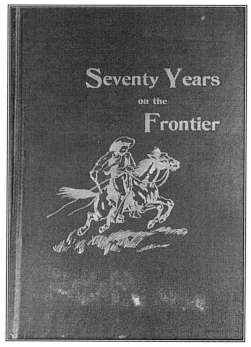

PLATE 173
Seventy Years on the Frontier
By Alexander Majors
Published by Rand, McNally & Company, Chicago & New York
Year – 1893
Pages – 325

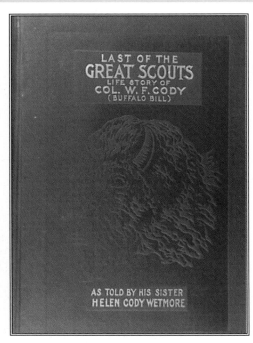

PLATE 174

The Last of the Great Scouts Life Story of Col. W.F. Cody (Buffalo Bill)
By Helen Cody Wetmore
Published by The Duluth Press Printing Co., Duluth, Minnesota
Year – 1899
Pages – 267
1st edition

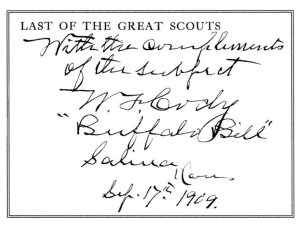

LAST OF THE GREAT SCOUTS

PLATE 174A
Autographed example

This book was written by one of Cody's younger sisters. The recounting of his boyhood years is the real asset of this book. In the preface we are told that many incidents of his later life were retrieved from other sources. So we have a continuation of the many myths that surround Cody's life. The book was printed over and over with many different covers and styles. It was continuously sold at the Wild West Show for about a dozen years. Some of the later issues had a special page in front for Cody to autograph. Helen Cody Wetmore had her volume copyrighted in Great Britain and France. The author has seen a copy in German and French and feels it was also done in Italian. Other languages are a strong possibility. This book was heavily advertised in The Wild West Programs.

The front cover is attractive and a frontispiece of the famous painting by Rosa Bonheur was utilized. Unfortunately, no other illustrations were used.

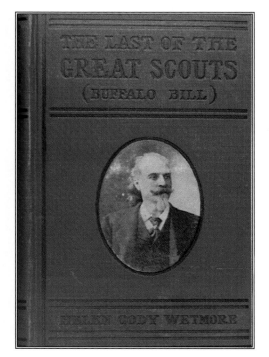

PLATE 175

The Last of the Great Scouts Life Story of Buffalo Bill
By Helen Cody Wetmore
Published by International Book and Publishing Co., New York
Year – 1900
Pages – 296
Lakeside Press
R.R. Donnelley & Sons Co., Chicago
Grosset and Dunlap

PLATE 176

Last of the Great Scouts
By Helen Cody Wetmore
Published by Methuen & Company,
30 Essex St. W.C. London
Circa – 1901
Pages – 296

This edition was printed and sold
in England. Naturally, they were
sold during the Britain touring
seasons of 1903 and 1904.

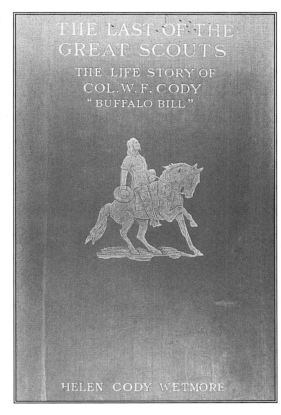

This is basically a rehash of Cody's book
*Story of the Wild West and Campfire
Chats* from 1888. The cover is nice and
many variations are seen. One hundred
and fifty illustrations are included, but the
paper quality is lacking. After the cover,
there is not much to get excited about.

PLATE 177

*History of Our Wild West &
Stories of Pioneer Life*
By D.M. Kelsey
Published by The Charles C.
Thompson Co., Chicago
Year – 1901
Pages – 542

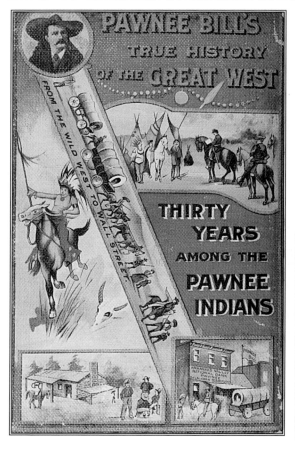

PLATE 178

Pawnee Bill's True History of the Great West
By J.H. DeWolff
Published by Pawnee Bill's Historic Wild West Company
Year – 1902
Pages – 108

The covers are colorful and the layout interesting. The text is fair with some very informative facts about the beginning of Pawnee Bill's Buffalo Ranch. There are several illustrations, however the paper quality is poor.

PLATE 178A
Back cover

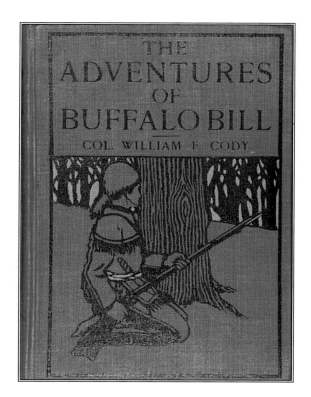

Juvenile editions like this one are not included on too many collector's want lists. The author would recommend however, that all period material should be collected to help preserve these interesting artifacts. The front cover is interesting because we find Cody with a "Daniel Boone" look.

PLATE 179

The Adventures of Buffalo Bill
By Col. William F. Cody
Published by Harper And Brothers, New York & London
Year – 1904
Pages – 156

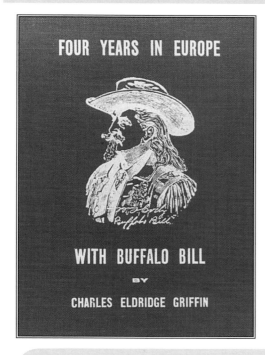

PLATE 180

Four Years in Europe with Buffalo Bill
By Charles Eldridge Griffin
Published by Stage
Publishing Co., Albia, Iowa
Year – 1908
Pages – 94

PLATE 181

True Tales of the Plains
By Buffalo Bill
(Col. W.F. Cody)
Published by
Cupples & Leon
Company, New York
Year – 1908
Pages – 259

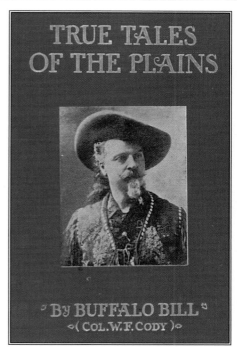

The author's selection of the best period written book on Cody and his Wild West Show. Charles Eldridge Griffin was an intelligent and articulate man. We are fortunate that he wrote of his experiences and reflections of the last of the European tours. A wealth of information is written in a way that leaves the reader convinced he is getting factual information. One of the best and a must for the serious Cody collector. This is not an easy find.

This book contains 33 chapters of different frontier events, most are about Cody and unfortunately reads like dime novels. The illustrations are fine with two exceptional ones of Iron Tail. The attractive front cover makes this a worth while collectible.

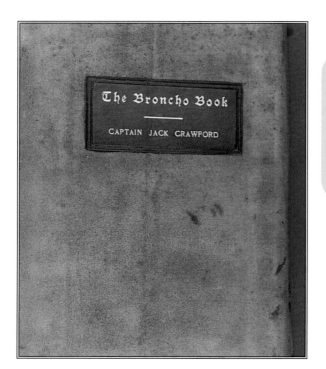

More poetry being characterized as Buck-Jumps in verse by Jack Crawford. He also claims that this book was roped for the relief of the author, the divertissement of tenderfeet and for the joy of all those who love God's great out-of-doors. Enough said!

PLATE 182

The Broncho Book
By Captain Jack Crawford
Published by The Roycrofters
Year – 1908
Pages – 143

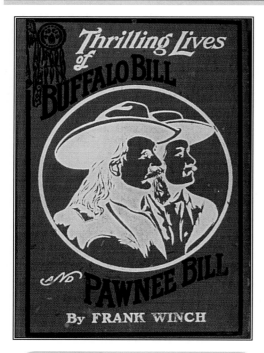

PLATE 183
Thrilling Lives of Buffalo Bill and Pawnee Bill
By Frank Winch
Published by S.L. Parsons & Company, Inc., Publishers and Printers, No. 45 Rose Street, New York, New York
Year – 1911
Pages – 224

PLATE 184
Stirring Lives of Buffalo Bill and Pawnee Bill
By Frank C. Cooper
Published by S.L. Parsons & Company, Inc., Publishers and Printers, No. 45 Rose Street, New York, New York
Year – 1912
Pages – 224

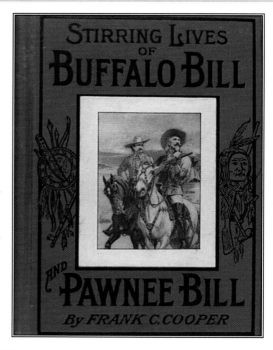

This book and its near copy *Stirring Lives of Buffalo Bill and Pawnee Bill* were both sold at the show for $1.00 each. The front cover and illustrations are the only reasons for collecting this book. The covers come in blue and green and most likely in other colors.
The illustration showing a few reasons why Buffalo Bill wants to retire is neat. Another good one is of Iron Tail making a war bonnet of eagle feathers. Fortunately, this book and its near copy are still plentiful.

A typical Cody history including many errors. Part two is about Pawnee Bill. Here again we find fiction. The attractive front cover combined with the many photo illustrations makes this book worth seeking. The cloth covers have been seen in red and yellow. Two of the better photo illustrations are Buffalo Bill on his favorite charger Omar, and a super portrait of Johnny Baker.

PLATE 185
Anecdotes of Buffalo Bill The Original Boy Scout
By Dan H. Winget
Published by Press Of The Merry War, Clinton, Iowa
Year – 1912
Pages – 224

Dan Winget was a boyhood friend of Bill Cody. He received permission from Cody to write this book. However, Winget was instructed by Cody to stick to the facts. Unfortunately, this author, like so many others, just could not write it straight. Most of the so called anecdotes are not believable. This is just another period book disappointment.

PLATE 186

The Great Salt Lake Trail
By Colonel Henry Inman and Colonel
William F. Cody
Year – published first in 1898
The example shown is a 1914 reprint
Published by Crane and Company of
Topeka, Kansas
Pages – 524

Col. Inman received information from Cody about Cody's life and therefore included Cody as co-author. The author feels the real reason he included Cody as co-author was to help him sell the book. Regardless, the book is interesting. Touching on the many incidents that occurred along this famous trail. A very nice fold-out map of the Salt Lake Trail is an added special touch that makes this book worth seeking. There are also footnotes and an index which enhances the usefulness of the book.

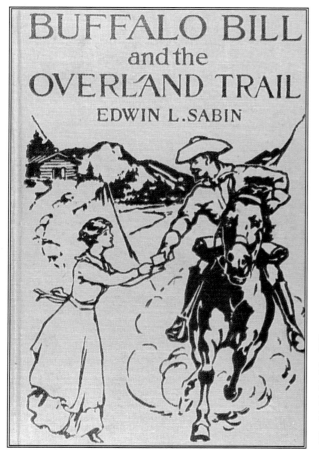

This book is from a series called *The American Trail Blazers*. The publisher explains that these books present in the form of vivid and fascinating fiction the early and adventurous phases of American history. A fine 1871 image of Cody and a chronological table are the only highlights contained within this volume.

PLATE 187

Buffalo Bill and the Overland Trail
By Edwin L. Sabin
Published by J.B. Lippincott Company,
Philadelphia & London
Year – 1914
Pages – 349

LATER BOOK REFERENCES

1. *The Lives and Legends Of Buffalo Bill*
   By Don Russell, 1960
   The very best available and still in print. A copy can be ordered from
   the University of Oklahoma Press, 1-800-627-7377 for ordering information.

2. *Buffalo Bill, His Family, Friends, Fame, Failures and Fortunes*
   By Nellie Snyder Yost
   The Swallow Press
   Chicago 1979

3. *The Wild West – A History of the Wild West Shows*
   By Don Russel
   Amon Carter Museum of Western Art, 1970

4. *Buffalo Bill and the Wild West*
   By Henry Blackman Sell and Victor Weybright
   Oxford University Press, 1955

5. *This Way to the Big Show – The Life of Dexter Fellows*
   By Dexter W. Fellows and Andrew A. Freeman
   The Viking Press
   New York, 1936

6. *Buckskin and Satin*
   By Herschel C. Logan
   The Stackpole Co.
   Harrisburg, Pennsylvania, 1954

7. *Buckskins, Bullets, and Business – A History of Buffalo Bill's Wild West*
   By Sarah J. Blackstone
   Greenwood Press, Inc.
   Westport, Connecticut, 1986

8. *The Business of Being Buffalo Bill – Selected Letters of William F. Cody*
   By Sarah J. Blackstone
   Praeger Publishers
   New York, 1988

9. *Buffalo Bill and His Wild West – A Pictorial Biography*
   By Joseph G. Rosa and Robin May
   University Press of Kansas, 1989

10. *Ten Days on the Plains*
    By Henry E. Davies, edited by Paul Andrew Hutton
    Reprinted by Princeton University Press, 1985

PLATE 188
Letterhead 1887

A fine example of the marvelous quality that can be expected when collecting Cody memorabilia. The fact that a letterhead was issued for the shows winter quarters in Madison Square Garden is fascinating. The author might add, that this letterhead is proof positive that color is not always necessary to create something special.

William Cody was without a doubt a prolific letter writer. This could have been one of his personal escapes from the demanding everyday nature of his business. There exists at least one photo of Cody in his traveling tent by his desk with pen in hand. It is known that he enjoyed receiving letters as he mentioned this more than a few times. Keeping in touch with family, friends, and business associates was important to this fascinating man.

Today it is interesting to note the amount of exciting W. F. Cody handwritten and typed letters, is incredible. For example, The Butterfield and Butterfield auction of Cody memorabilia in 1988, sold 84 of his letters. Most of those letters were saved by his sister, Julia. She was not alone, as it seems most people who received a letter from Buffalo Bill were inclined to keep it and for obvious reasons. In 1996 a large portion of a private Buffalo Bill collection was put on the auction block. One hundred and seventy lots were offered which included 38 Cody letters.

Wild West Show letterheads are in demand and it is easy to understand why. The colorful interesting logos of Buffalo Bill's Wild West Show are just what collectors are looking for. Actually, most have letters written on them, however, unused letterheads are available. It seems there are between 20 and 30 different Cody Wild West Show related letterheads.

Being an entrepreneur is one aspect of Cody's life many people are unaware of or may find difficult to understand. The many different business ventures he was a part of clearly points out he was broad minded and willing to take financial gambles. A variety of intriguing letterheads associated with him as a fortune seeker are available. The Buffalo Bill Combination, Scout's Rest Stock Ranch, Cody, Powell Coffee Co., The Cody Military College and International Academy of Rough Riders, and The Cody Enterprise are a few of the more appealing examples. Cody also used hotel stationery on many occasions.

Matching Wild West Show logo envelopes are also available. They can be found in several sizes and they are just as impressive as the letterheads. Unfortunately, not all letterheads have matching envelopes, however, there are enough to keep collectors busy.

Courtesy Buffalo Bill Historical Center, Cody, Wyoming

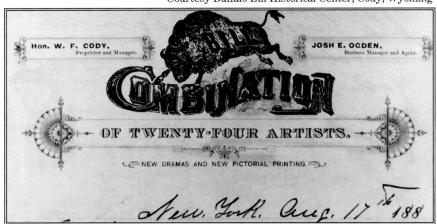

PLATE 189
Letterhead, 1881

The Buffalo Bill Combination of 24 artists was still scheduling performances in 1883, even as Cody and Carver's Wild West Show was about to open. Cody actually made stage appearances into 1885. This was sure money and he needed it until the Wild West became profitable.

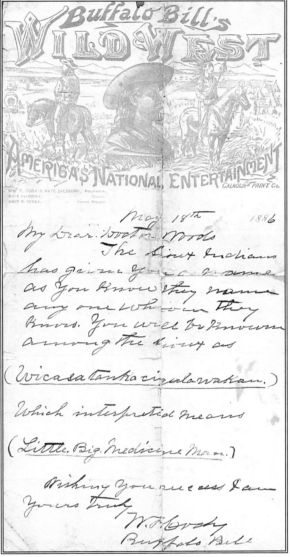

PLATE 190
Letter and letterhead, 1886

A letter to Dr. Frank Wood from Buffalo Bill is interesting because the Sioux Indians named Dr. Wood the "Little Big Medicine Man." In the Peoria, Illinois, city directory for 1886, W. Frank Wood was listed as the manager for the Lighthall Indian Medicine Company. This letterhead design may be the first used by the show's management.

PLATE 190A
Cabinet photo of W. Frank Wood, "The Little Big Medicine Man"

This fascinating group of items belonged to W. Frank Wood. He carried Cody's letter in his wallet for some years, as it is glued to one of Wood's own letterheads from the 1890s. The wallet contained his formulas and recipes, plus other related paper material. His little gold-plated Remington No. 1, revolver with engraving and pearl grips cost $11.50 back in the 1880s.

PLATE 190B

137

Courtesy Buffalo Bill Historical Center, Cody, Wyoming

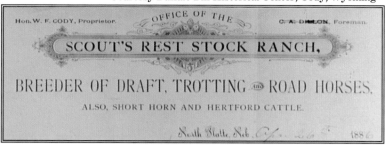

PLATE 191

Letterhead, 1886

Cody started ranching in 1878 with his friend Major Frank North. The location was on the Dismal River near North Platte, Nebraska. In 1886 Cody had the Scout's Rest Ranch built in North Platte. This letterhead is from the ranch's first year.

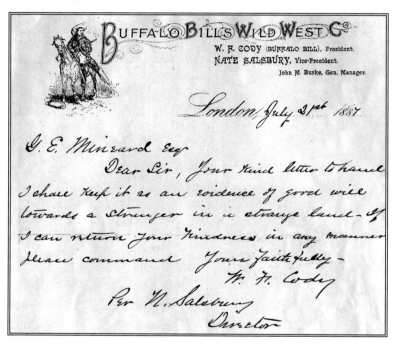

PLATE 192

Letter and letterhead, 1887

A thank you letter written for Cody by his astute business partner, Nate Salsbury. This letterhead has a matching envelope.

Little is known of this venture except that it was an attempt to market a substitute drink for coffee. Doctor Frank Powell, a close friend of Cody's, would lure him into investments that were for the most part failures. Most likely profits from the very successful Chicago 1893 season were lost on this endeavor. This example is page three of a letter written by an unidentified individual.

PLATE 193

Letterhead, 1893

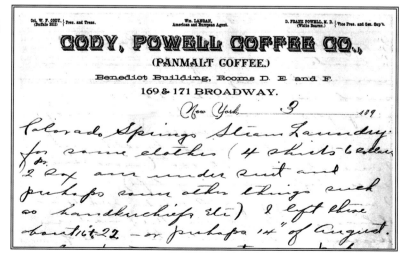

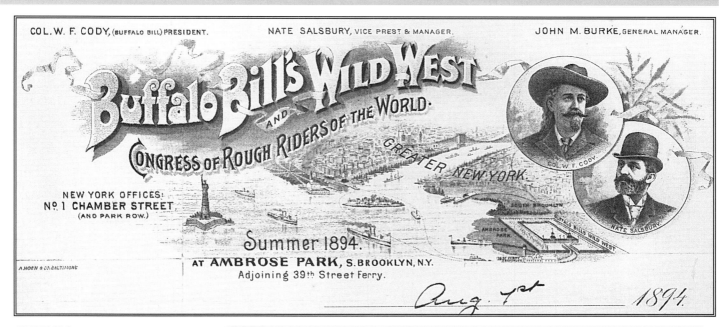

COL. W. F. CODY, (BUFFALO BILL) PRESIDENT.   NATE SALSBURY, VICE PREST & MANAGER.   JOHN M. BURKE, GENERAL MANAGER.

Buffalo Bill's Wild West
AND
CONGRESS OF ROUGH RIDERS OF THE WORLD.

GREATER NEW YORK.

NEW YORK OFFICES:
No. 1 CHAMBER STREET
(AND PARK ROW.)

Summer 1894.
AT AMBROSE PARK, S. BROOKLYN, N.Y.
Adjoining 39th Street Ferry.

A. HOEN & CO. BALTIMORE

Aug. 1st   1894.

PLATE 194
Letter and letterhead, 1894

This letterhead should be on any serious Buffalo Bill collector's wanted list. The striking logo is quality artwork at its finest. The letter mentions 21 days of rain, followed by the hottest spell of weather New York had ever known. Cody is also asking for more time to pay back a loan from his friend Harrington. He talks of selling his cattle to settle up. After the 1893 season, with all the money that was brought in, why would Cody owe a friend $3,500.00 by the summer of 1894?

Courtesy Buffalo Bill Historical Center, Cody, Wyoming

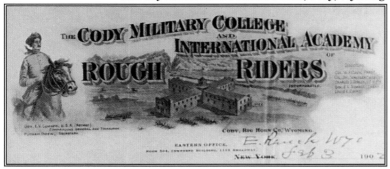

PLATE 195
Letterhead, 1902

Cody was involved in a variety of ventures, and it seems they all deserved letterheads. The author didn't have time to look into this Military College of Rough Riders, but most likely it didn't last long. The 1901 Wild West program had a great advertisement on this academy.

PLATE 195A
Ad from 1901 program

CODY MILITARY COLLEGE
AND INTERNATIONAL ACADEMY
OF
·· Rough Riders ··
(INCORPORATED)
BIG HORN BASIN, WYOMING.

COL. W. F. CODY, President.
COL. JNO. SCHUYLER CROSBY, Vice-President.
C. D. GURLEY, 1st Vice-President.
GEN. E. V. SUMNER, U. S. A. (Retired),
Commandant and Treasurer.
PUTNAM DREW, Secretary.

A TACTICAL SCHOOL for the teaching of horsemanship, marksmanship, cavalry and infantry drill, rough riding, scouting, camp-life, hunting, fishing, golf and physical perfection in out-door life. Located at an altitude of about 5,000 feet, in a magnificent climate, thirty-five miles from Yellowstone National Park. The buildings will be modeled after the old-fashioned blockhouse fort style, constructed of logs, and containing bathrooms, gymnasiums, libraries, diningrooms and sleeping quarters. Membership, $250 for first three months, $550 per year, which includes one railroad fare from student's home to the College; also, use of horse, gun, Khaki suit, tent, and all the accoutrement of the regular U. S. Cavalry; food, quarters and tuition. (Ordinary educational branches taught, if desired.) Address, for further information,

COL. JNO. SCHUYLER CROSBY,
EASTERN OFFICE:
ROOM 504, TOWNSEND BUILDING,
1123 BROADWAY, NEW YORK.
OR
GEN. E. V. SUMNER,
1123 Broadway, NEW YORK, or CODY, Big Horn County, WYOMING.

Personal application for enlistment may be made to COL. W. F. CODY (Buffalo Bill), IMMEDIATELY following the Afternoon Performances of Wild West.

COPYRIGHT 1900
BY
The Courier Co.
BUFFALO, N.Y.

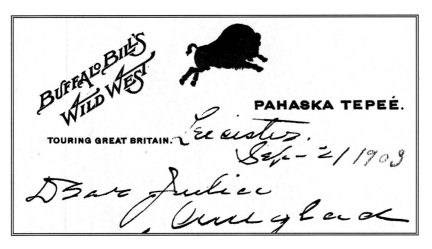

PLATE 196
Letter and letterhead, 1903

The Pahaska Tepee stationery is the smaller tablet size. This letter, from Leicester, England, to sister Julia, is a fine example of Cody's personal feelings. He is happy sister Julia's house if finally paid off. He writes of feeling better but must keep working. On the second page, not shown, he writes of becoming the sole owner by buying the Salsbury interest.

Pawnee Bill writes:
"Friend Hartly
Enclosed is our route. You will observe us at Beaver Falls, Monday we will be close to you. Would be very pleased to have you call and see the show if it is convenient for you. As I believe you did not get to see us this spring.
With best wishes
Your true friend
G. W. Lillie
"Pawnee Bill"

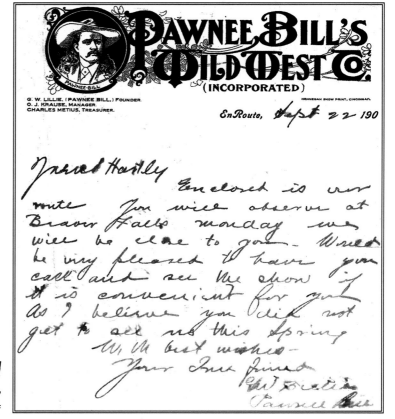

PLATE 197
Letter and letterhead, enroute Sept. 22, 1904

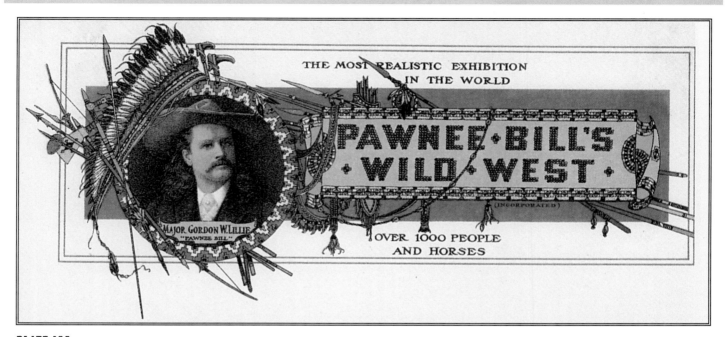

PLATE 198
Letterhead, c. 1905

Unused letterheads are indeed out there waiting for collectors. This Pawnee Bill example is one of the finest Wild West Show letterheads ever produced. The artwork, color, and layout are simply fantastic.

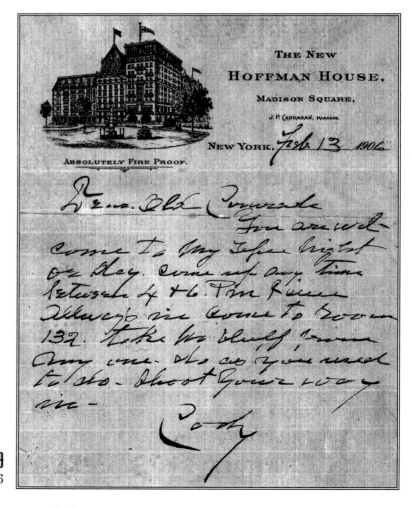

The Hoffman House was one of Cody's main working offices away from home. His old comrade was Oscar Sachs, an old scouting companion. Cody writes, "You are welcome to my tepee night or day. Come up anytime between four and six p.m. Always in, come to room 132. Take no bluff from anyone. Do as you used to do, shoot your way in." Another interesting letter written by a unique man, who never forgot an old acquaintance.

PLATE 199
Letter and letterhead, 1906

BUFFALO BILL'S WILD WEST

THE BAILEY BUILDING 27 EAST 22D ST.
NEW YORK CITY.

Feb 25th, 07.

Lewis Mortimer.
2I9 Barrett Street.
Syracuse, N. Y.

    Dear Sir:---

        There is a chance for you to get a job in the Cavalry

squad with the Buffalo Bill's Wild West, if you can do the Monkey

Drill. Let me know what you can do in this line, what experience

you havehad etc;   Yours truly

AddrewssJohn Baker.
    27 E. 22d Street.
    New York City, N' Y.
        Room 45

J.M Baker

BUFFALO BILL'S WILD WEST

THE BAILEY BUILDING 27 EAST 22D ST.
NEW YORK CITY.

March 5th, 07.

Mr Lewis Mortimer.
2I9 Barrett Street.
Syracuse, N. Y.

    Dear Sir:--

        Replying to your favor of March 4th, I can place you in

the Cavalry to do theRoman riding and Monkey Drill, The Salary

we pay the Cavalry boy, is $35, per month and board and the usual

transportation while on the road, also we furnish them their costu

etc.   I f you consider this offer we will want you at Bridgeport

Conn March 20th for rehearsals. Of course we do not pay a salary

for rehearsals, but we take care of you while you are learning the

work. Let me have your reply as so on as possible.
            Yours truly *J.M Baker*

W. F. CODY, PROPR.
L. E. DECKER, MGR.
OSCAR F. SWENSON, M'GR.

The Irma
BUFFALO BILL'S
HOTEL IN THE ROCKIES
EUROPEAN PLAN
$1.00 PER DAY & UP

E. Raucke
Cody, Wyo. DEC 27 1910

PLATE 200
Letters and letterhead, 1907

Here we have two wonderful typed letters by John Baker, who took over the arena director's responsibilities after the death of Nate Salsbury. These two letters were trimmed in half and mailed in a smaller sized matching Wild West logo envelope. We learn of the Cavalry Boy's salary and how they are cared for by the show. No doubt letters contain important information.

The Irma Hotel was named for Cody's daughter and built in Cody, Wyoming. The official opening was on the evening of Nov. 18, 1902. The local newspaper stated the hotel cost Buffalo Bill $80,000 to build. The reality was that it was just too large for the town and area and would consistently lose money while Cody was alive.

PLATE 201
Letterhead, 190?

This wonderfully designed letter-head, with excellent color and layout, makes one striking impression. Pawnee Bill also appreciated quality advertising and art. Many of his program covers and lithographs were of the same high standards that Cody always insisted on.

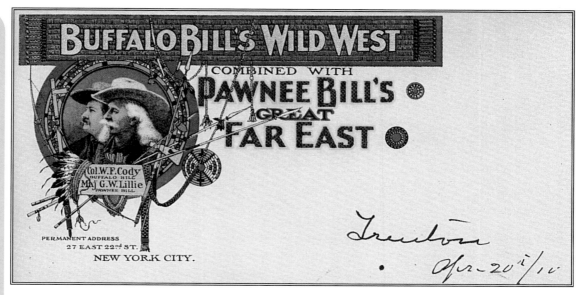

PLATE 202
Letter and letterhead, 1910

PLATE 203
Letter and letterhead, date unknown

A letter to Cody asking for free tickets. The reply, "Give Joe Webber the Garden," signed W. F. Cody. This letter was then returned to Mr. Weber by way of John M. Burke. The notation at bottom reads, "I thought I would send Col. Cody's endorsement, Yours truly Burke." Cody and Burke's signatures together makes this letter very unique. Cody misspelled Mr. Weber's name but the recognition more than offset that little embarrassment.

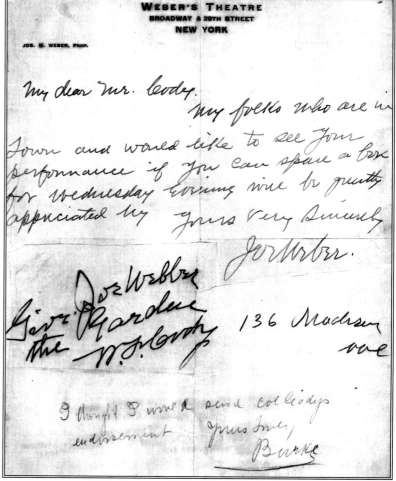

143

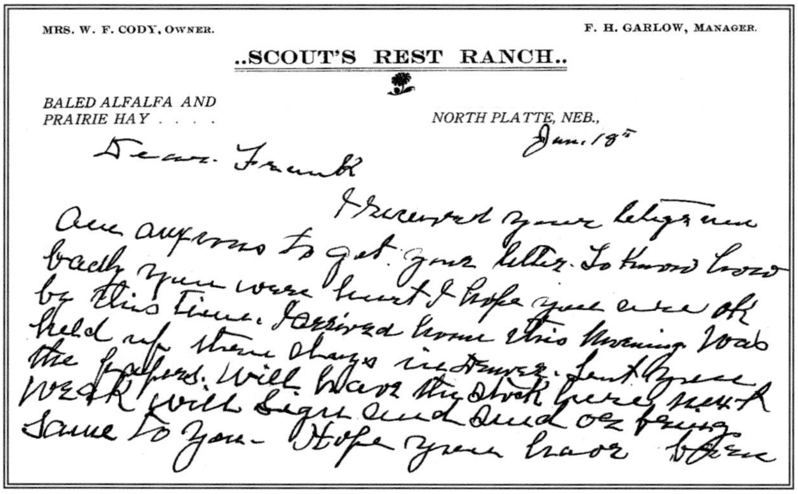

MRS. W. F. CODY, OWNER.   F. H. GARLOW, MANAGER.

..SCOUT'S REST RANCH..

BALED ALFALFA AND
PRAIRIE HAY . . . .   NORTH PLATTE, NEB.,
                             Jan. 18

Dear Frank

[handwritten letter text]

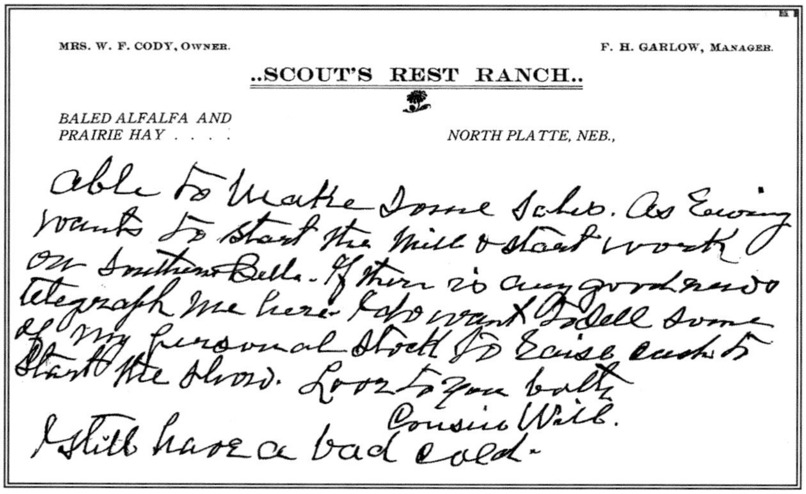

MRS. W. F. CODY, OWNER.   F. H. GARLOW, MANAGER.

..SCOUT'S REST RANCH..

BALED ALFALFA AND
PRAIRIE HAY . . . .   NORTH PLATTE, NEB.,

[handwritten letter text]

PLATE 204
Letter and letterhead

This letter to his cousin, J. Frank Cody touches on personal concerns and of course business. He closes with "Love to you both, Cousin Will." He included Frank's wife Nellie, showing his considerate feelings for his family.

PLATE 205
Letter and letterhead, 1913

"Dear Sister Julia:
Here is ten shares of my mining stock, which will be worth fair value someday. Am still guesting, will go to North Platte for Christmas if I can get through here. Will be here until 22nd. Do hope you are well and happy. I am feeling fine but a days rest would do me good.
Love Brother"

NEW YORK CABLE ADDRESS "WALDORF, NEW YORK."
PHILADELPHIA CABLE ADDRESS "BELLEVUE, PHILADELPHIA."

THE WALDORF.   THE BELLEVUE-STRATFORD.   THE ASTORIA.

THE WALDORF-ASTORIA, NEW YORK.
THE BELLEVUE-STRATFORD, PHILADELPHIA.

The Waldorf-Astoria,
New York, Dec. 14   1913

Dear Sister Julia.

PLATE 206
Letter and letterhead, 1913

A letter typed by Harry H. Tammen. Tammen was responsible for forcing Cody's show to be shut down. Cody toured with the Sells-Floto Circus for two seasons. The 1914 and 1915 seasons had to be very difficult for our western legend.

October Sixth
1913

W. J. Langer,
Warsau, N. C.
% Howe's Great London Shows.

Dear Sir:

Replying to your letter of September 30th, for engagement with SELLS FLOTO 1914, we would be inclined to send you a contract for next season but do not wish to pay you $50. a week. If $50. or thereabouts for the acts you name is satisfactory, we will seriously consider sending you a contract.

As always,

H H Tammen

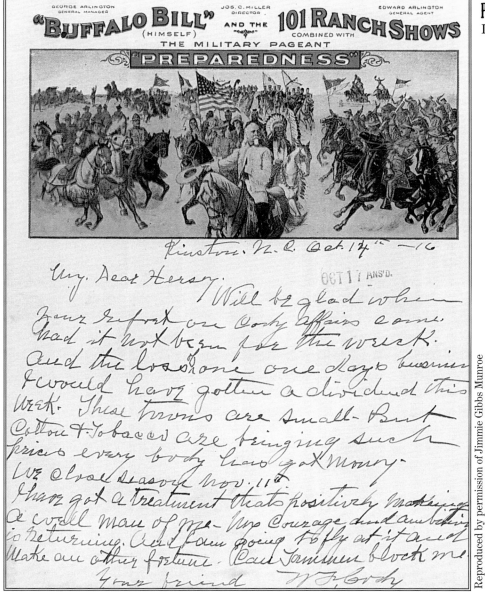

PLATE 207
Letter and letterhead, 1916

A letter to Henry Hersey, who was Cody's attorney. He writes, "I have got a treatment that's positively making a well man of me. My courage and ambition is returning, and am going to fly at it and make another fortune. Can Tammen block me?" Even in 1916 Cody was still worrying about Harry Tammen. Sadly, Buffalo Bill would not have to worry very long as he passed away on Jan. 10, 1917.

PLATE 208
Envelope, 1890
Size – 4¼" x 5½"

A very interesting envelope because it was first mailed in Bologna, Italy, to Frankfurt, Germany, where it missed Nate Salsbury. It was then forwarded to Paris, France. Unfortunately, no letter was retrieved with this envelope.

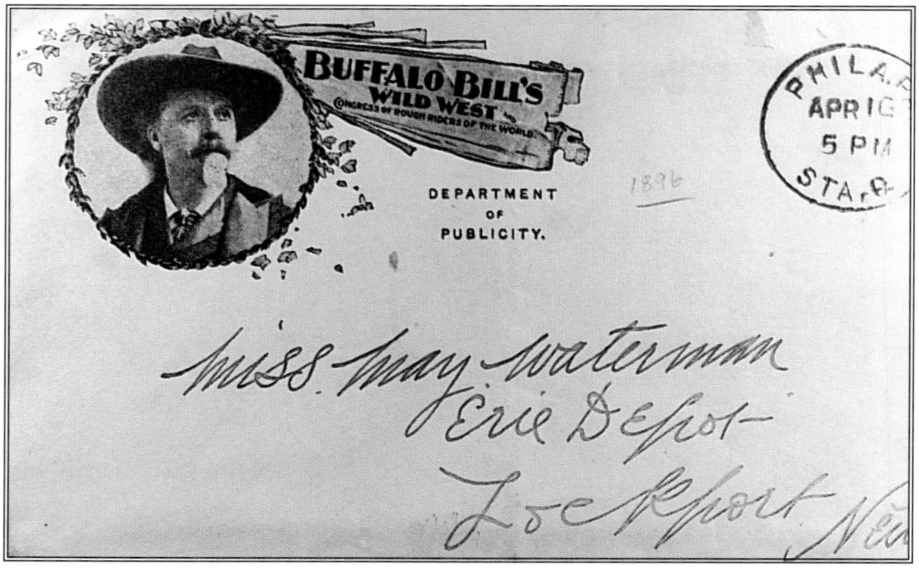

PLATE 209
Envelope, 1896
Size 3⅝" x 6½"

This envelope was mailed by Paul J. Staunton who was a principal orator of the side show. He was courting May Waterman and they would get married in 1899.

Courtesy Buffalo Bill Historical Center, Cody, Wyoming

PLATE 210
Envelope, 1899
Size 3⅝" x 6½"

May Waterman is now Mrs. P. J. Staunton. Paul wrote home on a regular basis. There is a letterhead to match this envelope.

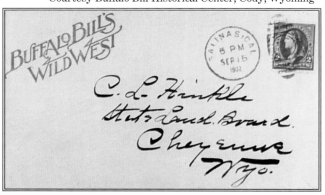

PLATE 211
Envelope, 1902
Size – 3⅝" x 6½"

This logo was used from 1902 to at least 1908. The matching letterhead has The Bailey Building, 27 East 22nd Street, New York City address as part of the logo.

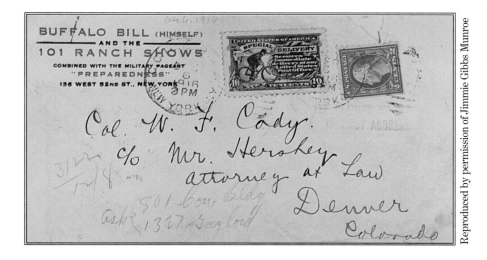

Reproduced by permission of Jimmie Gibbs Munroe

PLATE 212
Envelope, 1916
Size – 3⅝" x 6½"

The post mark reads Dec. 6, 1916, and that is only five weeks before Cody's death. Touring that last season simply robbed Cody of his seemingly eternal energy. He died just a few weeks before his 71st birthday.

Courtesy Buffalo Bill Historical Center, Cody, Wyoming

PLATE 213
The New York Weekly
March 25, 1872
Published by Street & Smith
Size – 14" x 21" approximately

PLATE 213A
Our dime novel hero

Buffalo Bill's Best Shot appeared nine months before Cody started his stage acting career. It may be concluded that the early dime novel style of writing actually was responsible for setting Cody's entertainment career in motion. The dime novel format would run unabated until long after Cody's death in January 1917.

The term dime novel is basically a collector's description of any early fiction pulp publication that tells a complete story, regardless of issue price. The main rush of dime novels occurred in the 1880s and would continue until about 1919. The author enjoys the early illustrations and title banners. The later color front covers are exciting and interesting. The variety of different style title banners should keep collectors busy. Since there are literally hundreds of dime novels it is suggested to focus on different style title formats. Even this method of collecting will yield many examples.

Classifying dime novels into three distinctly different groups is helpful. All pre-1900 issues are basically tabloid style or the more typical comic book size. All these are black print on a very inexpensive paper. In 1901 color front and back covers became standard. These dime novels were issued weekly until mid-1919 and are about the same size as today's comic books. The third group are what we would call paperback book size. Here again this style, like the color cover group is still easy to find.

Back in the 1940s a dime novel club reprinted many of the rarer and interesting dime novels. All were marked on the outside back cover on the bottom border. A rubber ink stamp was used with the club name, address, and price. Naturally a number of Buffalo Bill stories were reprinted. Should the reprint stamping be removed, it is almost impossible for the average collector to know if it is an original or the reprint. When purchasing dime novels always check to see if any of the bottom back cover is missing.

Don Russell's near masterpiece *The Lives and Legends of Buffalo Bill* has a complete chapter on dime novels. With help from two dime novel experts, he has covered this subject as well as possible. Chapter 27 is where the information may be found.

PLATE 214

The Star Journal, New York,
March 29, 1879
Published by Beadle & Adams
Size – 14¾" x 21½"
Pages – 8 numbered

Tabloid size, multiple story issues are early variations of dime novel material. A column titled "Topics of the Time" is included and actually is excellent. The author has seen at least 20 different *Star Journals* with Buffalo Bill stories.

PLATE 215

*The Boys of New York – A Paper for
Young Americans*
Published by Frank Tousey, No. 18
Rose Street, New York
Size – 14⅛" x 20⅛"
Pages – 8 numbered
Issue Date – September 4, 1880

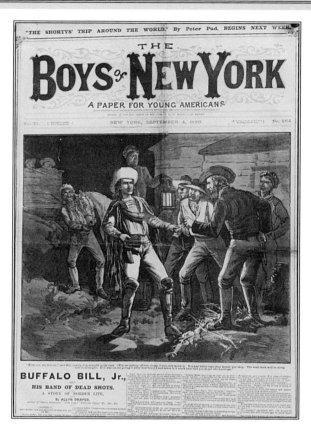

Competition for dime novel readers
was keen back in the 1880s and Frank
Tousey did very well. Buffalo Bill, Jr.,
by author Allyn Draper was just
another way to jump on the Cody
bandwagon. Frank Tousey offered the
subscribers of this paper free postage
for the year of 1880. Back issues were
also available for five cents each.

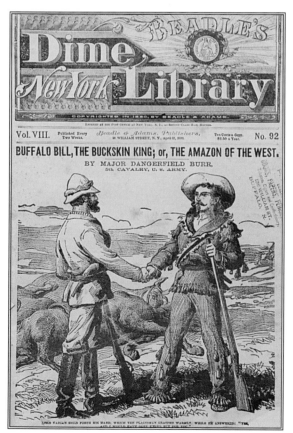

PLATE 216

Beadle's New York Dime Library
Published by Beadle & Adams
Size – 8⅜" x 12"
Pages – 23 numbered
Issue Date – April 21, 1880
Story by Major Dangerfield Burr,
5th Cavalry, U. S. Army.

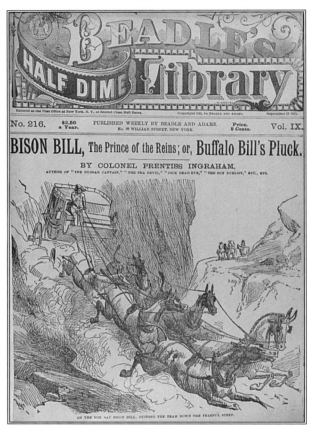

PLATE 217
Beadle's Half Dime Library
Published by Beadle & Adams, No. 98 William St., New York
Size – 8⅛" x 11"
Pages – 14 numbered
Issue Date – September 13, 1881
Story by Colonel Prentiss Ingraham

PLATE 217A
Colonel Prentiss Ingraham

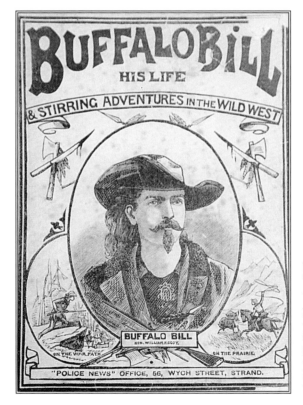

The first two pages of this British dime novel depicts Cody's Wild West Show plus interesting information about the preparations for the actual exhibition grounds.

PLATE 218
Buffalo Bill, His Life & Stirring Adventures in the Wild West
Published by "Police News" Office, 56 Wych Street, Strand
Size – 7¼" x 9¾"
Issue Date – 1887
No author's credit or price

HON. WILLIAM F. CODY,
(BUFFALO BILL)
The Great Scout, Guide, and Hunter-Author.

PLATE 219
Trade card
Published by
Beadle & Adams
Issue Date –
Unknown
Size – 3½" x 5½"
approximately

Removing glued in paper material from scrapbooks, will always result in various degrees of damage. On the other side can be read a short note from Cody to the publishers. This serial would start in number 287 of the *New York Saturday Journal*. A full-page portrait of Buffalo Bill was also included.

Buffalo Bill's Last and Best Serial.

DEADLY-EYE,

The Unknown Scout;
OR,
THE BRANDED BROTHERHOOD.

Regarding this splendid story the author writes:
MESSRS. BEADLE AND ADAMS:

My serial, "Deadly-Eye," much the best story I have yet produced, draws largely upon my own wild western experience, and, exciting and romantic as it may seem, old pards and friends on the plains will recognize it as "true to the life." I as greatly enjoyed its composition as I would a good buffalo chase or a "scrimmage" with the Sioux, and was vai ugh to think my revolvers had found a rival in my pen! I ... Deadly-Eye" will answer the "great expectations" creat ... he story.
Yo
m. F. CODY, ("Buffalo Bill.")

It is a romance of the l ... tographing life there, and on the Plains, as only a geni ... ffalo Bill can do it. It is like living in the very midst of ... s to read his story. Everybody will be delighted and thi ... ne author that *his revolver has found a rival in his pen!* The opening chapters c ... ndid serial, together with a **full- page portrait of Bu** ... sill, are given in No. 287 of the NEW YORK SATURDAY JOUR: ... Best Story Paper, the Best Family Paper, the Best Boys' ... e Best Girls' Paper, the Most Popu- lar of all the Weeklie ... e by all newsdealers, price six c ...ts; or sent, postage p ... scribers, four months for $1.00 – six months, $1.50 – one ... BEADLE AND ADAMS, Publishers, 98 William Street, Ne

Alber? W ... .'s Dick Talbot Ser

Owing to the immense popularity of the four romance ... which Dick Talbot ("Injun Dick") is the center of interest, and t ... ir in ability to keep these most noted of all Mr. Aiken's productions in print, as *serials*, \a the SATURDAY JOURNAL, the publis ... care im- pelled to put them into volumes of convenient size ... active style, each volu me to be a complete story. The ... he or- der of issue ... Rocky Mountain Rob," now ... , the Sport," b ready. "Injun Dick." ... land Kit," Re y Oct. 30th. For sale ... t, post- age pa' , to any address, on re ... s of ... TW ... ts each. BEADL : AND AD ws, Publishers, 98 Willia ... street, New York. The NEW ... SATURDAY JOURNAL, together with all other current i ... umbers of BEADLE AND ADAMS' publica- tions, are for s ...

Trevor Baxter, Norwalk, Ohio.

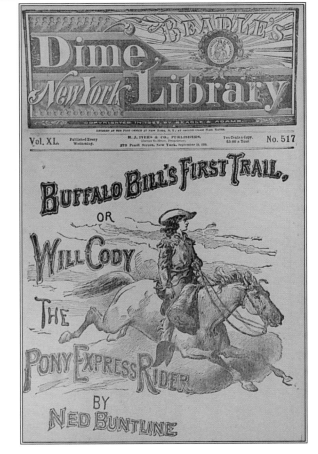

PLATE 220
Beadle's New York Dime Novel
Published by M. J. Ivers & Company, James Sullivan Proprietor, 379 Pearal St., New York
Size – 8½" x 11⅜"
Pages – 29 numbered
Issue Date – September 19, 1888
Story by Ned Buntline

PLATE 221
Log Cabin Library
Published by Street & Smith, 31 Rose Street, N.Y., P.O. Box 2734
Size – 8¾" x 12"
Pages – 48 numbered
Issue Date – August 27, 1891
Price – 10 cents
Story by Ned Buntline

PLATE 222
New York Five Cent Library
Published by Street & Smith
Size – 8¼" x 11¾"
Pages – 16 numbered
Issue Date – September 24, 1892
Story by Harry Hart

PLATE 223
Beadle's New York Dime Library
Published by Beadle & Adams
Size – 8¼" x 12¼"
Pages – 30 numbered
Issue Date – January 20, 1892
Story by Col. Prentiss Ingraham

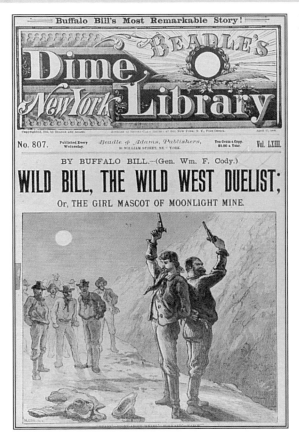

PLATE 224
Beadle's New York Dime Library
Published by Beadle & Adams
Size – 8¼" x 12"
Pages – 32 numbered
Issue Date – April 11, 1894
Story by Buffalo Bill (General Wm.F. Cody)

PLATE 225
Beadle's Half Dime Library
Published by Beadle & Adams
Size – 8" x 11½"
Pages – 15 numbered
Issue Date – November 10, 1896
Story by Colonel Prentiss Ingraham

PLATE 226
The Half Dime Library
Published by Beadle & Adams
Size – 8" x 11¼"
Pages – 15 numbered
Issue Date – June 15, 1897
Story by Buffalo Bill

PLATE 227
Beadle's Boy's Library of Sport, Story and Adventure
Original Issue Date – December 14, 1881

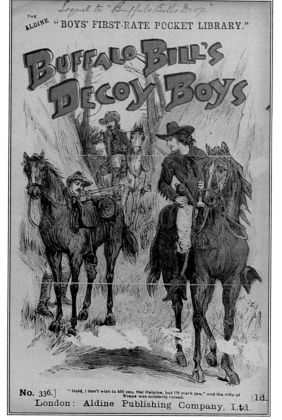

This volume one number one issue is a reprint from 1946. It is included here for information. Keep in mind that several pre-1900 Buffalo Bill dime novels have been reprinted.

PLATE 228
Boy's First Rate Pocket Library
Published by Aldine Publishing Company, 9 Red Lion Court, London, England
Size – 5⅞" x 9"
Pages – 32 numbered
Issue Date – circa 1899
Price – 1 penny
Author anonymous

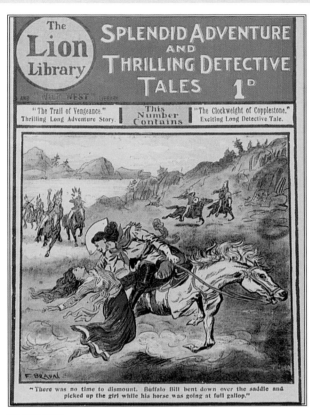

"There was no time to dismount. Buffalo Bill bent down over the saddle and picked up the girl while his horse was going at full gallop."

PLATE 229

The Lion Library and Wildwest Library
Published by James Henderson & Sons, Ltd.,
Red Lion House, Red Lion Court,
Fleetstreet, London E.C.
Size – 6¼" x 9¾"
Pages – 32 numbered
Issue Date – Circa 1902
Price – 1 penny
Author anonymous

PLATE 230

The Buffalo Bill Stories
Published by Street & Smith, 238 William Street, N.Y.,
Size – 8¼" x 10½"
Pages – 32 numbered
Issue Date – July 12, 1902
Story by – The author of *Buffalo Bill*.
Today this means anonymous

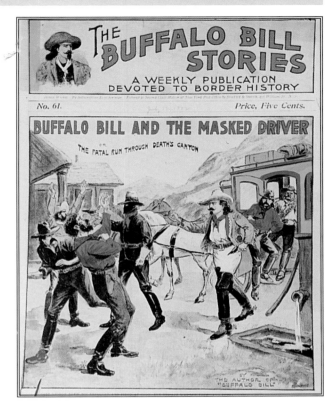

PLATE 231

Pluck and Luck
Published by Frank Tousey,
24 Union Square, New York
Size – 8" x 11¼"
Pages – 29 numbered
Price – five cents
Story by Pawnee Bill
Issue Date – August 19, 1903

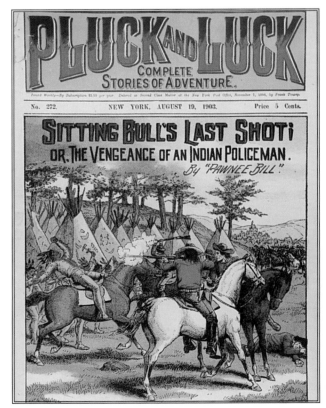

PLATE 232

Buffalo Bill Stories
Published by Street & Smith
Size – 8" x 11⅛"
Pages – 28 numbered
Issue Date – October 7, 1905
Author anonymous

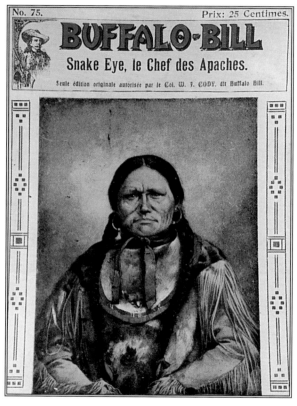

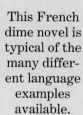

This French dime novel is typical of the many different language examples available.

PLATE 233

Buffalo Bill: Snake Eye – Chief of the Apaches
Published by A. Eichler, Paris,
41, Rue Dauphine
Size – 8⅝" x 10⅞"
Pages – 32 numbered
Issue Date – circa 1908

This Italian dime novel has one of the more brutally graphic front covers.

PLATE 234

Buffalo Bill, Kenton King
Size – 8½" x 11"
Pages – 32 numbered
Issue Date – 1908

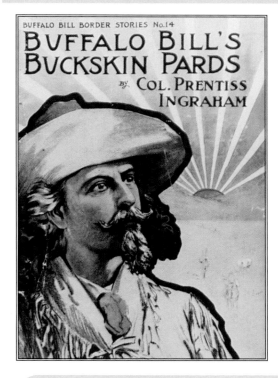

PLATE 235
Buffalo Bill Border Stories No.14
Published by Street & Smith
Size – 4⅞" x 7"
Pages – 320 numbered
Issue Date – 1908
Story by Col. Prentiss Ingraham

Paperback style novels are plentiful and may number in the hundreds. They continued for years after Cody's death in January of 1917.

PLATE 236
The Buffalo Bill Stories
Published by Street & Smith
Size – 8" x 11"
Pages – 32 numbered
Issue Date – March 28, 1908
Author anonymous

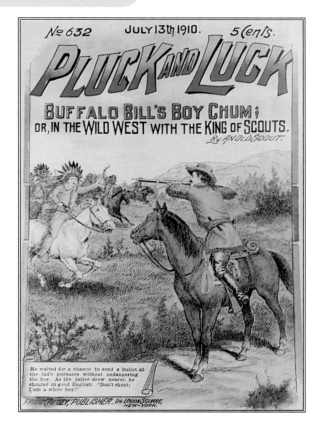

PLATE 237
Pluck and Luck
Published by Frank Tousey, 24 Union Square, New York
Size – 8" x 11"
Pages – 32 numbered
Issue Date – July 13, 1910
Story by an Old Scout – anonymous

PLATE 238
The Buffalo Bill Stories
Published by Street & Smith
Size – 8" x 11"
Pages – 31 numbered
Issue Date – October 29, 1910
Author anonymous

This series titled *The Buffalo Bill Stories* has 591 titles.

One interesting aspect of these Buffalo Bill dime novels is the fact that the last few pages contain articles about current events plus news of the world.

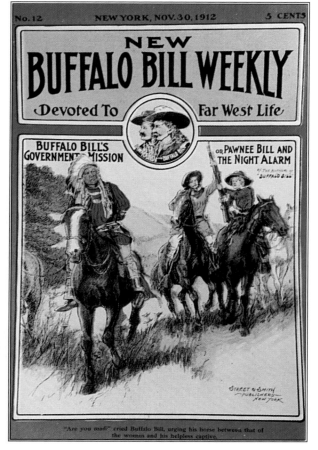

PLATE 239
New Buffalo Bill Weekly
Published by Street & Smith
Size – 8" x 11"
Pages – 32 numbered
Issue Date – November 30, 1912

PLATE 240
New Buffalo Bill Weekly
Published by Street & Smith
Size – 7¼" x 11"
Pages – 32 numbered
Issue Date – April 4, 1914
Author anonymous

The New Buffalo Bill Weekly series has 364 titles. The series would run to mid 1919.

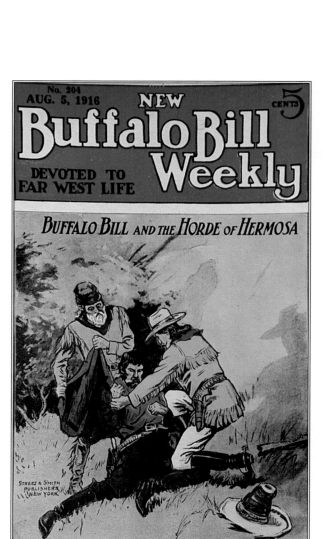

PLATE 241
New Buffalo Bill Weekly
Published by Street & Smith
Size – 7¼" x 11"
Pages – 32 numbered
Issue Date – August 5, 1916
Author anonymous

TOBACCO, OTHER INSERT CARDS & SILK PREMIUMS

Wm. F. Cody (Buffalo Bill).

PLATE 242
Celebrities and Actresses
Mrs. G.B. Miller's Company, 1885
Card size – 2¼" x 3¾"

The Mrs. G.B. Miller's Company of New York was established in 1876. The first series of insert cards they issued was in 1885. The cards are unnumbered and listed in the reference catalogs as "Celebrities and Actress." The total number of cards in this set is unknown.

Nineteenth century tobacco cards are indeed fine examples of the excellent lithography work done at this time. These mini cards are basically overlooked by most active Buffalo Bill collectors. Hopefully that will change after viewing the colorful and articulate cards to follow.

Tobacco insert cards were first used in the mid-1880s and enjoyed a very special popularity for many years. As many as 1,000 different sets may have been distributed by 1915. Most of the cards can be classified as advertising cards because that was one of their main purposes.

The variety of subjects depicted on these mini cards almost rivals that of postcards. Athletes were a favorite subject appearing on these insert cards and firearm shooters were considered athletes at that time. Naturally, Buffalo Bill and some of his companions were included in several sets.

Native Americans were also well represented on these extraordinary mini works of art. Actual photo cards were issued also and are popular. Mini booklets of intriguing people are yet another variation of insert material that we all have an opportunity to find.

By 1910, other products like coffee, chewing gum, and candy were using insert cards to help promote sales. Since Cody was still touring at this time he again appeared, and although the quality of cards had declined, they are still fun to collect.

In or about 1914, Tobacco silk premiums had a fine selection of Native Americans which included Sitting Bull. Buffalo Bill on horseback also appears on silk, from this time period. Most of the above mentioned cards and silks can be located within non-sport card collections and the cartophilic societies of Great Britain and the United States. These societies are devoted to promoting the hobby of cigarette and tobacco card collecting. For those collectors who would like to learn more abut this terrific subject matter visit the Museum of Tobacco Art and History in Nashville, Tennessee.

PLATE 243
Champions of Games and Sports
W. S. Kimball and Company,
Circa 1880s
Card size – 1½" x 2⅝"

Annie Oakley makes this set of 50 as Champion Lady Rifle Shot of the World. Lillian Smith was selected as The Champion Female Glass Ball Shooter, another interesting set from the 1880s.

CHAMPIONS

Base Ball,	Isaac Murphy,	Jockey.
Andrews, (C.F. Philadelphia).	Charles Wood,	do.
Anson, (1st Base, Chicago).	Beeckman.	Lawn Tennis
Brouthers, (1st Base, Detroit).	Dwight,	do.
Caruthers, (P. Brooklyn).	Sears,	do.
Dunlap, (Capt. Pittsburgh).	Taylor,	do.
Glasscock, (S.S. Indianapolis).		Marksman,
Keefe, (P. New York).	Captain Bogardus.	
Kelly, (C. Boston).	Beach,	Oarsman
Prince, Bicyclist.	Jake Gaudaur, do.	
Rowe, do.	Hanlan,	do.
Stevens, do.	Teemer,	do.
Wood, do.	James Albert, Pedestrian.	
Daly, Billiards.	Pat Fitzgerald,	do
Schaefer, do.	Rowell,	do.
Sexton, do.	D'oro,	Pool.
Slosson, do.	Jack Dempsey, Pugilist.	
Vignaux, do.	Jake Kilrain,	do.
Broadswordsman,	Mitchell,	do.
Duncan C. Ross,	Jem Smith,	do
Capt. Mackenzie, Chess.	Sullivan,	do.
Steinitz, do.	Myers,	Runner.
Zukertort, do.	Strongest Man in the World,	
Foot Ball,	Emil Voss,	
Beecher, (Capt. of Yale Team).	Wild West Hunter,	
W. Byrd Page, High Jumper.	"Buffalo Bill,"	
Snapper Garrison, Jockey.	Joe Acton, Wrestler.	
Mc Laughlin, do.	Muldoon,	do.

**GOODWIN & CO.
NEW YORK.**

PLATE 244
Champions
The Goodwin Company
Year – circa late 1880s
Card size – 1½" x 2⅝"

This very colorful set of 50 champions was issued in the late 1880s. Captain Bogardus was also included as The Champion Marksman. The Goodwin Company of New York produced many fine sets during the golden age of insert cards. George S. Harris and Sons of Philadelphia were the lithographers.

This is actually a mini booklet of 15 numbered pages. The text is excellent which is surprising. The lithography is extra fine and was done by Knapp & Company of Park Place, New York. An exciting variation insert example from the late 1880s.

PLATE 245
Histories of Poor Boys
Who Have Become Rich
and Famous People
Duke's Cigarettes
Year – circa late 1880
Booklet size – 1½" x 2¾"

Histories of Poor Boys
WHO
have become rich,
AND
Other Famous People.

Alger	Irving
Anderson	Jefferson
Astor	Kilrain
Barnum	Longfellow
Bernhardt	Materna
Billings	Meissonier
Blaine	Millais
Booth	Modjeska
Buffalo Bill	Morton
Carnegie	Nilsson
Childs	Ole Bull
Claflin	Parnell
Cornell	Patti
Depew	Peabody
Eads	Poe
Edison	Salvini
Ericsson	Stanley
Field	Stanford
Gerster	Sullivan
Gladstone	Talmage
Gould	Tennyson
Harrison	Twain
Hofmann	Vanderbilt
Huxley	Wanamaker
Ingersoll	Whittier

PACKED IN
Duke's Cigarettes

HON. W. F. CODY (Buffalo Bill)
ALLEN & GINTER'S
RICHMOND. Cigarettes VIRGINIA.

PLATE 246
The World's Champions
Allen & Ginter
Year – 1888
Card size – 1½" x 2¾"

The Allen & Ginter Company of Richmond, Virginia, started selling cigarettes in 1875. by 1888 an insert card was included in every box of ten Richmond Straight Cut No. 1 cigarettes. The other tobacco products this company made may have also had cards. The 50-card set of The World's Champions included Rifle Shooters, Buffalo Bill, Dr. W.F. Carver, Captain A. Bogardus, and Miss Annie Oakley and were excellent selections. It is interesting that Bogardus was included simply because he was a noted shotgun exhibitionist. Allen & Ginter also made magnificent albums for each set. Occasionally cards can be found that have been cut out of the albums. The examples show the actual insert cards and the cards cut from The World's Champions album. The album cards have blank backs and only the names of the shooters. Linder, Eddy and Clauss of New York did the lithographic work on both the inert cards and the album. The album cards have a slightly darker tone.

MISS ANNIE OAKLEY.
ALLEN & GINTER'S
RICHMOND. Cigarettes VIRGINIA.

DR. W. F. CARVER.
ALLEN & GINTER'S
RICHMOND. Cigarettes VIRGINIA.

THE WORLD'S CHAMPIONS
ONE PACKED IN EACH BOX OF
TEN CIGARETTES

BASE BALL PLAYERS.	PUGILISTS.
CHAS. W. BENNETT.	JOHN L. SULLIVAN.
JOHN M. WARD.	JAKE KILRAIN.
MIKE KELLY.	JEM SMITH.
JOHN CLARKSON.	CHARLIE MITCHELL.
TIMOTHY KEEFE.	JIMMY CARNEY.
JOSEPH MULVEY.	JACK DEMPSEY.
ADRIAN C. ANSON.	IKE WEIR.
CAPT. JACK GLASSCOCK.	JACK McAULIFFE.
R. L. CARUTHERS.	JOE LANNON.
CHARLES COMISKEY.	JIMMY CARROLL.

OARSMEN.	RIFLE SHOOTERS.
WM. BEACH.	CAPT. A. H. BOGARDUS.
JOHN TEEMER.	DR. W. F. CARVER.
E. A. TRICKETT.	HON. W. F. CODY (Buffalo Bill)
ED. HANLAN.	MISS ANNIE OAKLEY.
WALLACE ROSS.	
JACOB GAUDAUR.	BILLIARD PLAYERS.
GEO H. HOSMER.	WM. SEXTON.
ALBERT HAMM.	M. VIGNAUX.
JOHN McKAY.	J. SCHAEFER.
GEO. BUBEAR.	JOS. DION.
	MAURICE DALY.
WRESTLERS.	GEO. F. SLOSSON.
JOE ACTON.	YANK ADAMS.
WM. MULDOON.	
THEO. BAUER.	
MATSADA SORAKICHI.	POOL PLAYERS.

CAPT. A. H. BOGARDUS.
ALLEN & GINTER'S
RICHMOND. Cigarettes VIRGINIA.

PLATE 247

The Rifle Shooters

The Rifle Shooters page from Allen and Ginter's terrific World's Champions Album. The background artwork on each page is striking.

CHIEF JOSEPH,
NEZ PERCES.

RED CLOUD,
DAKOTA SIOUX.

SITTING BULL,
DAKOTA SIOUX.

PLATE 248
American Indian Chiefs
by Allen & Ginter
Circa 1888

SPOTTED TAIL,
BLACKFEET SIOUX.

RED SHIRT,
DAKOTA SIOUX.

CELEBRATED
AMERICAN INDIAN CHIEFS
ONE PACKED IN EACH BOX OF TEN
CIGARETTES

Agate Arrow Point.	John Grass.
Always Riding.	John Yellow Flower.
Arkikila.	Keokuk.
Big Bear.	Keokuk's Son.
Big Chief.	King of the Crows.
Big Elk.	Lean Wolf.
Big Razor.	Mad Bear.
Big Snake.	Man and Chief.
Black Eye.	Many Horns.
Black Hawk.(Sioux)	Noon Day.
Black Hawk(Sac&Fox)	Red Bird.
British.	Red Cloud.
Bull Head.	Red Shirt.
Cayatanila.	Red Thunder.
Chief Gall.	Rushing Bear.
Chief Joseph.	Sitting Bull.
Clam Fish.	Spotted Tail.
Crow's Breast.	Striker.
Deer Ham.	True Eagle.
Geronimo.	White Shield.
Great Bear.	White Swan.
Great War Chief.	War Captain.
Grey Eagle.	Wetcunie.
Hairy Bear.	Young Black Dog.
Iron Bull.	Young Whirlwind.

ALLEN & GINTER,
RICHMOND, VIRGINIA.
LITH. LINDNER, EDDY & CLAUSS N.Y.

The Allen & Ginter set of 50 American Indian Chiefs, is considered by many collectors to be the finest insert set ever made. The subject, color, and outstanding lithography is a combination that is hard to match. Linder, Eddy & Clauss of New York did themselves proud with this effort. Four of the cards from this set were used to decorate the title pages of the 1894 and 1895 Wild West Show programs. Those were done in black and white and didn't show the real beauty of these cards. A large Wild West Show lithograph also used these same four cards. The fifth card of Red Shirt is included because Queen Victoria wanted to meet this Indian Chief after the performance she attended in 1887.

Also shown is the impressive album of The American Indian Chiefs. The artwork, color, and lithography is magnificent. Both the cards and album are from 1888. Beware! This complete set has been reproduced and they are excellent.

PLATE 249
American Indian Chiefs album
Card Size – 1½" x 2¾"

PLATE 250
Civil War Generals
Mini Booklet Series
1888

Knapp and Company, Lithographers and Printers of Park Place, New York, produced this excellent series of 50 short histories of Civil War generals. Union Private W.F. Cody fought against troopers under the command of Confederate General Sterling Price. A notation included in this booklet tells us that the album for this series will be ready March 1, 1889.

This very small photo card was issued in England in 1901. The Ogden Company may have been the most prolific producers of cigarette insert cards at the turn of the century. There seems to be an unlimited supply of these wonderful mini cards. The Guinea Gold Cigarette cards have blank backs.

PLATE 251
Ogden's (Guinea Gold Cigarettes)
Card Size – 1½" x 2⅛"

Buffalo Bill

John M. Burke

PLATE 252
Wild West Caramels
The American Caramel Company
Circa 1910
Card size – 1½" x 2¾"

John M. Burke strikes again. Remember he slipped his likeness into the cowboy logo on the front of the 1896 Wild West Show program. The only way he would end up in a western set of cards would be by his own doing. It is obvious he must have supplied the names for this set. This 20-card set shows the lack of quality printing that became common with twentieth century cards. These cards were made by The American Caramel Company.

Pawnee Bill

Texas Jack

Wild West Caramels

THIS CARD IS ONE OF A SET OF 20 WILD WEST CARDS, ONE OF WHICH IS WRAPPED WITH EVERY WILD WEST CARAMEL :: ::

Texas Jack
Kit Carson
Pawnee Bill
Daniel Boone
Jim Bridger
David Crockett
California Joe
Buffalo Bill
John M. Burke
Gen. Geo. A. Custer
Always Riding
Black Swan
Rocky Bear
Black Bear
Left Hand Bear
Rushing Bear
Chief Lone Wolf
Shot in the Eye
Sitting Bull
Yellow Hair

MADE BY THE
American Caramel Co.

COL. W. F. CODY,
"Buffalo Bill."

MAJ. GORDON W. LILLIE
"Pawnee Bill."

SITTING BULL.

Gen. Geo. Armstrong Custer

GEN. NELSON A. MILES.

Brevet Maj.-Gen. E. A. Carr

PLATE 253
Wild West Gum
Circa 1910
Card size – 1½" x 2¾"

The Wild West Gum set of 24 western characters has impressive artwork. Undoubtedly the finest image of Cody on insert cards made after 1900. John H. Dockman and Son manufactured these colorful cards, circa 1910.

COL. THEODORE ROOSEVELT,
Col. of 1st U. S. Vol. Cavalry

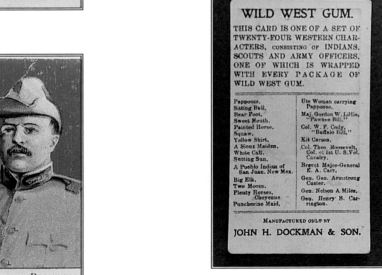

WILD WEST GUM.

THIS CARD IS ONE OF A SET OF TWENTY-FOUR WESTERN CHARACTERS, CONSISTING OF INDIANS, SCOUTS AND ARMY OFFICERS, ONE OF WHICH IS WRAPPED WITH EVERY PACKAGE OF WILD WEST GUM.

Pappoose,
Sitting Bull,
Bear Foot,
Sweet Mouth,
Painted Horse,
Squaw,
Yellow Shirt,
A Sioux Maiden,
White Calf,
Setting Sun,
A Pueblo Indian of San Juan, New Mex.
Big Elk,
Two Moons,
Plenty Horses, Cheyenne,
Puncherine Maid,

Ute Woman carrying Pappoose,
Maj. Gordon W. Lillie, "Pawnee Bill,"
Col. W. F. Cody, "Buffalo Bill,"
Kit Carson,
Col. Theo. Roosevelt, Col. of 1st U. S. Vol. Cavalry,
Brevet Major-General E. A. Carr,
Gen. Geo. Armstrong Custer,
Gen. Nelson A. Miles,
Gen. Henry B. Carrington.

MANUFACTURED ONLY BY
JOHN H. DOCKMAN & SON.

PLATE 254
Indian Life in the 60s
Copyrighted 1910
by American Tobacco Company
Size – 2½" x 3¼"

A fine set of 50 cards that has excellent color and fine artwork. Like Cody, this set of Hassan insert cards celebrated with respect the Native Americans.

PLATE 255
Cowboy Series
Size – 2½" x 3¼"
Circa 1914

This Hassan set of 50 cards is excellent and very popular with collectors. Unfortunately, only 49 cards can be accounted for. It is believed one card may have been objectionable and therefore not issued. Hopefully, examples exist and the author would love to see one. The image of the American cowboy was in large part given to us by Buffalo Bill and his wonderful Wild West Exhibition. Insert cards, as this set proves, can assist the romantic image of our American cowboy.

A BUCKING BRONCO

Before a round-up it is essential that all the horses to be used should be well rested and well fed. If it is in the spring the best behaved pony, after having run free all winter, is liable to display tricks he never showed before. Each cowboy, therefore, likes to try out all the animals in his string before actual work begins. If a man has an especially vicious horse he is sure of a lively performance and interested and unkind onlookers. A "bad" bronco generally has to be thrown before he can be bridled and saddled. Then, with the cowboy once in the saddle, the real fight begins. The bucker makes an arch of his back, with all the power of his lithe body in it, and putting his head down, jumps repeatedly with his legs stiff. If this fails, he has other tricks, but in the end is almost always conquered. In exceptional cases a ranch will have in its outfit a "bronc" that only one or two of the boys dare tackle.

COWBOY SERIES
1-50
HASSAN
CORKTIP
CIGARETTES
The Oriental Smoke

THE LARGEST SELLING BRAND OF CIGARETTES IN AMERICA
FACTORY No 649 1ST DIST. N.Y.

Factory No. 21, 5th Dist. N.J.

Sitting Bull the Greatest War Chief

NEBO CIGARETTES

PLATE 256
Tobacco Silk
Circa – 1914
Size – 3¼" x 5" approximately

Indian Silks were very popular when they were introduced and are even more popular today. The likeness of Sitting Bull is excellent and is yet another example of the quality available regarding early tobacco giveaways.

Col. W.F. Cody was included in a set of mounted generals. This silk plus four others from The Generals set was incorporated in a large pillowcase from the same time period. The example shown was cut from the pillowcase. The silk from The Generals set is exactly the same except for a small number 200 printed in the upper left-hand corner.

COL. W. F. CODY
(BUFFALO BILL)

PLATE 257
Tobacco Silk
Circa – 1915
Size – 7" x 9"

TICKETS, TRAIN PASSES & BUSINESS CARDS

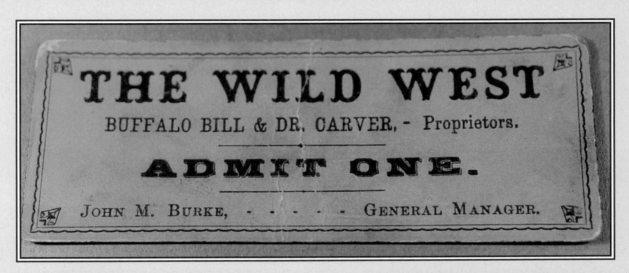

PLATE 258
Complimentary ticket
Size – 1¾" x 4¼" approximately
Year – 1883

The first Wild West touring season of 1883 was indeed an exciting and educational experience for both Cody and John M. Burke. Burke understood early on the importance of giving out free tickets or passes to the press and other prominent people. This ticket was made thicker than usual so it could be reused.

The show started touring in 1883 and was sold at auction in the summer of 1913. Cody would tour with the Sells-Floto Show in 1914 and 1915 followed by his final touring season with The 101 Ranch Wild West. That is 34 consecutive touring seasons which makes a remarkable run.

It is virtually impossible to comprehend how many tickets must have been printed and sold and handed out by this Wild West entertainment. The author has found that tickets for some reason are difficult to acquire. This does not make sense since so many were used. Hopefully, more will surface soon. There is however, a fair supply of complimentary show tickets around and many are signed by Cody.

Train or transportation passes started most likely in 1895 when the real aggressive circus style touring began. The year is printed on these passes and the employees name was normally written in.

Business cards used by Cody are available, however, they are tough to find. We can also find business cards used by some of the show Indians, plus many other performers with the show. The author would like to make an appeal for collectors to share with him any different tickets, passes, or business cards.

Courtesy Buffalo Bill Historical Center, Cody, Wyoming

PLATE 259
Ticket statement
Year – 1886

This show admission ticket seller's statement tips off how many tickets were issued to a seller and how many were sold. The ratio of five adult tickets issued to one child's is also interesting. With other entries added on this statement it appears that just over 3,900 tickets were sold on August 11, 1886.

John M. Burke, the show's general manager, understood completely the importance of the newspaper media. Certainly, these free press tickets helped to get the show extra newspaper coverage.

PLATE 260
Press ticket
Year – 1893

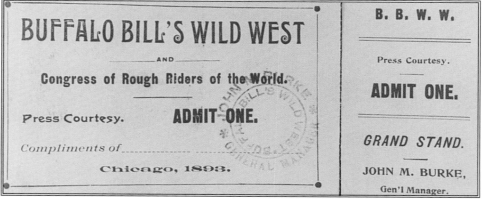

PLATE 261
Complimentary ticket
Year – 1893

The official closing of the Columbian Exposition was on October 31, 1893. The Wild West Show played their last two performances that day and tickets show it to be "Buffalo Bill Day."

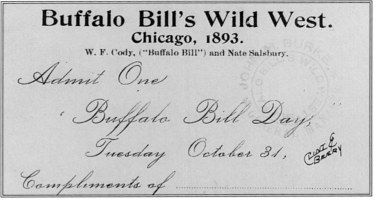

Buffalo Bill's Wild West.
Chicago, 1893.
W. F. Cody, ("Buffalo Bill") and Nate Salsbury.

Admit One
'Buffalo Bill Day,'
Tuesday October 31,
Compliments of

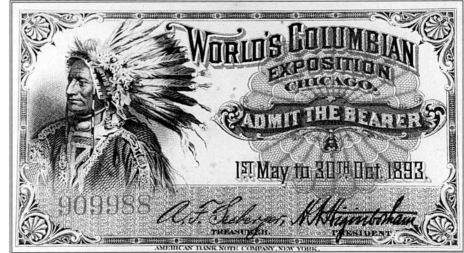

PLATE 262
World's Columbian Exposition ticket
Year – 1893
Size – 2½" x 3¾"

The American Indian was honored by the Columbian planners by including a representative image of these proud people in the official set of admission tickets. The other five appearing on this set of six are Christopher Columbus, Ben Franklin, George Washington, Abe Lincoln, and then popular musician and composer, George Handel. This ticket represents one adult admission and cost 50 cents.

177

TICKET STATEMENT.

F. 104—1,000.

Place .... Date .... (1899)

	AFTERNOON.		EVENING.		TOTAL.
	RES.	REG.	RES.	REG.	
W. F. Cody, ...					
Nate Salsbury, ...					
Fred. Hutchinson, ...					
L. E. Cooke, ...					
Jule Keen, ...					
M. Coyle, ...					
F. J. O'Donnell, ...					
John M. Burke, ...					
S. H. Semon, ...					
John McLaughlin, ...					
P. S. Mattox, Car No. 1, .					
Alf Riel, Car No. 2, . . .					
Fred Beckman, Car No. 3, .					
Show Press Agent, . . .					
Lithographs, ...					
Wagon Tickets, ...					
Extra Help, ...					

PLATE 263
Ticket statement
Year – 1899

A list of show personnel who were able to give out complimentary show tickets. Here again it was important to keep a record of how many were being issued. Cody was often criticized by show management for handing out too many free tickets.

S.H. Semon was the general contracting agent for the publicity department. Fred Beckman, who issued this free ticket, was the manager of advance advertising. Generally, these free tickets were issued for allowing lithographs of the show to be posted in storefront windows.

Courtesy Circus World Museum, Baraboo, Wisconsin

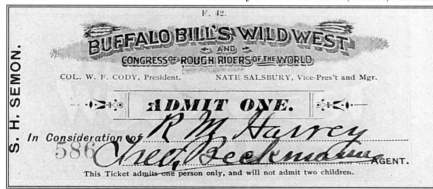

PLATE 264
Complimentary ticket
Year – 1901

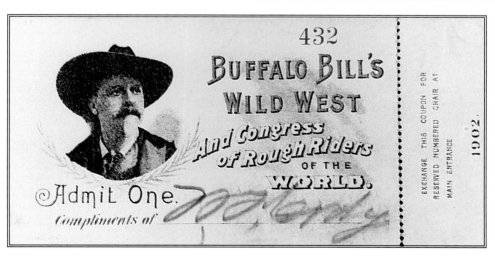

This design was used from 1897 to at least 1902. This example was signed by Cody and he gave out many. They are not as rare as some collectors believe.

PLATE 265
Complimentary ticket
Year – 1902

PLATE 266
Employee ticket
Year – 1902 – 1903
Size – 2" x 4⅛"

BUFFALO BILL'S WILD WEST
AND
CONGRESS OF ROUGH RIDERS OF THE WORLD,
OLYMPIA.
EMPLOYÉ'S TICKET.

LONDON
1902—1903.

This ticket will be honored only at the Blythe Road entrance.

Name   *E. Phillips*
Dept.   *Wild West*
No. _____ Issued } *A D Starr*
                by }

Cowboy Ed Phillips was issued this ticket by Alfred D. Starr, a staff member of The Barnum and Bailey Company. The Bailey group directed the touring seasons in England and Europe during this last overseas tour. The Olympia was a large indoor arena in London. These tickets allowed employees of The Wild West free admission to the arena.

The Wild West played here from December 26, 1902, to April 4, 1903, for a total 172 performances. Even King Edward and Queen Alexandra visited the show insuring a successful stand.

PLATE 267
The Olympia
Year – circa 1903

PLATE 268
Complimentary ticket
Year – 1908

This design was used in
1907 and 1908. Another
Cody signed ticket. Even
damaged examples are
welcomed into collections.

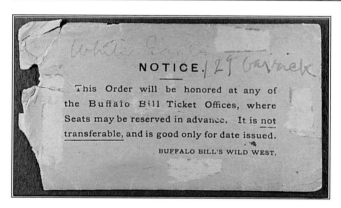

Courtesy Circus World Museum, Baraboo, Wisconsin

This ticket was
issued and signed
by G.W. Lillie,
Pawnee Bill.

PLATE 269
Complimentary ticket
Year – 1909 – 1913

PLATE 270
Annual pass
Year – 1910
Size – 2⅜" x 4"

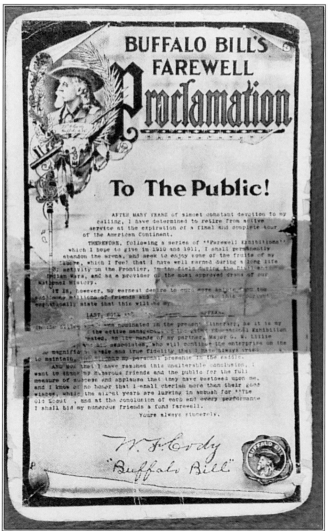

The annual pass is yet another variation of the many ways management gave out free admissions. G. W. Lillie signed and surely issued this colorful and attractive annual pass. The back has the Buffalo Bill farewell proclamation.

PLATE 271
Side show ticket
Year – 1909 – 1913

The side shows were unusually well attended during these years. One interesting question is why there are no side show performer postcards from these years.

PLATE 272
Complimentary ticket
Year – 1910 – 1913

Unsigned complimentary tickets could very easily become a problem. It is interesting to note that they were even used.

At least someone saved this partial ticket. Naturally there are better examples waiting to be found by collectors.

PLATE 273
Reserved seat ticket
Year – circa 1909 – 1913

Reproduced by permission of Ringling Bros. – Barnum & Bailey Combined Shows, Inc.

PLATE 274
Reserved seat ticket

A Sells-Floto ticket marked Saturday, August 8.

Reproduced by permission of Ringling Bros. – Barnum & Bailey Combined Shows, Inc.

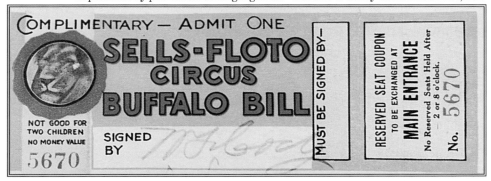

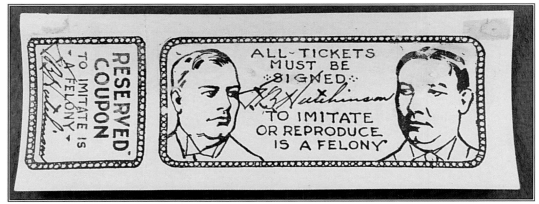

PLATE 275
Complimentary tickets
Year – 1915
Size – 2⅛" x 5½"

This Sells-Floto ticket was signed by Cody. The back has the show owners' Harry Tammen and Fred Bonfils illustrated. NOTE — All tickets must be signed.

No. **108** _____ 1902.

BUFFALO BILLS WILD WEST

Pass *E. Phillips*

Positively not Transferable.

MEMPHIS, TENN.
— TO —
BRIDGEPORT, CONN.

GOOD ON SHOW TRAIN ONLY.

PLATE 276
Train pass
Year – 1902
Size – 2" x 3½"

Employee train passes were first issued in 1895 and were used at least until 1902. E. Phillips was in fact Ed Phillips a cowboy with the show. He can be seen in the photography section.

This six page flyer for The North British Railway Company's servants is another example of the interesting ephemera associated with Cody. It was issued by the superintendent of the line in Edinburgh on August 4, 1904.

1049

North British Railway Company

PRIVATE.
No. E. 39–43.

OFFICE OF SUPERINTENDENT OF THE LINE,
EDINBURGH, 4th *August* 1904.

ADVICE OF SPECIAL PASSENGER TRAINS AND
SPECIAL ARRANGEMENTS.

For the information of the Company's Servants only.

SPECIAL TRAINS IN CONNECTION WITH

BUFFALO BILL'S "WILD WEST" SHOW

(*Under the direction of Messrs Barnum & Bailey, Limited*).

For General Instructions to be observed in connection with the Running of Special, Excursion, and Relief Trains, the Staff are referred to pages 76, 77, and 78 of the "General Appendix to the Book of Rules and Regulations and to the Working Time Tables," dated 1st May 1901.

SUNDAY, 7th August.

1-3.   Special Train—Haymarket West Junction to Gorgie.
(*Buffalo Bill's Show from Gushetfaulds, Cal.*)

		1		2		3	
		a.m.		a.m.		a.m.	
Haymarket West Junction	{ arrive	2 49	} No. 2 Section	3 19	} No. 3 Section	3 34	} No. 1 Section
	{ depart	2 54		3 24		3 39	
Gorgie	arrive	2 58		3 28		3 43	

Trains to be stored at Haymarket West Down Lines Siding and Up Loop.

MONDAY, WEDNESDAY, and FRIDAY, 8th, 10th, and 12th August.

4.   Buffalo Bill's "Wild West" Show—Cheap Return
Tickets to Edinburgh.

On Monday, Wednesday, and Friday, 8th, 10th, and 12th August, Return Tickets at Single Journey Fares—plus factions of a penny; no less charge than 2s. First Class and 1s. Third Class—will be issued to Edinburgh (Waverley or Gorgie) from all North British Stations within a radius of thirty miles of Edinburgh by Ordinary trains. The Tickets will be valid for return on day of issue only by Special or Ordinary trains.

PLATE 277
Train schedule flyer
Size – 6" x 9¼"

A photo postcard from the 1903 – 1904 English touring seasons shows the show train parked in a train station somewhere in England. The half penny stamp for inland and one penny foreign markings on the back gives us the time period for this early postcard.

PLATE 278

FIGURES TELL THE STORY.

From The " Walsall Advertiser."
April 30th, 1904.

BUFFALO BILLS show on Wednesday caused the tramways to be tested in a way they have not been tested before, particularly on the Pleck section; and large as was the number of passengers carried, it would have been more than doubled had there been double the number of cars. Fourteen cars were running continually in the afternoon and evening, and practically everything went off without a hitch. During the day 11,193 passengers travelled on the Pleck route, the receipts being £44 17s. 3d.; whilst the number on all the Corporation routes for the day was 19,964, and the receipts £101 8s. 4d. The figures for the corresponding day last week were—Pleck section, 2,695; receipts £10 14s. 4¼d.; all sections 8,843, and receipts £47 14s. 3d.

PLATE 279

Size – Approximately the same as today's

Cody even turned business cards into complimentary tickets. Keep in mind that Cody signed his name so many times it can not be considered a rare autograph.

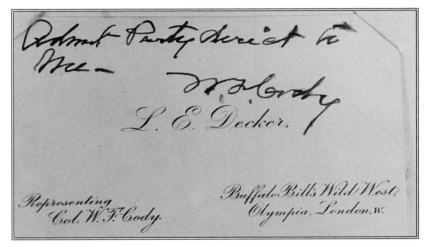

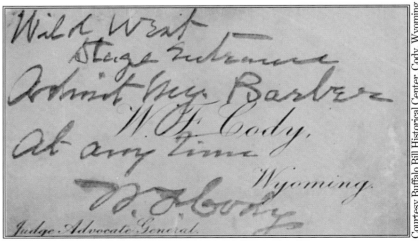

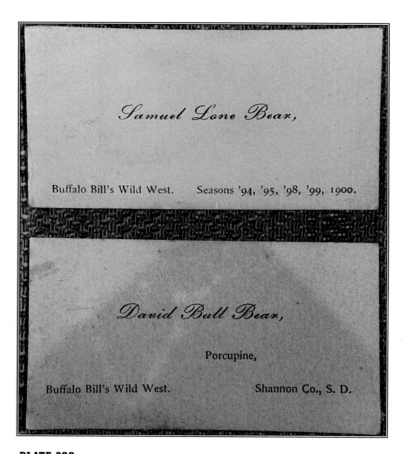

PLATE 280
Business cards
Size – standard

Samuel Lone Bear was also listed in the 1902 route book and indeed was a veteran performer. David Bull Bear was listed as an interpreter in the 1899 route book. Many other performers used business cards.

PLATE 281
"Buffalo Bill" No. 71
Cast Iron Cap Gun
Year – 1878
Length – 6⅞"

This cast-iron toy gun was made by the Ives, Blakeslee and Williams Company of Bridgeport, Connecticut. The opposite side is marked "US PAT Dec 1878." The Ives Company would become one of the very successful early toy manufacturers. This is possibly the first toy made using Buffalo Bill's name.

The American toy industry was developing in the 1870s and would become and still is a major industry. During the 1870s, 1880s, and 1890s the majority of toys were made of either cast iron or paper. Tin, wood, cast alloys, cloth, glass, and other materials were also used to make toys, but to a lesser degree. Collectors today have a wide variety of interesting juvenile items to search for.

During the last half of the nineteenth century autograph books were very popular with children. The autograph book included here is very significant because it has three Cody family autographs. Buffalo Bill signed autograph books are out there just waiting to be discovered. Most of the examples in this section can be found at antique toy shows. Book and ephemera shows are other good searching grounds.

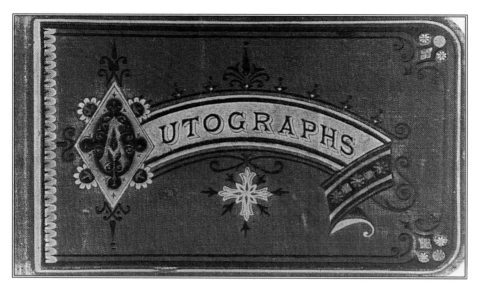

PLATE 282
Autograph book
Year – 1876 – 1877
Size – 3¼" x 5¼"
Pages – 50

This wonderful autograph book belonged to Daisy Dwight of Quincy, Illinois. Little Daisy as she is referred to on many pages was most likely from a prominent Quincy family. Apparently they stayed at the same hotel in St. Louis that Buffalo Bill, his wife, and daughter stayed or took in his stage performance on April 8, 1877. The fact that Buffalo Bill and his wife and daughter all signed Daisy's little book is very unique in terms of autographed material. Note the sharp crisp look of Cody's writing.

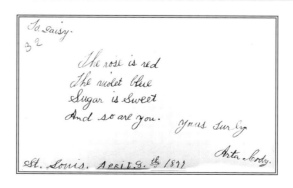

PLATE 283
Paper cutouts
Year – 1894

The McLoughlin Brothers of New York City produced these colorful paper cutouts. The three strips shown are representative of at least 12 different strips included in a very colorful and attractive box. Each individual strip measures 4" x 21". The instructions read, "How to make the figures stand without blocks. Take pieces of the white paper about ½ x 1¾ inches. Fold to the back, at the bottom edge, leaving the other to project as a support." Each strip is marked "amusement for boys to cut out. Buffalo Bill and The Wild West. Copyrighted 1884 by McLoughlin Brothers, New York."

PLATE 284
Buffalo Bill,
wooden rifle
Year – 1885
Length – 35½"

This advertisement appeared in the July 1, 1887, publication titled *The Farm And Fireside*. There is also a rather nice advertising envelope associated with this toy. The hammer, or actually the release hook and trigger, is of one piece cast iron. Directly under Buffalo Bill on the stock we find the markings "Patented March 3D. 1885."

PLATE 285
Painted tin plateform pull toy
Maker – James Fallows of Philadelphia
Size – 9" x 5"
Dated – August 3, 1886

Pre-1900 American made tin toys are scarce and eagerly pursued by antique toy collectors. This example was obviously made to cash in on Buffalo Bill's popularity. As a youngster pulled this toy down the sidewalk both bison would bob up and down.

PLATE 286
"Texas Jack" cast-iron cap gun
Year – 1886
Length – 9⅜"

This "Texas Jack" toy gun was made by The Ives, Blakeslee and Williams Company of Bridgeport, Connecticut. Texas Jack was a close friend of Cody's until they had some problems during their stage acting days. Jack split with Bill and started his own little acting group but died prematurely in 1880. "Texas" appears on one side and "Jack" on the opposite side. This toy gun was also made with a round barrel.

PLATE 287
"A Peep at Buffalo Bill's Wild West"
By McLoughlin Bros.,
New York
Copyrighted 1887
Size – 10" x 12"
Pages – 8

The artwork in this large soft-cover booklet is excellent. The prose style text is interesting and a different approach to Cody's Wild West. McLoughlin Bros. of New York were leaders in producing quality paper artwork during the 1880s and 1890s.

PLATE 288
The Terrors of America &
their Doings
Size – 1½" x 2¾"
Circa – 1889

Playing Buffalo Bill "Just
See Me Lassoo The
Dude" is the caption for
this cigarette insert card.
During the 1890s many
newspapers reported
that young boys were
getting into all sorts of
mischief after viewing
Cody's Wild West Show.
This set of cards, had to
be popular with the
youngsters of the day

PLAYING BUFFALO BILL
"Just see me lassoo the dude".

The
Terrors of America
and their Doings.
┿◇┿

The Umpire	"Extra! Extra!"
The Pitcher	Rabbit Hunting
Foot Ball	"Please come home"
A Stunt	Maud S
The Catcher	Spread the Eagle
Swimming	"Hit a fellar yer
Kite Time	size"
Snow Balling	"Knuckle down!"
The Figure Eight	"Get off there"
Election Night	In the First Class
"Pot a Boilin'"	Leap Frog
Big Bite	"Let her go slow"
Hide and Seek	De Boss of de Gang
Save the Core	Boss Whistler
The Dude	Tappy-on-the-window
A Turkish Bath	My New Duds
"Wid me one hand"	Out in left field
"What a find"	Me galluses is gone
Before Election	wrong
Tug of War	Playing Buffalo Bill
Fishing	Out on first
"Watch me hit him"	The Boss Short Stop
"Line up back there"	"I didn't steal no
The Boss Fighter	apples"
Playing Nurse	"Clean it for a
Brick in Hat	quarter"
"Ain't she a beauty"	

┿◇┿
Packed in
Duke's Cigarettes
KNAPP & CO. LITH. N. Y.

PLATE 289
"Buffalo Bill"
cast-iron cap gun
Year – 1890
Length – 11¾"

This wonderful long barrel Buffalo Bill toy gun was
made by The J. & E. Stevens Company of Cromwell,
Connecticut. Long barrel cap guns are favorites of
many early style cap gun collectors. The author is
happy to report that this example is in decent supply.
Buffalo Bill is embossed only on one side and there are
no other markings. The J. & E. Stevens Company were
still selling cast-iron cap guns in the early 1950s. One of
their last selling cast-iron toy guns was a "Buffalo Bill"
which came in a nicely designed yellow and red box.

This very small puzzle box with nine square pieces was sold at the show for five cents during the Chicago 1893 stand. Other markings that appear on this box, are "Buffalo Bill's Wild West, 62nd and 63rd streets." The end flap is marked "summer 1893, twice daily 3 p.m. and 8 p.m." Unfortunately no instruction sheet was retrieved with this example.

PLATE 290
The "Buffalo Bill" puzzle
Year – 1893
Box size – 1½" x 2¼"
Puzzle piece size – 1⅜" square

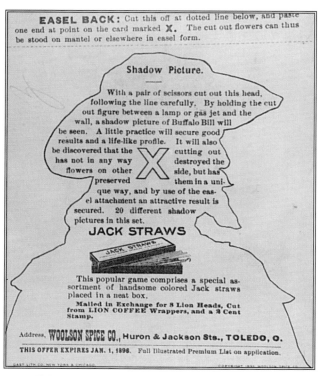

PLATE 291
Shadow card
Year – 1895

Entertainment came in many simple forms back in the 1890s. This shadow picture was most likely cut out by a youngster and Mom would end up with a pretty flower arrangement to set on the table. The Jack Straws game offer expired on January 1, 1896.

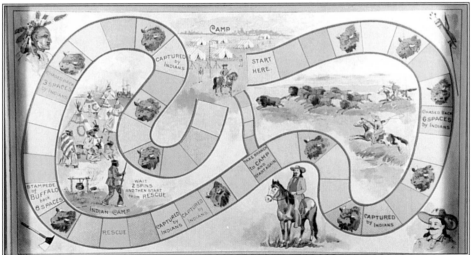

PLATE 292
The game of "Buffalo Bill"
Year – 1898
Box size – 9" x 15⅛"

Early games are eagerly pursued by game collectors and it is easy to understand the reason. The colorful and interesting box artwork coupled with an equally attractive game board makes two excellent reasons to seek out these wonderful early American games. The game of "Buffalo Bill" by Parker Brother's of Salem, Mass., is a choice example of a nineteenth century game.

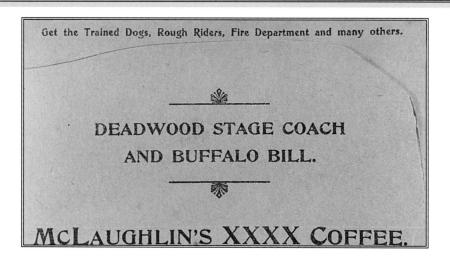

Get the Trained Dogs, Rough Riders, Fire Department and many others.

DEADWOOD STAGE COACH
AND BUFFALO BILL.

McLAUGHLIN'S XXXX COFFEE.

W.F. McLaughlin and Company made a series of foldout and stand up heavy paper toys during 1903 and 1904. This example and another called the "Buffalo Hunt" fit our interests just fine.

Get the Buffalo Hunt, Fox Chase and many others.

DIRECTIONS.

Fold back the lines where this Novelty has been folded so that it will lay flat, carefully break the little catches which hold the cutout in position, then holding the fingers of one hand at the bottom of the picture, bend up the figure on the lines indicated until it stands perfectly straight, when the procession will be complete. If desirable to pull this with a string, take a needle and make a little hole in the front margin and tie a string through it. You can also tie these different processions together by putting a hole in the back margin and tying another on to it. This will make a full parade and is particularly interesting in case of the various circus parades, etc.

PLATE 293
Premium foldout
Circa – 1903
Size – closed 2⅜" x 4",
opened 2⅜" x 16"

194

PLATE 294
Die cuts
Three of six
Year – circa 1903 –
1908
Size – 4¼" x 6"

This set of six colorful die cuts was sold at the show in a paper envelope. The fact that Indians dominate this set is a tip off they were produced in either England or Europe. The Indian village is one of the author's favorite Cody collectibles. The white banner proclaims, "Buffalo Bill or The Wild West."

PLATE 294A
Die cuts
Three of six

PLATE 295
Writing tablet
Year – circa 1907
Size – 6¾" x 8¼"

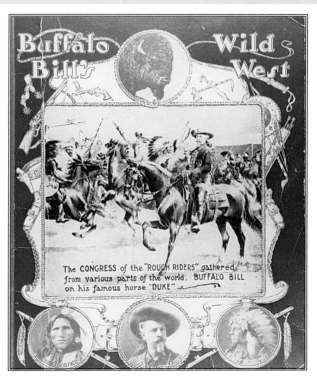

There is a strong possibility that these writing tablets were sold on the show grounds during the 1907 and 1908 seasons. Three different center pictures have been used on these attractive ruled paper tablets.

PLATE 296
Dexterity game
Year – circa 1910
Size – 1⅝" in diameter
Glass front and a mirror back

Roll the mini white beads into the indentations on the headdress and the goal has been achieved of this novelty. It's easier said than done. There is no doubt that most people came to "The" Wild West Show to see Buffalo Bill. The American Indians were the second most important aspect of the show. The concession stands sold a wide variety of items and it would stand to reason that Indian related novelties would be good sellers. The inclusion of this dexterity game is speculation.

PLATE 297
Tin whistle
Year – circa 1915
Size – 1⅝" square

The unmistakable image of Buffalo Bill on this "Solophone," qualifies it for inclusion. The Cracker Jack Company, makers of the popular caramel coated popcorn confection, not only sold Cracker Jack on the show grounds but also advertised in several Wild West Show programs. In 1912 a prize was included inside each box of Cracker Jack, and still is to this day. This tin whistle was used as a prize in Cracker Jack boxes and perhaps they were sold as novelties on the show grounds. According to author Charles Eldridge Griffin, one of Cody's favorite sayings was "He's a Cracker Jack."

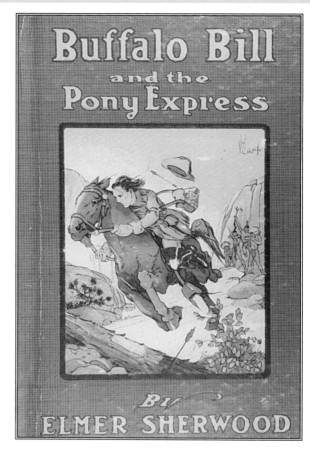

PLATE 298
Juvenile books
Year – circa 1915
By Elmer Sherwood
Published by Whitman Publishing Company,
Racine, Wisconsin
Illustrations by Neil O'Keeffe
Size – 4¾" x 6⅞"
Pages – 125

Elmer Sherwood was an author of adventure stories for boys. These efforts are pure fiction, but the covers are colorful and fun. In 1918 he added another book on Cody called *Buffalo Bill, The Boys Friend*. This book is slightly larger in size and contains 245 pages.

Courtesy Jimmie Gibbs Munroe

PLATE 299
Felt pennant
Year – 1916
Size – 24" long, approximately

Research turned up a felt pennant from the 1908 season. The Two Bills Show, and the Sells-Floto Circus also sold felt pennants of Buffalo Bill.

PINBACK BUTTONS, MEDALS & ADVERTISING TOKENS

PLATE 300
Pinback buttons
Circa – late 1890s
Size – 1¼" in diameter

This trio of buttons exemplifies the variation possibilities regarding Cody collectibles. As mentioned before variations are common and encountered often when collecting Buffalo Bill.

Pinback buttons first appeared in the mid 1890s and were very popular then and still receive special attention by collectors today. The Whitehead and Hoag Company of Newark, New Jersey, produced most of the buttons from this early period. Listed in the 1902 route book is Mr. Harry Ramsey in charge of selling Col. Cody's photographs and buttons. There is no doubt pinback buttons were sold at the show.

Advanced Columbian Exposition collectors estimate there are well over 300 different medals associated with that fair. This fact is solid evidence that medals were in demand back in the 1890s. Naturally, Buffalo Bill was included in this medium. Advertising tokens using Buffalo Bill's name and image are few, however they are excellent examples of the diverse material to be collected.

PLATE 301
Year – circa late 1890s
Size – 1¼" in diameter

Pinback buttons were a new novelty back in the mid-1890s and of course were popular. We can find a decent variety of these really nice Cody mini photographs. Look at the button on Cowboy Ed Phillips's scarf in photograph section.

PLATE 302
Pinback button
Year – circa 1900
Size – ⅞" in diameter

This button lacks a quality image, however it is a period example. The smaller size leads one to believe they were targeted for children. The printing along the periphery on the back reads "Patented July 21 1896."

PLATE 303
Pinback buttons for the ladies
Year – circa late 1890s to 1908
Size – ¹⁵⁄₁₆" overall
Image – ½" in diameter

PLATE 304
Pinback buttons for the ladies
Year – circa late 1890s to 1908
Size – 1¼" in diameter

The look of fine jewelry was just as alluring back in the 1890s as it is today. The appearance of gold will always be magical and definitely helped to sell these attractive buttons.

PLATE 305
Pinback button
Year – circa late 1890s
Size – 1¼" in diameter

This Annie Oakley button appears to be original and it would seem obvious that her image would be used on these popular novelties. Unfortunately, collectors today have to use caution when buying items they have little knowledge of, as fakes abound.

Pawnee Bill also insisted on quality with regards to show-related material. This attractive button holder is proof of that excellent policy. Most of these buttons will be found without the fancy holder.

PLATE 306
Pawnee Bill, pinback button
Size – 1¼" in diameter
Year – 1904 – 1913

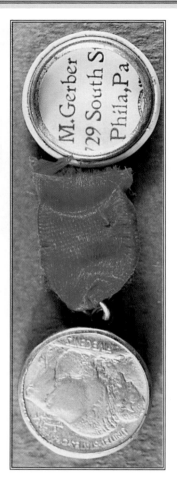

PLATE 307
Pinback button
Year – 1913
Size of Button – ⅞" in diameter

A unique design for the last of the pinback period buttons. Iron Tail was one of three Indian models used by the artist who created this wonderful nickel. Most people would agree the profile definitely favors Iron Tail. Iron Tail was with Cody from 1899 to 1913. He then joined The 101 Ranch Wild West and was also advertised as the Indian that made the nickel famous. This interesting novelty was made by M. Gerber, 729 South Street, Philadelphia, Pennsylvania.

PLATE 308
Novelty mirrors
Size – 2¼" in diameter
Year – Kicking Bear, 1903 – 1906;
Wenona, 1914 – 1916

Kicking Bear's understandable look of contempt was his trademark. Wenona, was in fact Lillian Smith and she was performing with the 101 Ranch Show when this mirror and others were sold on the show grounds.

The show was playing London in 1892 and these exciting medals were likely sold as souvenirs. The high relief and articulate design adds up to one of the finer Cody collectibles. Striking medals in different alloys was a common practice back in the 1890s.

PLATE 309
Medals – Bronze & Brass
Year – 1892
Size – 1½" in diameter
Made by Baddeley & Reynolds,
London

PLATE 310
Advertising token
Year – circa 1895
Size – 1⁹⁄₁₆" in diameter
Maker unknown

The face of this ad token reads "Alaroma," "Bunola" with Buffalo Bill at the bottom. The obverse reads "The Union Coffee Co. Limited, New York" and has the company's letter logo in the center. Examples have been seen in green, brown, black, and a mustard yellow. The material appears to be a compressed composition similar to today's phenolic resin.

PLATE 311
Worlds Fair Medal
Made by Childs of Chicago
Size – 1½" in diameter
Year – 1893

The London medal of 1892 may have inspired the idea for the 1893 souvenir medal. Examples can be found in gilt bronze, brass, and aluminum. The souvenir hanger was optional and very popular as many Columbian medals can be found on a variety of hangers.

The medal making company of N.J. Schloss of New York City used Buffalo Bill as so many others did to help bring attention to their products. The obverse is marked with the company's name and boasts of good quality, originality, fine style, and excellence.

PLATE 312
Brass advertising token
Year – circa 1900
Size – 1¼" square
Maker by N.J. Schloss & Co., New York

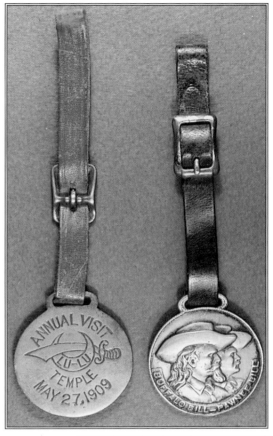

PLATE 313
Buffalo Bill
Pawnee Bill
Brass watch fob
Maker unknown
Size – 1⁹⁄₁₆" in diameter
Year – 1909 – 1913

This fob is one of the more easy to find Cody collectibles. Many different finishes are available and a Masonic Logo on the back is also common. These have been reproduced and are flooding the market.

PLATE 314
Buffalo Bill
Himself
Brass watch
fob
Maker
unknown
Size – 1⁹⁄₁₆"
in diameter
Year –
1914 – 1916

The Buffalo Bill/Pawnee Bill watch fob was undoubtedly a good seller. We know because of the many examples existing today. It stands to reason that the Sells-Floto Show and or The 101 Ranch Wild West Show would sell a fob of Buffalo Bill.

Tex Crane was listed in the 1910 – 1911 route flyer as a groom. His I.D. tag was most likely on his tool box. Where are other I.D. tags?

PLATE 315
Brass identification tag
Year – 1912
Size – 2" in diameter

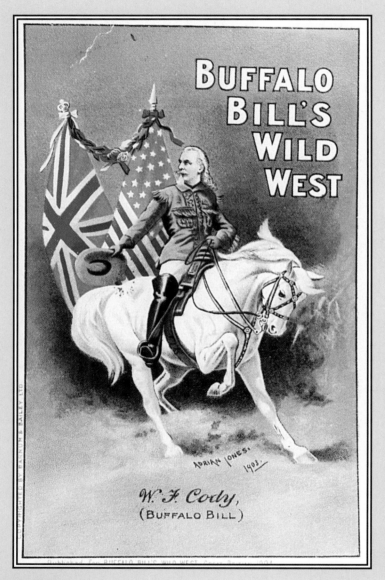

PLATE 316
Postcards
1 of 8
1903 – 1904

The first postcards sold at the show during the 1903 and 1904 Great Britain touring seasons are some of the finest examples of early postcards to be found anywhere. The color and quality is outstanding. The color postcards were done by Weiners Ltd. of London. The actual photo cards are marked "Rotary Photographic Series."

Charles Eldridge Griffin's wonderful book *Four Years in Europe with Buffalo Bill* pinpoints the exact time the postcard craze struck England and the United States. He wrote, "When I left America, four years ago, the souvenir postcard craze had not yet struck New York, but upon my arrival in England, I found it was all the rage there. Upon my return to New York I found the disease, after a careful diagnosis, to be far more acute than it ever was in Europe." He arrived in England in 1903 and returned home after the 1906 season.

The first Wild West Show postcards were produced in England in 1903 and 1904. This explains why we do not find Annie Oakley on period postcards. She left the show after the 1901 season. The four-year overseas tour produced a variety of postcards from several countries. A good guess would be that there are at least 100 different postcards from this four-year tour.

To be found are actual photo postcards, color printed cards, and of course black and white cards from this very interesting last overseas tour. When Cody returned home and began his 1907 season, postcards were being sold at the show and would be until the last season in 1916.

Four different sets were produced by The Wild West Show plus an unknown amount sold by other postcard vendors from 1907 through 1916.

Many cards have interesting reading with complimentary comments about The Wild West Show and even comments on Buffalo Bill's appearance. One puzzling aspect of postcards is why Johnny Baker isn't to be found on a period postcard.

A troubling development with postcards is that many dealers mistakenly sell museum postcards from the 1920s and 1930s as original period postcards. Most are easy to identify, simply by the back design. Study the backs of the original period postcards to improve buying savvy.

Another unhappy report is that there are phony postcards. Some devious individuals cleverly glue a paper printed picture to a period postmarked postcard. So please be observant when purchasing postcards. Postcards undoubtedly give collectors a significant image record of Cody and his Wild West Show during the last 14 years of this extraordinary entertainment enterprise.

2 of 8

3 of 8

4 of 8

5 of 8

6 of 8

7 of 8

8 of 8

Sample back
of postcard

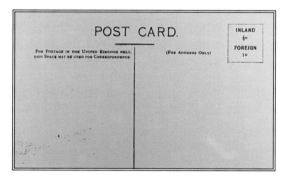

Actual photo postcards like
these two examples, will always
be in demand. We also see a
touch of vanity as Cody dyed his
hair and mustache to help
impress the British public.

PLATE 317
Postcards
Year – 1903 – 1904

Mᵈˡˡᵉ OCTAVIA,
BUFFALO BILL'S YANKEE SNAKE CHARMER,
Touring Great Britain 1903-4.

CHIEF STANDING BEAR.
With BUFFALO BILL'S WILD WEST.

CHIEF SANDS ROCK.
With BUFFALO BILL'S WILD WEST.

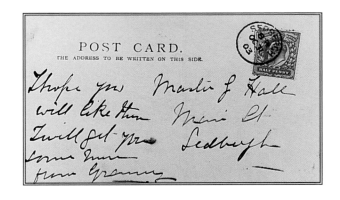

POST CARD.
THE ADDRESS TO BE WRITTEN ON THIS SIDE.

PLATE 318

More examples of postcards
Year – 1903 – 1904

LAURA STANDING BEAR.
With BUFFALO BILL'S WILD WEST.

An explosion of post-cards occurred during these two seasons. Europe was going through a postcard craze and Cody and his show were excellent subjects. Enjoy the following examples as many are exciting.

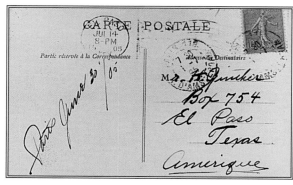

PLATE 319
Postcards
Year – 1905 – 1906

2 of 17

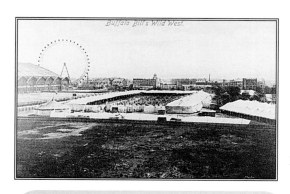

1 of 17

3 of 17

This 17 card set shows The Wild West set up in Paris for the opening of the 1905 season. The postcards are numbered one through seventeen. W. Schinkmann apparently published this wonderful set.

PLATE 320
Postcards
Set of 17

4 of 17

5 of 17

6 of 17

7 of 17

8 of 17

9 of 17

10 of 17

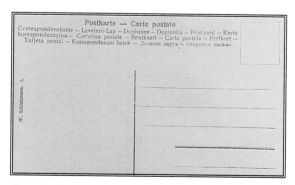

Sample back of postcard

The "Wild West „ in the Eternal city.
Buffalo Bill's Indians in the Caffè Greco, Rome.

PLATE 321

John M. Burke on right and Iron Tail in the headress enjoy the good life in Rome in 1906.

PLATE 322

Italian photo postcards dated March 13, 1906, were taken in Geneva.

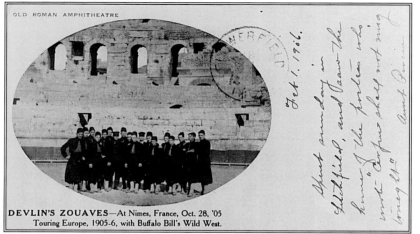

OLD ROMAN AMPHITHEATRE

DEVLIN'S ZOUAVES—At Nimes, France, Oct. 28, '05
Touring Europe, 1905-6, with Buffalo Bill's Wild West.

PLATE 324

PLATE 323

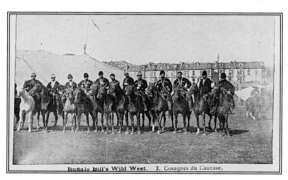

Buffalo Bill's Wild West.   3. Cosaques du Caucase.

The popular
Cossacks
line up in
1906.

PLATE 325

The show set up in Bordeaux, France. A typical crowd on it's way to see Buffalo Bill.

23. — Visite du Roi et de la Reine d'Angleterre chez Buffalo Bill's
à l'Olympia de Londres

PLATE 326

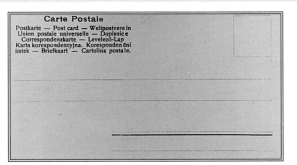

PLATE 327

Kicking Bear lets us know how he feels one more time.

PLATE 328

Side show performers were popular subjects during the four years touring in England and Europe.

Charles E. Griffin wrote and signed this card. It is hard to imagine this intelligent and articulate man would earn a living by putting swords down his throat. His terrific book *Four Years in Europe with Buffalo Bill* is one of the finest ever written about The Wild West Show.

PLATE 329

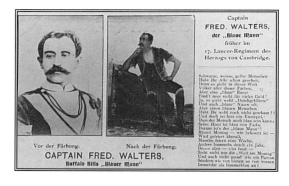

PLATE 330

More side show
postcards from Europe

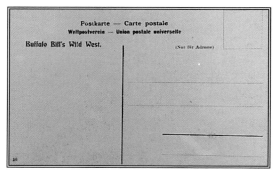

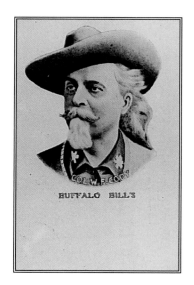

Postcards from this period are eagerly pursued by avid collectors. There is no question that postcards are important examples of Cody collectibles. Postcard shows are the best places to locate these cards and the prices are still reasonable.

PLATE 331

U.S. postcards
1907 – 1916
Black and white
Set of 6

IRON TAIL
THE FAMOUS INDIAN CHIEF.

This set of six black and white postcards were the first U. S. produced postcards sold at Cody's show. They were offered during the 1907 and 1908 seasons. The backs are undivided and an orange-brown color ink was used for the postcard logo. The simulated autograph on the Buffalo Bill card was obviously done by someone other than Cody. Collectors take note, this set is still relatively easy to acquire.

U. S. ZOUAVES.
WITH BUFFALO BILL'S WILD WEST.

INDIAN WAR DANCE AT BUFFALO BILL'S WILD WEST.

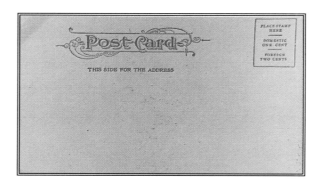

SKILL WITH THE LARIAT.
AT BUFFALO BILL'S WILD WEST.

"BUFFALO BILL"
By Rosa Bonheur

COW GIRL
WITH BUFFALO BILL'S
WILD WEST

SIOUX INDIAN CHIEF
WITH BUFFALO BILL'S WILD WEST

MAJOR GORDON W. LILLIE
"PAWNEE BILL"

BUFFALO BILL'S BUCKING BRONCHOS

CHIEF IRON TAIL, INDIAN SQUAWS AND PAPOOSES
AT BUFFALO BILL'S WILD WEST

The first U.S. produced color set of six was introduced during the 1908 season. They can be found with undivided and divided backs. They were made by the same company that made the 1907 black and white set. We find the same simulated autograph which of course is not correct. In 1909 Pawnee Bill was added to this set and the cowgirl card was eliminated. The first set came in a matte or flat finish. The second set with Pawnee Bill came in the same flat finish but was also available with a glossy finish. The envelope example contained the glossy set and the price was fifteen cents.

PLATE 332
Color set of 6

BUFFALO BILL'S DEADWOOD STAGE COACH

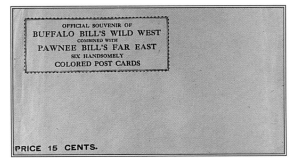

OFFICIAL SOUVENIR OF
BUFFALO BILL'S WILD WEST
COMBINED WITH
PAWNEE BILL'S FAR EAST
SIX HANDSOMELY
COLORED POST CARDS

PRICE 15 CENTS.

Winter Home of the Wild West Show, Bridgeport, Conn.

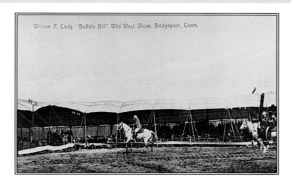

William F. Cody, "Buffalo Bill" Wild West Show, Bridgeport, Conn.

Indians, Buffalo Bill's Wild West Show, Bridgeport, Conn.

W. F. Cody, "Buffalo Bill" Shooting Glass Balls at Wild West Show, Bridgeport, Conn.

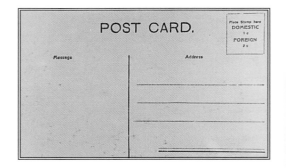

Buffaloes Running, Buffalo Bill's Wild West Show, Bridgeport, Conn.

Winter Quarters Barnum and Bailey Circus and Buffalo Bill's Wild West Show, Bridgeport, Conn.

POST CARD.

Message   Address

Place Stamp here
DOMESTIC
1 c
FOREIGN
2 c

PLATE 333
Second color set of 6

H.H. Jackson of Bridgeport, Connecticut, published this interesting set of six post-cards. The earliest postmark the author found on these cards is from 1908. Four of the views are in the show arena during a performance at Bridgeport, Connecticut, during the 1907 season. Since the show's winter quarters were in Bridgeport, it is possible that these cards were associated with The Wild West touring season of 1908.

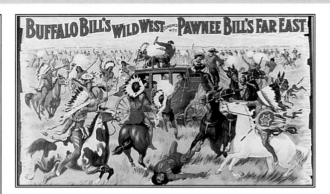

Simulated autograph

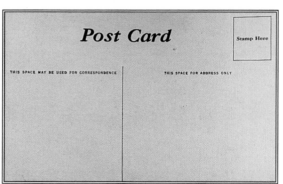

PLATE 334

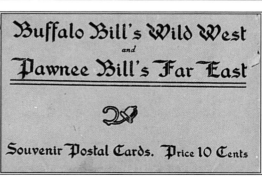

The Gerlach-Barklow Company of Joliet, Illinois, made this colorful set of six postcards for the 1912 season. They were sold on the show grounds in a light brown envelope marked "Buffalo Bill's Wild West" and "Pawnee Bill's Far East" souvenir postal cards, price 10 cents. It is possible that these same cards were sold during the 1913 season.

The portrait of Cody has the proper simulated autograph. The Gerlach-Barklow Company were leaders in producing qulaity art calendars, direct mail advertising, holiday greetings, and paragon leather gifts.

PLATE 335

There are many variations of the North Platte home.

Residence of W. F. Cody, (Buffalo Bill) North Platte, Neb.

PLATE 336

This Hiscock photo card reads "The Irma, Buffalo Bill's hotel in the Rockies, Cody, Wyoming." The doors in the Irma originally had buffalo head door knobs, which today are highly prized.

PLATE 337

A terrific card from 1908.

PLATE 338

Notation at top reads "former residence of Buffalo Bill, North Platte, Neb." His wife still lived there, but Cody's home was The Irma Hotel in Cody, Wyoming. Information on back reads — "After March 1, 1907, this space can be used for a written message." Before this date the backs were exclusively for the address, as noted.

PLATE 339

Cody and wife Louisa in front of The Irma Hotel. Note postcard published for Bennett's Drug Store. Surely more than one view of Buffalo Bill was offered by the local drug store.

PLATE 340

Cody visits Wild Bill Hickok's grave. There are variations of this postcard.

PLATE 341

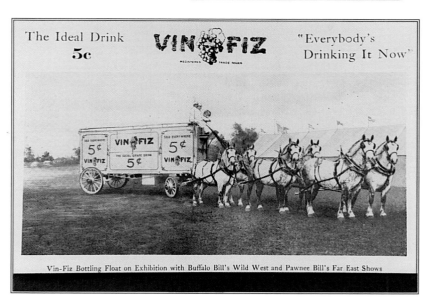

The Vin-Fiz float was also advertised in the 1912 Wild West program.

PLATE 342

Early bison cards are a must for any real Buffalo Bill collector.

Col. Cody, "Buffalo Bill", in Office of Irma Hotel, Cody, Wyo. Copyrighted 1910, by F.J. Hiscock.

PLATE 343

This postcard is an excellent example of the interesting information that can be found on postcards. F.J. Hiscock was the town of Cody's resident photographer. He is credited with many late views of Buffalo Bill.

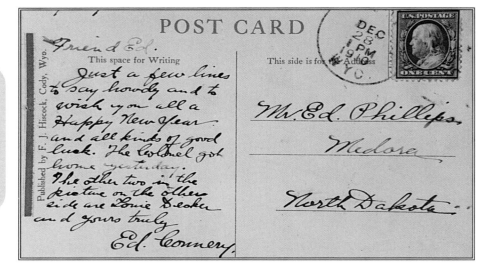

PLATE 344

The route sheet for 1910 tells us the show played Winnipeg in August and now we know when this view was taken.

BUFFALO BILL, DAUGHTER, GRANDSON AND SON-IN-LAW

The importance of postcards can be proved by this very significant example. Cody, with his daughter Irma and her husband Fred Garlow. The youngster is William Cody Boal, the son of Cody's daughter Arta who died in 1904.

PLATE 345

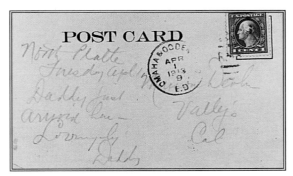

This example is a U.S. period pirated postcard taken from a 1904 English actual photo postcard. This practice was common during the early years of photography and postcards.

PLATE 346

Col. W. F. Cody. (Buffalo Bill)   The Famous Scout.

"Curley," Sole Survivor of Custer Battle.

PLATE 347

"Curley," sole survivor of the Custer battle is the caption for this postcard. He is included simply because he is listed in the 1886 Wild West program. He was just one of many interesting people to appear with Cody's Wild West.

A late Picture of Col. Cody (Buffalo Bill).

A fine example of an F.J. Hiscock postcard. By now you should have noticed the stamp box markings, domestic one-cent postcard, foreign – two-cents. These designations are helpful period indicators.

PLATE 348

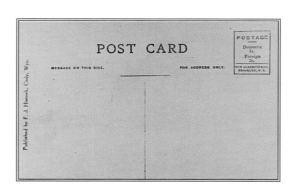

PLATE 349

A great image of a Western trio. A Buffalo Jones advertisement postcard for his book *The Last of the Plainsmen*. The caption reads in part "This book is more startling than fiction and facts from cover to cover." The reality is that the book is fiction from cover to cover with only a few facts sprinkled here and there.

BUFFALO BILL
World's Greatest Scout

PAWNEE BILL
White Man Raised by Indians

BUFFALO JONES
Preserver of the Buffalo

"THE LAST OF THE PLAINSMEN"
This book is more startling than fiction and facts from cover to cover.
Sale Price $1.50 Net.
Published by A. C. McClurg & Co., Chicago, Ill.
COPYRIGHTED, 1909, BY C. J. JONES

PLATE 350

First peace council ever held between Chippewas and the Sioux, "Buffalo Bill" peace maker. This event took place in September of 1896 when the show was playing Ashland, Wisconsin. The 1896 route book mentions this interesting affair.

PLATE 351

Black Fox and Iron Tail, two Wild West Show regulars.

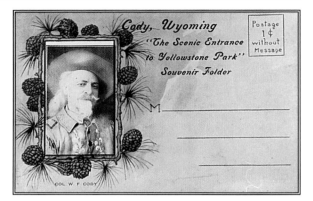

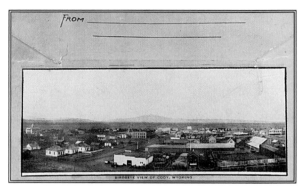

PLATE 352

Postcard souvenir folder
Year – c. 1916

This folder contains 20 scenic views along the Cody Road to Yellowstone Park. Individual postcards of each view were also available. Three views from the folder are shown in the actual postcard format.

PLATE 353

Black Fox, Iron Tail, Cody, and other show Indians visit the grave of Uncas in Norwich, Connecticut. This card was also printed in black and white.

PLATE 354

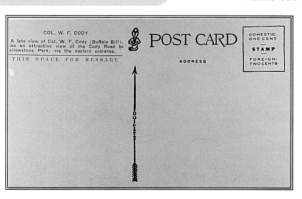

The original Pahaska Teepe Lodge still stands and the inside can be seen by chance if you can find a staff member with a little time to spare. The new Pahaska Teepe Lodge is excellent and its location is one of the best in the West. The lodge is situated about one mile east of the eastern entrance to Yellowstone National Park. The 52-mile ride from Cody, Wyoming, to the park's entrance is a beautiful scenic route.

PLATE 355

Buffalo Bill handed out these postcards while touring with The 101 Ranch Wild West Show in 1916. He was obviously promoting Cody, Wyoming, and Yellowstone National Park. This postcard is autographed, however, it appears that someone else signed these postcards for Cody. Even Abraham Lincoln had his secretary sign his name for him at times. It is possible that Johnny Baker or John M. Burke helped out with this function.

PLATE 356

OPERA HOUSE,

3 NIGHTS AND SATURDAY MATINEE,

THURSDAY, FRIDAY, SATURDAY, June 14, 15 & 16

Admission 50c.,75c. & $1. No extra charge for Reserved Seats. To be had at usual places.

THE RENOWNED HISTORICAL CELEBRITIES,

BUFFALO BILL AND CAPTAIN JACK

(Hon. W. F. CODY.)

(J. W. CRAWFORD.)

Chief Scout for Gen'ls TERRY and CROOK.

The "Poet Scout" of the Black Hills, direct from GEN'L CROOK'S command.

Hon. W. F. CODY — (Buffalo Bill.)

In the realistic Western Drama, written especially for BUFFALO BILL, in 5 Acts, entitled

LIFE ON THE BORDER

Supported by a Powerful Dramatic Organization.

CHANGE OF PROGRAMME NIGHTLY.

The Scalp and War Paraphernalia of YELLOW HAND, Chief of 800 Cheyenne Braves, KILLED BY BUFFALO BILL, at the Battle of Indian Creek, Black Hills, July 8th, 1876, are on Free Exhibition in the most prominent Show Window in this City on the advertised dates.

Francis & Valentine, Printers, 517 Clay Street, San Francisco.

PLATE 357

Stage Program
Printed by Francie &
Valentine, 517 Clay Street,
San Francisco, CA
Size – 6" x 9"
Pages – 2
Year – 1877

"Life On The Border" starring Cody and Captain Jack, who was J. W. Crawford, The Poet Scout, was one of two plays presented for the 1876 – 1877 season. "The Red Right Hand" was the other play. They alternated plays nightly. While playing in Virginia City, Nevada, at the end of June, Captain Jack accidentally shot himself with a blank which caused a nasty leg wound. Cody continued with the stage tour while The Poet Scout was in the hospital recovering. This incident ended the friendly association between Cody and Crawford.

The variety of Cody collectibles illustrated in this section exemplifies the broad range of material associated with this fascinating man. As mentioned before, no one will ever have access to every Cody related collectible, but at least here we have a good look at some different, interesting, and tantalizing examples.

The majority of available Cody material will be found in the ephemera and manuscript categories. We have seen that photography makes a strong and exciting showing when it comes to Buffalo Bill. Stereopticon cards and candid snapshots will appear in this section and are interesting. Glass paperweights, fine silk woven souvenirs, a felt pen wiper, and a terrific ink well plus much more all help to add diversity and fun to this Buffalo Bill collecting experience. This pasttime has exceptional educational benefits and also provides an intriguing link to a romantic historical past.

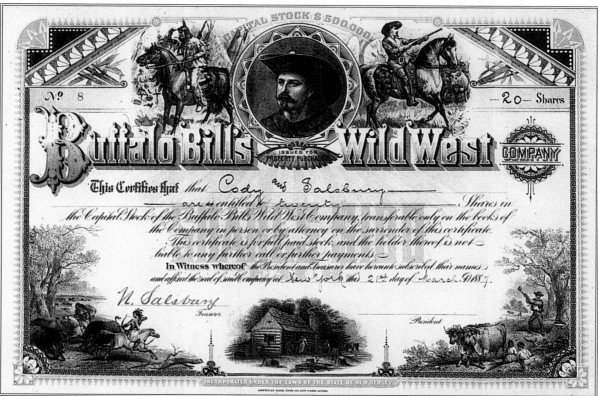

Courtesy Buffalo Bill Historical Center, Cody, Wyoming

PLATE 358
Stock Certificate
Year – 1887

A Certificate of Organization for "Buffalo Bill's Wild West Company" was issued in the state of New Jersey on Feb. 8, 1887. The incorporators were W.F. Cody, Nathan Salsbury, and Frank C. Maeder. Total capital stock was $500,000. The company commenced business with $10,000.
The original stockholders were

William F. Cody, North Platte, Nebraska	35 shares
Nathan Salsbury, Long Branch, New Jersey	35 shares
Frank C. Maeder, Long Branch, New Jersey	10 shares
Milton E. Milner, Fort Benton, Montana	15 shares
William D. Guthrie, New York City	5 shares

The company would commence on Feb. 10, 1887, and terminate on Feb. 10, 1912.

PLATE 359
Souvenir Silk
Year – 1887
Maker – Thomas Stevens,
Coventry, England
Silk Size – 3⅜" x 5½" approximately
Original card mounts vary in size

A superb souvenir from the 1887 Earl's Court triumph. The example shown is not in an original mount. The original mounts are marked. A small print credit line reads "Woven in pure silk by Thomas Stevens, Coventry, England." The mount is also marked with much larger print, souvenir of the "Wild West" Thomas Stevens wonderful silk creations are today referred to as Stevengraphs.

The church of England's Temperance Society and W.F. Cody brought together for a just cause. A fine example of the fascinating material associated with Buffalo Bill.

PLATE 360
Autograph Souvenir
Size – 3½" x 5" approximately
Year – 1887

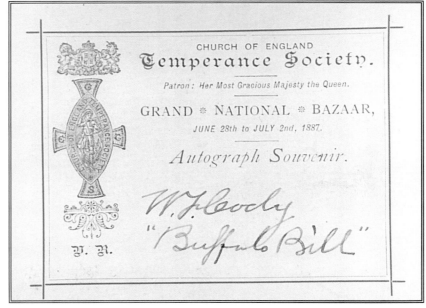

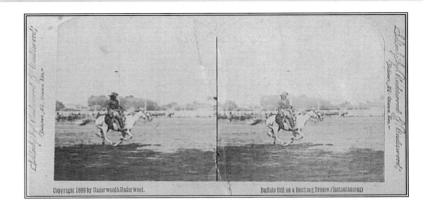

Copyright 1889 by Underwood & Underwood.   Buffalo Bill on a Bucking Bronco. (Instantaneous)

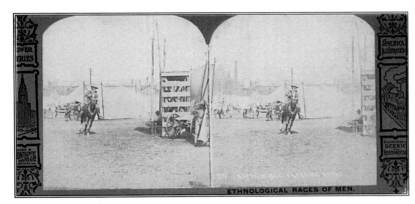

ETHNOLOGICAL RACES OF MEN.

PLATE 361
Stereoptican Cards
Years – 1880s – 1910

1892.   Buffalo Bill, Mounted.

COPYRIGHT 1889.   MISS HICOCK, GREATEST EQUESTRIENNE IN THE WORLD. -INST.

These stereo cards were as popular in the 1890s as video games are to children in the 1990s. Nearly every subject or geographic location seems to be depicted on stereo cards. Thankfully, Cody was well covered by this unique photographic medium.

PLATE 362
Drawings from
Life
Artist – Charles
Henckel
Size – 4⅝" x 6½"
Year – 1891

There are 11 fold out drawings and most are captioned in English, German, and French. The last fold out page has an ink stamp that reads original pictures – Buffalo Bill's Wild West – Cy. 1891.

The American Indians that toured with Cody's show were treated with respect and curiosity by most of the English and European publics. Invitations for a variety of affairs were extended to the Chiefs on a regular basis. Dinners were one of their favorite activities. The complimentary dinner notice to No Neck, Short Bull, and Kicking Bear is a prime example of an early dinner invitation. This dinner was held at Galloway's, 115 West Nile Street, Glasgow, Scotland. The time was at one p.m., Friday, December 4, 1891.
The back has an interesting advertisement for Liebig's Extract of Meat Company, Limited, 9 Fenchurch Avenue, London E.C.

Courtesy Circus World Museum, Baraboo, Wisconsin

PLATE 363
Dinner Invitation
Year – 1891

PLATE 364
Glass Paperweights
Makers – Barnes & Abrams
Co., Grapeville, PA
Abrams Paperweight Co.,
Pittsburgh, PA
Size – 2⅝" x 4"
Circa – 1892 – 1895

Most Cody related examples from this period are marked across the bottom PAT. SEPT. 5 82, Barnes & Abrams Company, Grapeville, PA. A variation reads Abrams Paperweight Company, Pittsburgh, PA., PAT. NOV. 29 92. The Grapeville, Pennysylvania, marked examples actually have a milk glass coating protecting the image. The Pittsburgh, Pennsylvania, examples have a thinner white coating covering the image. The major in London is John M. Burke. The popular Wild West Show general manager. The Cowboy Band had an impressive 27 members back in 1893. Annie Oakley and the Deadwood Stage Coach can also be found on paperweights from this time period.

PLATE 365
Felt Pen Wiper
Size – 2¾" x 4¼" approx.
Year – 1892

Pen wipers were common in England back in the 1890s. This wonderful example is as good as they get.

The Columbian Exposition had many vendors including at least four different silk makers including Thomas Stevens. This silk was introduced in 1887 but it did not have the simulated signature below the flags. The 1887 issues were in cardboard type mounts with the Thomas Stevens, Coventry, England, credit. The back labels had interesting facts about the subject presented. The many examples of this attractive silk that exist today would indicate excellent sales here in the United States. It is possible this attractive silk was made and sold at the fair. Cody may have also sold these as souvenirs during his 1893 Chicago stand.

PLATE 366
No. 10
Silk
Size – 2⅜" x 4½"
Year – 1893

One of the first marches composed and dedicated to Buffalo Bill.

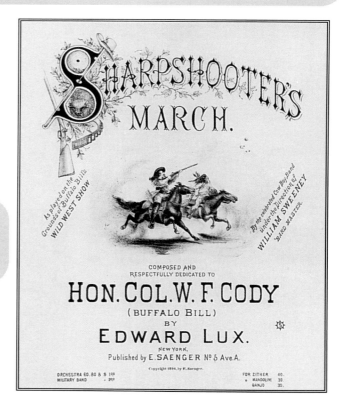

PLATE 367
Sheet Music
Year – 1894
The Sharpshooters' March
By Edward Lux.

ANNIE OAKLEY.

AMERICA'S REPRESENTATIVE LADY SHOT AND FANCY RIDER, WHO ALSO HOLDS THE "POLICE GAZETTE" MEDAL.

PLATE 368
Illustrations

Many fine examples are available in a variety of sizes and styles. This Annie Oakley is from *The National Police Gazette* issue of Saturday, June 30, 1894. Police gazettes from the 1880s and 1890s contain a good number of cuts including Buffalo Bill and numerous other Wild West characters. Photo type illustrations can be found in *Halligan's Illustrated World's Fair* magazine. Original engravings can be obtained from *Harper's Weeklys* and even color illustrations are available in New York's *Puck* magazine.

PLATE 369
Inkwell
Maker – Unknown
Size – Woodbase 6⅛" in diameter,
5¼" high
Year – circa 1890s

A delightfully whimsical characterization of W.F. Cody. His mustache will cradle a pen and the crown of his hat covers a small copper cup containing a small glass cup for the ink.

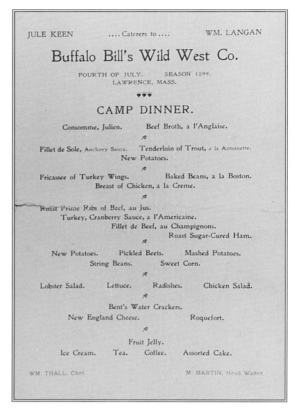

PLATE 370
July 4th Menu
Year – 1899

Cody's show celebrated the 4th of July with a special camp dinner every season. It is unclear exactly when the attractive menus were first used.

Five pages are sheet music and the remaining pages contain lyrics of songs copyrighted by a variety of artists.

PLATE 371
Songster
Year – c. 1899
Published by Frank Tousey, New York
Size – 4¾" x 6⅜"
Pages – 32 numbered

Courtesy Buffalo Bill Historical Center, Cody, Wyoming

Courtesy Buffalo Bill Historical Center, Cody, Wyoming

PLATE 372
Photos from Glass
Plate Negatives

Actual glass plate negatives
were common during Cody's
show years. Most collectors
do not realize that they occasionally turn up at antique
photographic shows.

PLATE 373
Cigar & Pipe Holder
Size – Base 7¾" x 8⅜" x 8¾" high
Maker – Unknown
Year – circa 1900

A ceramic or plaster type material was used to make this early tobacco product organizer. A small space for matches was also incorporated. Buffalo Bill is marked on the small plaque just below the rifle stock.

When Cody opened his show in London on December 26, 1902, this greeting card was utilized to introduce the staffs of The Wild West Show to the English public. James Bailey's staff and Cody's were pictured and an almost religious theme was tried. Another greeting card from this period with a Christmas tree design was also printed and designed by the same artist.

PLATE 374
Greeting Card
Designed by Alick P.F. Ritchie
Printed by Weiners Lts. London N.W.
Size – 8" x 11½"
Year – 1902 or 1903

PLATE 375
Checks

Cody, like many of his contemporaries, used
checks on a regular basis. Collecting his signature
on different items is a challenging endeavor.

Courtesy Circus World Museum, Baraboo, Wisconsin

DEWITT BALLARD, Caterer.

PLATE 376
July 4th Menu

The 1905, July 4th special dinner was held at Lille, France. The American flag design was a solid reminder of home.

BUFFALO BILL'S WILD WEST
JULY 4th, 1905.
LILLE. FRANCE.

Menu

ASPARAGUS CREAM SOUP

BOILED SALMON AND EGG SAUCE

OX TONGUE AND SPINACH
FRICASSEE OF CHICKEN
BANANA FRITTERS AND WINE SAUCE

FILET OF BEEF AND MUSHROOMS
VEAL AND DRESSING
YOUNG TURKEY AND GIBLET SAUCE

NEW POTATOES AND STEWED CORN

LETTUCE AND LOBSTER

PUMPKIN PIE AND ICE CREAM

CHEESE AND BISCUITS

ASSORTED FRUITS AND NUTS

COFFEE AND TEA

Courtesy Circus World Museum, Baraboo, Wisconsin

BUFFALO BILL'S WILD WEST
And Congress of Rough Riders of the World.
DAILY REPORT OF NEWSPAPER ADVERTISING.

Town _Bologna_   Date of Exhibition _April. 7-8-1906_

NAME OF PAPER.	AMOUNT OF SPACE.	No. OF TIMES.	DATE OF INSERTIONS.	AMOUNT OF MONEY.
"Resto del Carlino'	1 vol. 3 col	2	Mar. 28. Apr. 4.	
" "	60 " 2 "	4	" 5. 6. 7. 8.	4.20
'Avvenire di Italia'	120 " 4 "	2	April 1- 5-	
" "	60 " 2 "	4	Mar. 29. Apr. 6. 7. 8	4.00
Tickets: Libreria Treves, 6, Via Farini (8)				
TOTALS				

PLATE 377
Daily Reports of
Newspaper Advertising
Size – 8⅛" x 6½"
Year – 1906

All newspaper advertising was recorded on these informative forms during the 1906 European tour. This form tells us the show was to play Bologna, Italy, on April 7 and 8, 1906. We also see eight free tickets were issued.

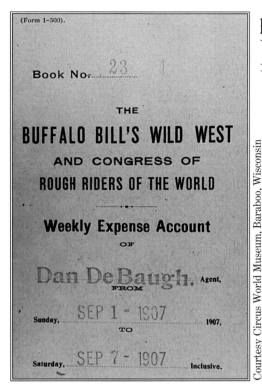

(Form 1–500).

Book No. 23

THE

BUFFALO BILL'S WILD WEST

AND CONGRESS OF

ROUGH RIDERS OF THE WORLD

Weekly Expense Account

OF

Dan DeBaugh. Agent,

FROM

Sunday, SEP 1 - 1907 , 1907,

TO

Saturday, SEP 7 - 1907 Inclusive.

Courtesy Circus World Museum, Baraboo, Wisconsin

PLATE 378
Weekly Expense
Account Booklet
Year – 1907

Keeping records of expenses was absolutely critical to the well being of an enterprise this large and complex. Dan DeBaugh was with the advance advertising crews and they all had to keep records of their expenditures.

BEFORE PRESENTING THIS ORDER FOR TICKETS
You will please affix, in this space, such notice as may appear in your columns.

EDITORIAL DEPARTMENT.

BUFFALO BILL'S WILD WEST

AND CONGRESS OF ROUGH RIDERS

OF THE WORLD

Editor of the *Pilot*,

Published at *Marion, Iowa.*

Upon Presentation of this Order, with a preliminary notice of our exhibition attached thereto as evidence of publication, TWO RESERVED SEATS will be granted in exchange for the courtesy of your columns,

Truly yours, LOUIS E. COOKE, General Agent.

NOTE.—It is understood that this is not an order for advertising, but merely an exchange of courtesy for publishing a local.

Two reserved seats were given to the editors of newspapers that presented this form with affixed notice about Cody's show that appeared in their columns.

PLATE 379
Press Ticket Order Form
Year – Circa 1907
Size – 3½" x 9"

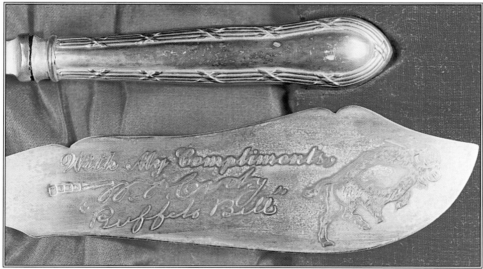

PLATE 380

Presentation Knife and Fork
Maker – Unknown
Year – Unknown

The knife is engraved "With my compliments W. F. Cody, Buffalo Bill." Can anyone help identify this set?

PLATE 381
Advertising Fan
Size – 8" x 8¼"
Year – 1907 – 1908

This fancy getup came to Cody by way of gifts received during the last overseas tour. At least three different advertisements on the back of this colorful fan have been seen. A fan would indeed come in handy during a hot humid summer day or evening while watching The Wild West Show.

Patriotism and Buffalo Bill make a fine combination. It is easy to understand why these menus are popular with Cody collectors.

PLATE 382
July 4th Menu
Year – 1908

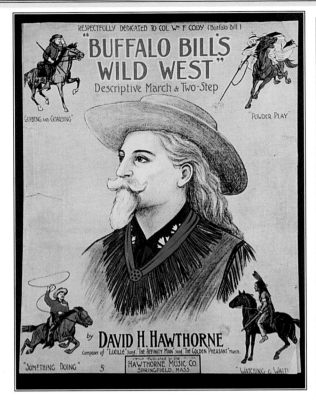

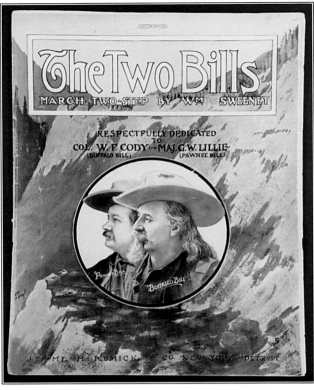

PLATE 383
Sheet Music
Size – 10¼" x 13⅜" approximately

Buffalo Bill's Wild West descriptive march and two-step by David H. Hawthorne is from 1908. *The Two Bill's* march and two step by William Sweeney is from 1910.

PLATE 384
Buffalo Bill's Farewell March and *Two Step*
Sheet music, cover
by Wm. Sweeney

PLATE 385
Playing Cards
Circa 1909 – 1913
Made by United
States Playing
Card Co.,
Cincinnati, Ohio

Cody enjoyed hunting, smoking cigars, and playing cards. A variety of different decks were advertised in the Wild West programs for many years.

PLATE 386
Outer Cigar Box Label
Size – 4¼" x 4¾"
Circa – 1910

A superb representation of Colonel Cody. Inner and outer cigar box labels were indeed some of the finest artwork and color lithography of the period.

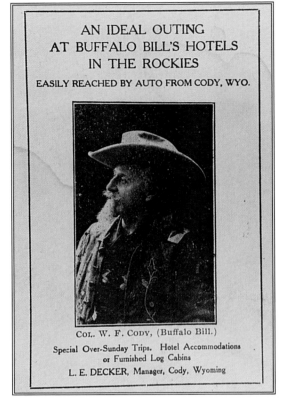

PLATE 387
Advertisement Booklet
Year – 1910
Printed by Enterprise Print, Cody, Wyoming
Size – 3⅞" x 5¾"
Pages – 12 numbered

The Irma, Wapiti-Inn, and Pahaska Teepe were the hotels Cody owned and are described in this booklet.

Cody used telegrams as often as we now use the telephone. This example illustrates that the advance crews also used this form of quick communication.

PLATE 388
Telegrams

PLATE 389
The Indian Buffalo
Bill's Art Studies
with Portraits of
Himself
Year – 1910

Six 11" x 14" prints made up these portfolios. A young artist from Chicago named Joe Scheurle was attempting to make his presence known. The oval print of Cody was a Courier lithograph that surely Cody wanted included with these sets. A two-page spread of these prints were included in the 1910 Buffalo Bill – Pawnee Bill advance diecut courier.

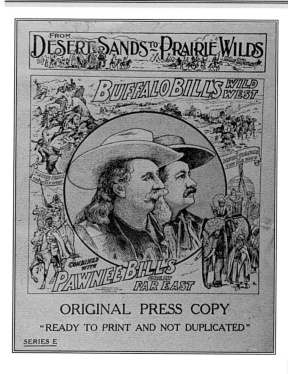

PLATE 390
Press Copy Booklet
Size – 5¼" x 6⁹⁄₁₆"
Pages – 6

Press notices on perforated pages made it very convenient for smaller town editors. Illustrations on the reverse side of the text were also provided. A quick check of the route sheets reveals that Tuesday, August 1, was in 1911. We also learn the show was playing at Burlington, Iowa.

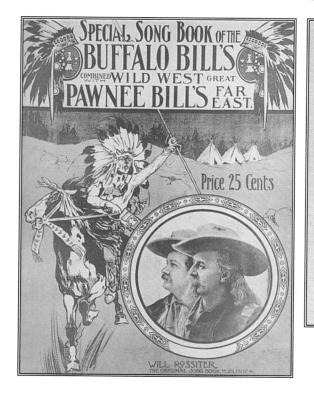

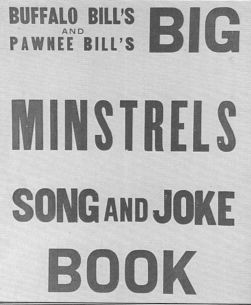

PLATE 391
Special Song Book
Published by Will Rossiter,
Chicago, IL
Size – 10¼" x 13½"
Pages – 8
Year – 1912

The inside front cover has Cracker Jack conundrums while the inside back cover has a dictionary of dreams and their meanings. The eight pages are basically sheet music.

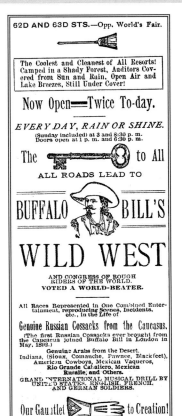
Virtually every aspect of Cody's active and fascinating life was covered by the newspaper media. Through his long distinguished career the public was always interested in his personal life as well as all of the different business ventures he was associated with. Many clippings are rich in illustration and most have worthwhile information. The good news about these newspaper columns is that the supply is unlimited and the variety remarkable.

PLATE 392
Newspaper Clippings

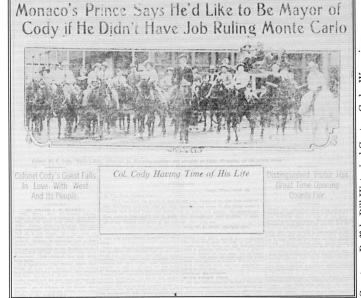

Like newspaper clippings, candid snapshots taken by anyone with a camera, are encountered often and no one knows how many may exist. The majority are not too clear or too distant, however some are indeed important links to help identify people and places.

PLATE 393

Four Candid Snapshots

A. Cody talking to Prince Albert, the First, of Monaco, who came to Wyoming in September 1913 for one of Cody's famous hunts. A terrific side rear view of Cody's saddle is the highlight here.

B. Laura Luther, Standing Bear, and son on Wild West Show lot, circa 1890s.

C. Cody and Iron Tail in a typical snapshot, circa 1913.

D. The Colonel receiving a report from his mining partner, D.B. Dyer, in dark shirt, at the mine site near Oracle, Arizona, circa 1910.

PLATE 394
Buffalo Ranch Souvenir
Published by The Courier Company,
Buffalo, New York
Size – 7¾" x 9"
Year – 1912
Pages – 18

Pawnee Bill and his wife May Lillie celebrated their twenty-fifth wedding anniversary in 1910. This interesting booklet also informs us of their just completed beautiful bungalow home on Blue Hawk Peak over looking Pawnee, Oklahoma. The Buffalo Ranch is highlighted along with other facets of the Lillie's holdings. Buffalo Bill, John M. Burke, Louis E. Cooke, Frank Winch, and Captain Jack Crawford all contributed to this fascinating souvenir. A page of famous artists who came to paint the Buffalo is a nice added touch.

PLATE 395
Stock Certificate
Year – 1913

The Cody-Dyer Arizona Mining & Milling Company of Tucson, Arizona, was the investment dream that kept Cody during this period in constant financial jeopardy. The old scout had too much faith in Mr. Dyer, his mining partner. Cody's relationship with this recognized mining expert started around 1902. No one knows the amount of capital Cody invested in this venture but we know it came close to ruining him financially. Cody also held stock in "Cody's Wyoming Coal Company," "The Roaring Fork Mining & Milling Company" and "The Cody Musical Association."

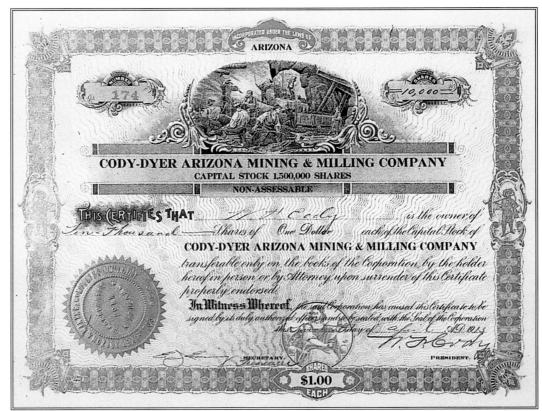

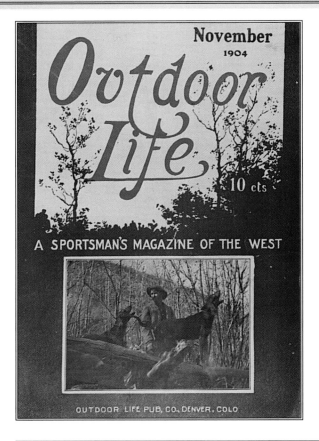

PLATE 396
Magazines

A fine selection of magazines is available from most periods of Cody's life. The *Cosmopolitan* from 1894 has a very good article written by Cody himself. The *Outdoor Life Sportsman's* magazine of the west has a terrific article by Irving R. Bacon. He writes of a never-to-be-forgotten hunting trip with Cody and friends. The *Billboard* for December 1913 has one of the better front covers of our western hero.

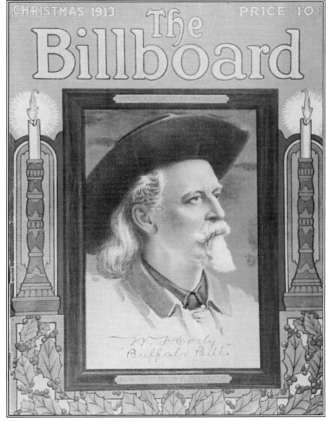

PLATE 397
July 4th Menu
Year – 1913

The people of Chicago and Buffalo Bill always had a special relationship. After New York City, Chicago was second on a list of favorite places to exhibit

Courtesy Circus World Museum, Baraboo, Wisconsin

First Public Presentation

AT THE

COLUMBIA THEATRE

WASHINGTON, D. C.

February 27
1914

UNDER AUSPICES
OF THE

National Press Club.

THE COL. W. F. CODY

(Buffalo Bill)

Historical Pictures Company

DEPICTING THE

LAST INDIAN BATTLES

AND FINAL SURRENDER TO

Lieutenant-General Nelson A. Miles

WITH

COLONEL W. F. CODY—BUFFALO BILL

as Chief of Scouts, under whose Personal Directions these Historical Moving Pictures Were Produced by the

ESSANAY FILM MANUFACTURING COMPANY, of CHICAGO, ILL.

Cody's film-making effort was actually an early attempt at documentary style entertainment. Unfortunately, the public was not ready for this very important aspect of film making. The movies depicting different Indian battles were not popular and faded away by the time the 1914 Sells Floto touring season began. Sadly, no known complete versions of these films have surfaced. However, this program states that a set of reels will be placed in the archives of the War Department for future use and educational purposes.

PLATE 398
Movie Announcement Program
Size – 6⅛" x 9½"
Pages – 7 numbered
Year – 1914

PLATE 399
Annual Farewell
Dinner Menu
Year – 1914

Annual Farewell Dinner
OF THE
Sells-Floto-Buffalo Bill Shows
(HIMSELF)

FORT WORTH, TEXAS, OCT. 14, 1914.

F. B. HUTCHINSON, Manager
DIXIE ENGLE, Steward

Menu

Oyster Cocktail

Deep Sea Turtle

Baked Red Snapper, Maitre D'Hotel

Olives   Sweet Pickles   Celery

Braised Veal Sweet Breads, Mushroom Sauce
Oyster Patties
Comport of Fruit

Prime Ribs, Au Jus
Young Turkey, Oyster Dressing, Cranberry Sauce
Suckling Pig, Candied Sweet Potatoes

Claret Punch

Asparagus   Green Lima Beans   Mashed Potatoes

Peach Sundae With Nuts

Assorted Cake

Tea   Cocoa   Coffee   Milk

The Season is over,
To our homes we must go.
We have had a good time,
With the Sells-Floto Show,
And now through the tents,
This sad cry does ring,
Goodby brother trooper,
I'll see you in the spring.

The larger outdoor traveling shows not only celebrated the 4th of July with a special camp dinner but also closed the touring season with a farewell dinner for everyone associated with the enterprise.

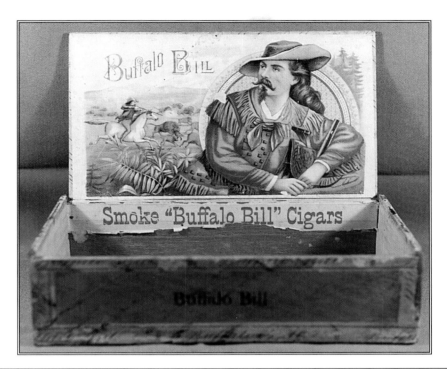

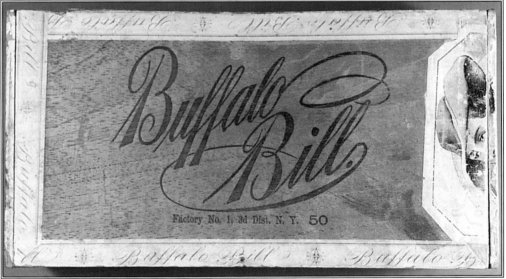

PLATE 400

Cigar Box
Size – 4¾" x 8¾" x 2⁵⁄₁₆" high
Year – circa 1915

Inner lid cigar box labels have some of the finest artwork ever produced. Another terrific image of our hero.

257

Reproduced by permission of Jimmie Gibbs Munroe

Reproduced by permission of Jimmie Gibbs Munroe

PLATE 401

Poster Stamps
Size – 1⅞" x 2⅝"
Bottom group from left to right –
Joseph C. Miller, Unidentified,
Etheyle Parry, Juanita Parry,
Martha Allen

Reproduced by permission of Jimmie Gibbs Munroe

Poster stamps were becoming popular about the time these 1915 101 Ranch examples were issued. This miniature form of advertising reached its zenith in the 1930s and covered as many subjects as any other advertising medium.

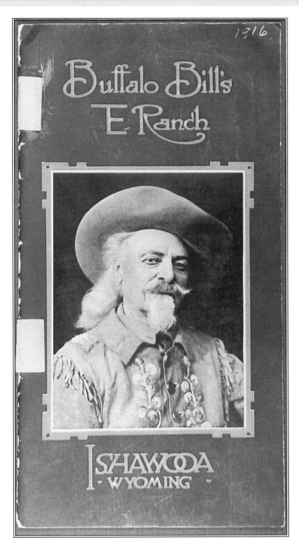

PLATE 402

Vacation Brochure
Year – 1916
Printed by Press of the Western
Newspaper Union, Denver
Size – 4⅝" x 9"
Pages – 6 numbered

This brochure informs us in detail about Cody's home ranch called the TE. Opening his beloved ranch to the tourist trade was an attempt to help with his money problems.

This advertising flyer's announcement turned out to be accurate. The 1916 season was indeed Cody's last campaign.

PLATE 403
Flyer
Year – 1916
Printed by Gazette Show Print
Company, Mattoon, IL
Size – 6" x 9"

Courtesy Buffalo Bill Historical Center, Cody, Wyoming

PLATE 404
Celebrity Memento
Year – 1916

A single cigar safely rests in this envelope. What is written on the front of this envelope explains its significance. "Cigar received from Col. W.F. Cody, Buffalo Bill in the lobby of The Library Park Hotel after being introduced to him by his cousin J.F. Cody April 5, 1916, Detroit, Michigan." Sadly, the individual who received this cigar is not identified. Let us keep in mind that other mementos given to people by Buffalo Bill are out there just waiting for collectors to round them up.

PLATE 405
Program
Year – 1917
Size – 7⅜" x 9½"
Pages – 8 full, tip in program of events with typical advertising

Johnny Baker teamed with Jess Willard, "The Heavy Weight Boxing Champion," and Edward Arlington, an outdoor amusement veteran, to keep the show in business. One full season of touring was accomplished, however, without Buffalo Bill and other factors like World War I, doomed the show.

Mrs. William F. Cody

Mrs. Irma Cody Garlow

Mrs. Julia Cody Goodman

Mrs. May Cody Decker

desire to express their

sincere thanks and appreciation

for your kind expressions of sympathy

in their deep bereavement

PLATE 406
Funeral Acknowledgement
Card

Buffalo Bill passed away on January 10, 1917, at his sister, May Cody Decker's, house in Denver, Colorado. His body would lie in state in the Capitol Rotunda on January 14th followed by an afternoon funeral. He was then taken to a mortuary and placed in a vault until late spring. Naturally time was needed to properly prepare the burial site. Early in June Cody was laid to rest on Look-Out Mountain. The postmark of January 16th on the envelope tells us this thank you acknowledgment was sent after the first and official funeral. The family responded quickly by sending thank you cards to family, friends, and those who participated in the funeral.

POSTSCRIPT

The impact William Frederick Cody has had on our Wild West heritage is truly fascinating. He was a man for all seasons and his legacy will be forever entrenched in America's extraordinary history. Collecting artifacts associated with Buffalo Bill is entertaining, educational, and rewarding. The items presented in this reference book illustrate the broad range of material that is available to the active collector. The focus was on collectibles that the average collector can still acquire. Cody authenticated firearms and other personal effects are basically accounted for in museums and very private collections. Since most of these items will never be on the open market they were omitted. The fact that Cody's popularity was so wide spread and lasted for 44 consecutive years explains why so much is still available. The diversity of items that can be credited to this man is yet another tribute to his long list of accomplishments.

Please do not make a very common mistake after viewing this work. Some collectors and dealers automatically assume that the example they own is rarer and more valuable simply because it is not in a reference book. Nine out of ten times this is not the case. Research your object before you decide on its value. Writing to The Buffalo Bill Historical Center in Cody, Wyoming, may yield important specific information. To find the value, you may talk with veteran dealers who cater to the western collector. Your best approach would be to talk with advanced Buffalo Bill collectors. It takes 15 to 20 years of active collecting to get a descent understanding of Cody collectible values. You will need at least three or four different opinions on value. You then average those figures to a fair level. You will then have achieved what many would consider a "fair market" value. Paying for an appraisal is another option. However, factor that information along with dealer, collector, and price guide opinions to achieve a fair value range. All this takes money, time, and effort but if you truly want to know the proper value, this is a good way to made that determination.

A thank you to all who have purchased this reference book. I sincerely hope that you have learned a few things and maybe enjoyed the effort. To those who may be disappointed, I offer this suggestion. The market place for Buffalo Bill information is wide open and we eagerly await your contribution. Helping collectors for the first 12 months after publication is my way of perpetuating the educational experience of collecting. Collectors with questions or information to share may contact the author but please include a self-addressed stamped envelope. Write to James W. Wojtowicz, P.O. Box 0042, Bensenville, IL 60106.

Final words come by way of Charles Eldrige Griffin from his book *Four Years in Europe with Buffalo Bill.* Griffin wrote, "It is really too bad that everybody can not know the Colonel as his friends know him. He is truly one of the best fellows in the world, open hearted and generous to a fault. Why, his managers have to hedge him in and keep people from him during the season, otherwise he would have his tents filled with free tickets." There is no doubt about it, *Buffalo Bill was special!*

PRICE GUIDE

The pricing structure collectors encounter as they pursue the collecting habit is often complex and at times confusing. We all know condition and geographic location can drastically affect prices. Many other common sense factors are understood, however, how do we explain the idiosyncrasies of some dealers who have prices in the stratosphere. The point being that every item has a fair market value to each collector. This fair market value can be determined by simply purchasing and or pricing a specific item at least three or four times. This process allows us to focus and average the different prices to an expectable level. Ascertaining this information can take years of active collecting.

A simple short cut will always be reference price guides, however, we must realize that none are absolute. The values listed here are an opinion of what prices should be when items in fine condition are being sold on the open market. It should only be used as a guide and everyone associated with this effort cannot be held responsible for anyone making or losing money because of the information it presents. Should you encounter Cody material at auction you will in general pay much more simply because that is the nature of that action. Exclusive galleries will also have higher prices. Please keep in mind that the expertise of gallery owners coupled with the fact that they offer mighty fine regalia are two exceptable reasons for higher prices. I believe it is clear no single price guide can properly represent all facets of the collecting world. Regardless of this belief, price guides still represent a way for collectors to help determine what they should pay for specific collectibles.

WILD WEST SHOW PROGRAMS

Wild West programs have always been popular with collectors, however, in the past three years the demand has increased to a level that is quickly using up the supply. A few collectors are trying to collect a complete run of programs. This is a real challenge but it is possible with one exception. The 1883 program is rare and most collectors will not own one. The programs from the 1880s are becoming scarce and the prices are increasing rapidly.

1883	$4,500.00	1900	$300.00
1884	$700.00	1901	$400.00
1885	$700.00	1902	$300.00
1886	$700.00	1903	$300.00
1887	$700.00	1903 (silk)	$1,500.00
1888	$700.00	1904	$500.00
1889	$700.00	1905	$500.00
1890	$800.00	1906	$600.00
1891	$600.00	1907	$300.00
1892	$500.00	1908	$300.00
1893 (first)	$400.00	1909	$400.00
1893 (second)	$300.00	1910	$300.00
1894	$300.00	1911	$300.00
1895	$300.00	1912	$400.00
1896	$300.00	1913	$400.00
1897	$300.00	1914	$300.00
1898	$300.00	1915	$300.00
1899	$300.00	1916	$300.00

Items have been assigned plate numbers.

PHOTOGRAPHY — CODY

The demand for photos of Cody and his contemporaries is at an all-time high. Pricing his photos is very difficult because of the rapidly increasing market. In general Cody photos are not rare. There is an abundent supply, but unfortunately, the demand has passed the supply. This demand has driven prices up and some dealers and collectors confuse these high prices with rarity. Large format photos of Copdy that he autographed have become very expensive. These are at the top of the demand list and fit into the scarce category.

Plate #	Item	Price
1	CDV, signed to Julia	$1,600.00
2	CDV, Sarony	$500.00
3	CDV, Sarony	$500.00
4	CDV, no credit	$400.00
5	CDV, no credit	$400.00
6	Photo card, no credit	$500.00
7	CDV, no credit	$400.00
8	Cabinet card, Mosher	$600.00
9	Large photo, Scott	$900.00
10	Large photo, Chickering	$800.00
11	Imperial cabinet card, Platz	$800.00
12	Cabinet card, Notman	$700.00
13	Cabinet card, Sarony	$800.00
14	Cabinet Card, Elliott & Fry?	$700.00
15	Photo card, Lauvy, signed	$2,500.00
16	Large format cabinet card, Lauvy	$900.00
17	Large format cabinet card, Piron, signed	$3,000.00
18	Cabinet card, Brisbois	$600.00
19	Cabinet card, Newsboy	$600.00
20	Cabinet card, Prince	$600.00
21	Cabinet card, Brisbois	$500.00
22	Cabinet card, Newsboy	$600.00
23	Cabinet card, Stacy	$500.00
24	Cabinet card, Stacy	$500.00
25	Cabinet card, Stacy, signed	$1,000.00
26	Cabinet card, Stacy	$500.00
27	Cabinet card, Stacy	$500.00
28	Photo card, Stacy	$400.00
29	Photo card, Stacy	$300.00
30	Photo card, Stacy	$200.00
31	Printed card, Stacy	$80.00
32	Large format photo, Prince, signed	$2,500.00
33	Large format photo, Bodim	$1,000.00
34	Vertical format, Modiano	$800.00
35	Large format photo, Hemment	$1,000.00
36	Large format, Marccau	$800.00
37	Cabinet card, no credit	$400.00
38	Large format, Black	$500.00

PHOTOGRAPHY — COMPANIONS

Plate #	Item	Price
39.	General Phil Sheridan, CDV	$125.00
40.	Ned Buntline, cabinet card	$750.00
41.	Duke Alexis, CDV	$100.00
42.	George A. Custer, CDV	$900.00
43.	Texas Jack, cabinet card	$900.00
44.	Dr. Powell "White Beaver," cabinet card	$600.00
45.	John M. Burke, cabinet card	$600.00
46.	Doc Carver, cabinet card	$900.00
47.	Bogardus & Sons, cabinet card	$600.00
48.	John Nelson, photo card, trimmed	$400.00
49.	Buck Taylor, cabinet card	$700.00
50.	Johnny Baker, cabinet card	$600.00
51.	Sitting Bull, cabinet card	$700.00
52.	Annie Oakley, cabinet card	$900.00
53.	Annie Oakley, cabinet card	$900.00
54.	Annie Oakley, cabinet card	$900.00
55.	Lillian Smith, cabinet card	$600.00
56.	Red Shirt, cabinet card	$600.00
57.	Notman ground photo, 8" x 8"	$800.00
58.	Vicente Orapezo, cabinet card	$500.00
59.	Bronco Bill Irving & Family, cabinet card	$600.00
60.	Deadwood Stagecoach, cabinet card	$400.00
61.	Bennie Irving, cabinet card	$400.00
62.	William Sweeny, cabinet card	$400.00
63.	Little Bull, cabinet card	$600.00
64.	Pawnee Bill & May Lillie, cabinet card	$600.00
65.	Alfred Heimer, cabinet card	$150.00
66.	Ed Phillips, cabinet card	$600.00
67.	May Lillie, printed card	$100.00
68.	Cy Compton, large photo	$300.00

WILD WEST ROUTE BOOKS AND ROUTE SHEETS

Plate #	Item	Price
69	1896 Route book, cloth or leather cover	$450.00
70	1896 Route sheet, monthly	$50.00
71	1899 Route book and map	$450.00
72	1900 Route book and map	$450.00
73	1902 Route book and map	$400.00
75	1902, 1903, 1904 Route map	$400.00
76	1904 Route postcard	$75.00
77	1905 Route map	$400.00
	1906 Route map, not illustrated	$350.00
78	1908 Route sheet, monthly	$40.00

Plate #	Item	Price
79	1909 Route postcard	$125.00
80	1910 Route sheet, monthly	$40.00
81	1910 – 1911 Route flyer, complete seasons	$500.00
82	1914 Route flyer, complete season	$75.00
83	1916 Route card	$40.00
	Example shown with Cody's writing	$250.00
84	1915 Route card, monthly	$40.00
85	1916 Route sheet, complete season	$75.00
	Plates 86 – 107	no price

HERALDS & ADVANCE COURIERS

Plate #	Item	Price
108	1893 Herald paper, 4-section style	$200.00
109	1895 Herald paper, multi–foldout	$200.00
110	1895 Herald, 10" x 28"	$250.00
111	1896 Ad. Courier, blue & white	$400.00
112	1895 Ad. Courier, green & gold cover	$500.00
113	1897 Ad. Courier, 9" x 12"	$300.00
114	1898 The Daily Scout	$250.00
115	1898 – 1899 Courier Buffalo Head, each	$400.00
116	1899 Rough Rider, 1st issue	$200.00
117	1901 Herald, 7½" x 27½"	$200.00
118	1901 Rough Rider	$125.00

Plate #	Item	Price
119	1902 Rough Rider, color covers	$300.00
120	1902 The Wild West Illustrated, beware of reprints	$125.00
121	1906 Roughriders (foreign)	$200.00
122	1903 Endorsement Herald, 25" x 39½"	$350.00
123	1906 Window Herald (foreign), 6⁵⁄₁₆" x 29⅝"	$250.00
124	1907 – 1908 Courier, Indian head (each)	$500.00
125	1909 – 1910 Courier, two bills diecut (each)	$400.00
126	1913 The Overland Trail, beware of reprints	$200.00
127	1913 Herald, postcard style	$300.00

LITHOGRAPHS

The lithograph market is one of the most difficult to track. Most examples show up at auction and this does not help the average collector. Because of the rapidly fluctuating lithograph market these values should be considered with caution. When lithographs are found glued or pasted to boards or some other hard material it would decrease the overall value by at least 25 percent. The examples without values were done so by request of the contributor.

Plate #	Item	Price
128	1885 W.F. Carver	Rare
129	1879 Herald lithograph	Scarce
130	1873 – 1876 Three sheets, rare, each	$5,000.00+
131	1883 Hon. W.F. cody	$4,000.00
132	1886 Buffalo Bill's Wild West	$3,000.00
133	1888 Lillian F. Smith	Rare
134	1892 General Miles & Buffalo Bill	$1,500.00
135	1893 Wild West, Russian Cossack	$1,800.00
136	1890 – 1893 Pawnee Bill	Rare
137	1890 – 1893 Pawnee Bill	Rare
138	1895 May Lillie	$3,000.00
139	1895 Buffalo Bill's Wild West	Rare
140	1896 Buffalo Bill's Wild West Cowboy	$2,500.00
141	1898 Buffalo Bill's Wild West	$5,000.00
	Date banner	$200.00
142	1898 Buffalo Bill's Wild West Virginia Reel	$4,000.00
	Date banner	$200.00
143	1907 Col. W.F. Cody	$3,000.00
144	1907 Buffalo Bill's Wild West	$3,500.00
145	1907 Lillian Shaffer, three sheet	$4,000.00
146	1908 Johnny Baker, three sheet	Rare
147	1909 Buffalo Bill's Wild West and P.B.	$4,000.00
148	1909 Buffalo Bill's Wild West and P.B.	$2,000.00
149	1910 Buffalo Bill's Wild West and P.B.	$4,000.00
150	1910 The Life of Buffalo Bill	$1,600.00
151	1912 Iron Tail	$4,000.00
152	1913 Buffalo Bill's Wild West	$1,500.00
153	1916 Buffalo Bill & 101 Ranch	$1,200.00
154	1916 Buffalo Bill Himself, 101 Ranch	$2,000.00
155	1900 lithograph ticket order, 1900 & earlier	$75.00
156	1909 city bill, poster contract	$75.00
157	1911 lithograph ticket order	$60.00
158	Store front photos	$25.00 – 50.00

BOOK VALUES

Plate #	Item	Price
159	*Buffalo Land*, 1872	$150.00
160	*Life of Buffalo Bill*, autobiography, 1879	$250.00
161	*The Poet Scout*, 1879	$200.00
162	*Heroes of the Plains*, 1881 1st edition	$100.00
163	Later issues, fancy covers	$75.00
164	Later issues, plain covers	$50.00
165	*Famous Frontiersmen, Pioneers and Scouts*, 1883	
	1st edition	$100.00
	later editions	$60.00
166	*The Rifle Queen Annie Oakley*, 1887	$800.00
167	*Story of the Wild West & Campfire Chats*, 1888	
	1st edition	$150.00
	Variations	$75.00
	Advertising paper	$75.00
168	*Story of the Wild West*, sample book, 1888	$250.00
169	*Out West*, view book, c. 1890	$90.00
170	*Sitting Bull and the Indian War*, 1891	$110.00
171	*Campfire Sparks*, 1893	$110.00
172	*Buffalo Bill from Prairie to Palace*, 1893	
	Hard cover	$200.00
	Paperback	$125.00
173	*Seventy Years on the Frontier*, 1893	$175.00
174	*Last of the Great Scouts*, 1899, 1st edition	$75.00
175	Later editions	$60.00
176	London edition	$75.00
177	*History of Our Wild West & Stories of Pioneer Life*, 1901	$45.00
178	*Pawnee Bill's True History*, 1902	$175.00
179	*The Adventures of Buffalo Bill*, 1904	$75.00
180	*Four Years in Europe with Buffalo Bill*, 1908	$300.00
181	*True Tales of the Plains*, 1908	$125.00
182	*The Bronco Book*, 1908	$100.00
183	*Thrilling Lives of Buffalo Bill & Pawnee Bill*, 1911	$75.00
184	*Stirring Lives of Buffalo Bill & Pawnee Bill*, 1912	$75.00
185	*Anecdotes of Buffalo Bill*, 1912	$150.00
186	*The Great Salt Lake Trail*, 1898 1st edition	$125.00
	1914 reprint	$75.00
187	*Buffalo Bill and the Overland Trail*, 1914	$60.00

LETTERS, LETTERHEADS, ENVELOPES

Plate #	Item	Price
188	1887 Wild West (winter quarters), unused	$200.00
	with letter signed by Cody	$2,000.00
189	1881 Combination letterhead, unused	$250.00
	with letter signed by Cody	$2,500.00
190	1886, Wild West, unused	$200.00
	with letter signed by Cody	$2,000.00
191	1886 Scout's Rest Stock Ranch, unused	$200.00
	with letter signed by Cody	$2,000.00
192	1887 Wild West (London), unused	$200.00
	with letter signed by Cody	$2,000.00
	with letter signed by Nate Salsbury	$600.00
193	1893 Cody, Powell Coffee Co., unused	$125.00
	with letter signed by Cody	$1,200.00
194	1894 Wild West, unused	$200.00
	with letter signed by Cody	$1,800.00
195	1902 Cody Military College, unused	$150.00
	with letter signed by Cody	$1,200.00
196	1903 Pahaska Tepee, unused	$75.00
	with letter signed by Cody	$1,000.00
197	1904 Pawnee BIll';s Wild West Co., unused	$75.00
	with letter signed by Lillie	$600.00
198	1905 Pawnee Bill, unused	$150.00
	with letter signed by Lillie	$750.00
199	1906 Hoffman House, unused	$20.00
	with letter signed by Cody	$600.00

Plate #	Item	Price
200	1907 Wild West, unused	$75.00
	with letter signed by Cody	$800.00
	with letter signed by John Baker	$400.00
201	The Irma Hotel, unused	$75.00
	with letter signed by Cody	$800.00
202	1910 Buffalo Bill & Pawnee Bill, unused	$100.00
	with letter signed by Cody	$800.00
203	Double Signed Letter	$1,000.00
204	Scout's Rest Ranch, unused	$75.00
	with letter signed by Cody	$800.00
205	1913 The Waldorf Astoria, unused	$20.00
	with letter signed by Cody	$600.00
206	1914 Sells-Floto, unused	$75.00
	with letter signed by Cody	$900.00
	with letter signed by Harry Tammen	$200.00
207	1916 101 Ranch, unused	$100.00
	with letter signed by Cody	$1,000.00
208	1890 envelope	$75.00
209	1896 envelope	$60.00
210	1899 envelope	$60.00
211	1902 envelope	$50.00
212	1916 101 Ranch envelope	$60.00

Note: Letters with historic content or interesting personal highlights will increase the value.

DIME NOVELS

Plate #	Item	Price
213 – 215	Tabloid style, pre-1900	$60.00
216 – 218, 220 – 226	Regular size, pre-1900	$75.00
219	Trade card, pre-1900	$125.00
227	Pre-1900 reprints	$7.00
228	Foreign color covers, pre-1900	$50.00
none illustrated	United States color covers, pre-1900	$75.00
229 – 232, 236 – 241	Post 1900 Dime novels, color cover United States printed	$30.00
233, 234	Foreign	$30.00
235	Paper back styles	$20.00

PRICE GUIDE

INSERT CARDS, TOBACCO SILKS

Plate #	Item	Price
242	1885 G.B. Miller, Cody	$100.00
243	1800s Champions, Annie Oakley	$100.00
244	Champions, Goodwin Co., Cody	$90.00
245	1880s Histories of Poor Boys, Cody	$60.00
246	1888 World's Champions, Cody	$100.00
	Oakley	$100.00
	Carver	$100.00
	Bogardus	$100.00
247	Page from World's Champions album	$125.00
	Cards cut from album, each	$75.00

Plate #	Item	Price
248	American Indian Chiefs, each	$40.00
249	American Indian Chiefs album	$350.00
250	Civil War Generals, 1888, each	$30.00
251	Ogdens, 1901, Cody	$40.00
252	Wild West Caramels, each	$20.00
253	Wild West Gum, each	$20.00
254	Indian Life in the '60s	$15.00
255	Cowboy Series	$15.00
256	Indian Tobacco Silk, each	$30.00
257	Tobacco Silk, Cody mounted	$225.00

TICKETS, TRAIN PASSES, BUSINESS CARDS

Plate #	Item	Price
258	1883 Complimentary ticket	$700.00
259	1886 Ticket statement	$75.00
260	1893 Press courtesy ticket	$250.00
261	1893 Buffalo Bill Day ticket	$350.00
262	1893 Columbian ticket, Indian	$35.00
263	1899 Ticket statement	$40.00
264	1901 Complimentary ticket	$250.00
265	1902 Complimentary ticket, blank	$200.00
	signed by Cody	$600.00
266	1902 – 1903 Employee's ticket, Olympia	$150.00
267	1903 Photo, Olympia arena	$50.00
268	1908 Complimentary ticket, blank	$150.00
	signed by Cody	$600.00
269	1909 Complimntary ticket, blank	$100.00
	signed by Cody or Pawnee Bill	$700.00
270	1910 Annual pass, blank	$250.00
	signed by Cody or Pawnee Bill	$800.00

Plate #	Item	Price
271	1909 – 1913 Side show ticket	$75.00
272	1910 – 1913 complimentary ticket	$250.00
273	1909 – 1913 half or damaged ticket	$40.00
274	1914 Sells-Floto reseverted seat ticket	$75.00
275	1915 Sells-Floto complimentary ticket, blank	$75.00
	signed by Cody	$800.00
276	1895 – 1902 train passes, blank	$100.00
	filled in	$175.00
277	1904 train flyer	$50.00
278	1903 – 1904 train photo postcard	$35.00
279	Cody business cards, unsigned	$200.00
	signed by Cody	$800.00
280	Performer business cards, unsigned	$50.00
	signed	$150.00

PRICE GUIDE

TOYS & OTHER JUVENILE DELIGHTS

Plate #	Item	Price
281	1878 Cast iron cap gun, rare	$750.00
282	Autograph books, Cody signed	$500.00
	multiple Cody autographs	$800.00
283	1884 paper cutouts, original box, complete	$500.00
	single sheets, uncut	$40.00
284	1885 wooden rifle	$250.00
285	1886 painted tin platform pull toy	$7,000.00
286	1886 cast-iron cap gun, Texas Jack	$350.00
287	1887 A Peep at Buffalo Bill's Wild West	$150.00
288	1889 Terrors of America card, each	$40.00
289	1890 long barrel cast-iron cap gun	$350.00

Plate #	Item	Price
290	1893 Buffalo Bill mini puzzle, complete	$175.00
291	1895 shadow card	$35.00
292	1898 board game	$350.00
293	1903 premium foldout	$45.00
294	1907 – 1908 set of six diecuts	$120.00
	single diecut	$20.00
295	1907 – 1908 writing table	$100.00
296	1910 Indian dexterity game	$50.00
297	1915 tin whistle, solo phone	$30.00
298	1915 juvenile books by Elmer Sherwood	$25.00
299	1916 felt pennant, 101 Ranch	$350.00

PINBACK BUTTONS, MEDALS, ADVERTISING TOKENS

Plate #	Item	Price
300	Cody, red, white & blue	$150.00
	variations	$75.00
301	Cody, no markings on front	$125.00
302	Cody, smaller size	$100.00
303	Fancy jewelry style	$200.00
304	Plain jewelry style	$150.00
305	Annie Oakley	$250.00
306	Pawnee Bill jewelry style	$200.00
	Pawnee Bill	$75.00
307	Pinback with 1913 nickel	$250.00

Plate #	Item	Price
308	Novelty mirror, Indians	$200.00
	Novelty mirror, Wenoa	$500.00
309	London 1892 medals	$350.00
310	Ad. token 1895 composition	$90.00
311	1893 Columbian medals	$300.00
312	Ad. token 1900 brass	$150.00
313	Buffalo Bill & Pawnee Bill watch fob original, beware of copies	$125.00
314	Buffalo Bill himself, watch fob	$200.00
315	I.D. tags, brass	$60.00

POSTCARDS

Plate #	Item	Price
316 – 330	Foreign, 1903 – 1906	
	printed black & white	$25.00
	color	$35.00
	actual photo	$50.00
331 – 355	U.S. & foreign, 1907 – 1916	
	printed black & white	$15.00
	color	$20.00
	actual photo	$30.00
	Postcard set with envelope	$225.00
	Postcard set envelope only	$100.00
356	Cody autographed postcard	$400.00

MISCELLANEOUS SPECIALITIES

Plate #	Item	Price
357	1877 Stage program	$500.00
358	1887 Stock certificate, unsigned	$600.00
359	1887 silk	$350.00
360	1887 autograph souvenir	$600.00
361	Stereoviews, shown, each	$75.00
	scarcer views, not shown, each	$300.00
362	1891 drawings from life	$250.00
363	1891 dinner invitation	$200.00
364	1892 – 1895 glass paperweights, each	$250.00
365	1892 felt pen wiper	$900.00
366	1893 silk	$200.00
367	1894 sheet music	$200.00
368	Illustrations	$25.00
369	Circa 1890s inkwell	$600.00
370	1899 July 4th menu	$150.00
371	1899 songster	$150.00
372	Glass plate negatives, each	$200.00
373	Circa 1900 Cigar & pipe holder	$400.00
374	1902 or 1903 greeting card	$200.00
375	Checks, signed by Cody	$1,000.00
376	1905 July 4th menu	$150.00
377	1906 daily report form	$35.00
378	1907 account booklet	$250.00
379	1907 press order form	$75.00
380	Presentation knife and fork	$500.00
381	1907 – 1908 Ad fan	$150.00
382	1908 July 4th menu	$100.00
383	1908 – 1910 sheet music, each	$90.00

Plate #	Item	Price
384	Buffalo Bill Farewell March and 2-Step	$125.00
385	Circa 1910 playing cards	$600.00
386	1910 outer cigar box label	$150.00
387	1910 ad booklet	$75.00
388	Telegrams	
	nondescript, show related	$60.00
	Cody, sent & signed, not shown	$800.00
389	1910 art studies, complete	$500.00
390	1911 press copy booklet	$250.00
391	1912 song book, red or blue	$175.00
392	Newspaper clippings	$5.00 – 40.00
393	Candid snapshots	$15.00 – 100.00
394	Buffalo Ranch souvenir	$300.00
395	1913 stock certificate, unsigned	$500.00
396	1894 Cosmopolitan magazine	$60.00
	1904 Outdoor Life magazine	$50.00
	1913 Billboard magazine	$50.00
397	1913 July 4th menu	$100.00
398	1914 movie announcement	$100.00
399	1914 farewell dinner menu	$100.00
400	Circa 1915 cigar box	$450.00
401	1915 poster stamps, set of five	$200.00
402	1916 vacation brochure	$75.00
403	1916 flyer, last performance	$50.00
404	Cody-given mementos	$100.00+
405	1917 program	$250.00
406	Funeral card & envelope	$125.00

BIBLIOGRAPHY

Blackstone, Sarah J. *Buckskins, Bullets and Business - A History Of Buffalo Bill's Wild West.* Greenwood Press, 1986.

Buel, J.W. *Heroes of the Plains.* St. Louis, MO, 1881.

Burke, John M. *Buffalo Bill from Prairie to Palace.* Chicago, 1893.

Carroll, John M. *The Grand Duke Alexis in the U.S.A.* Reprint of 1872 Book, New York, 1972.

Cattermole, E.G. *Famous Frontiersmen, Pioneers and Scouts.* Chicago & New York, 1890.

Cody, W.F. *The Life of Hon. William F. Cody His Autobiography.* Hartford, 1879.

Cody, W.F. *Story of the Wild West and Campfire Chats.* Philadelphia & Chicago, 1888.

Davies, General H.E. *Ten Days on the Plains.* New York, 1871. Reprinted and edited by Paul Andrew Hutton, Dallas, 1985.

DeWolff, J.H. *Pawnee Bill's True History of the Great West.* 1902.

Fellows, Dexter W. with Andrew A. Freeman. *This Way to the Big Show.* New York, 1936.

Finerty, John F. *Warpath and Bivouac.* Chicago, 1890.

Griffin, Charles Eldridge. *Four Years in Europe with Buffalo Bill.* Albia, IA, 1908.

Inman, Col. Henry. *The Great Salt Lake Trail.* Topeka, 1914.

Logan, Herschel C. *Buckskin and Satin.* Harrisburg, 1954.

Majors, Alexander. *Seventy Years on the Frontier.* Chicago, 1893.

Miller, Broncho Charlie Broncho. *Charlie – A Saga of the Saddle.* His autobiography. London, 1935.

Monaghan, Jay. *The Great Rascal.* About Ned Buntline. Boston, 1952.

Nolan, Paul T. *John Wallace Crawford.* Boston, 1981.

Rennert, Jack. *100 Posters of Buffalo Bill's Wild West.* New York, 1976.

Russell, Don. *The Lives and Legends of Buffalo Bill.* Oklahoma, 1960.

Russell, Don. *The Wild West or a History of the Wild West Shows.* Amon Carter Museum of Western Art, 1970.

Sayers, Isabelle S. *Annie Oakley and Buffalo Bill's Wild West.* Dover Publication, soft cover, 1981.

Sell, Henry Blackman And Weybright, Victor. *Buffalo Bill and the Wild West.* New York, 1955.

Sheridan, P.H. *Personal Memoirs.* New York, 1888.

Spring, Agnes Wright. *Buffalo Bill and His Horses.* Colorado, 1948.

Standing Bear, Luther. *My People the Sioux.* Boston & New York, 1928.

Thorp, Raymond. *Spirit Gun of the West.* California, 1957.

Walsh, Richard J. *The Making Of Buffalo Bill.* Indianapolis, 1928.

Webb, W.E. *Buffalo Land* Cincinnati & Chicago, 1872.

Wetmore, Helen Cody. *The Last of the Great Scouts* Duluth, Minnesota, 1899.

Yost, Nellie Snyder. *Buffalo Bill His Family, Friends, Fame, Failures & Fortunes.* Chicago, 1979.

The Brooklyn Museum Exhibition book, *Buffalo Bill and the Wild West.* Soft cover, 1981.